ETHICAL ISSUES IN SPORT, EXERCISE, AND PERFORMANCE PSYCHOLOGY

Edward F. Etzel · Jack C. Watson II

Fitness Information Technology

A Division of the International Center for Performance Excellence
262 Coliseum, WVU-CPASS · P O Box 6116
Morgantown, WV 26506-6116

Library of Congress Card Catalog Number: 2013948940

ISBN: 978-1-935412-19-9

Production Editor: Rachel Tibbs

Cover Design: 40 West Studios

Typesetter: 40 West Studios

Copyeditor: Rachel Tibbs

Proofreader: Rachael Kelley

Indexer: Potomac Indexing

Printed by Data Reproductions Corp.

Front cover photos: Cover image courtesy iStockphoto

10 9 8 7 6 5 4 3 2 1

Fitness Information Technology
A Division of the International Center for Performance Excellence
West Virginia University
262 Coliseum, WVU-CPASS
PO Box 6116
Morgantown, WV 26506-6116
800.477.4348 (toll free)
304.293.6888 (phone)
304.293.6658 (fax)
Email: fitcustomerservice@mail.wvu.edu
Website: www.fitinfotech.com

Table of Contents

Acknowledgments

I want to thank all of the contributing authors who took time out of their very busy lives to share their thoughts and experiences for our readers. Also, I want to extend my sincere appreciation to everyone at FiT Publishing for their support, assistance and patience over the course of crafting this publication. Specifically, I want to thank FiT's Rachel Tibbs, Matt Brann, and Sheila Saab. I am grateful to ethics authority Dr. Gerry Koocher, who graciously crafted our foreword. Lastly, I want to recognize the constant support and patient ear of my wife, Dr. Anne Cather.

– Edward F. Etzel, EdD
West Virginia University
College of Physical Activity and
Sport Sciences

I would like to take this opportunity to thank all of the contributing authors who wrote outstanding chapters for this book. This is not always an easy topic to write about, but your persistence and dedication to this topic have helped to create a truly outstanding product. I would also like to thank my professional mentors and guide posts for their constant support of this and other endeavors. Specifically, I would like to mention Andy Ostrow, Edward Etzel, Sam Zizzi, Damien Clement, Dana Brooks, and Lynn Housner. I am also thankful for the efforts of the FiT staff for their support and patience throughout this very long process. Finally, I would like to thank my wife Joanne and children Matt, Alex and Katie for their constant support and humbling musings that always keep me grounded on what is really important in my life.

– Jack C. Watson II, EdD
West Virginia University
College of Physical Activity and
Sport Sciences

Foreword

ON GAMING THE GAMES

Amateurs and professionals, individual competitors and team players, deliberate strategists and instinctive responders, mentors and abusers, people who play with costly equipment and those whose only tool is their own body, winners and losers—the world of sports has all of these and more. Despite the range of athletic activity and dimensions of sport, the players are only human and some will always cheat or try to. The psychological research literature has taught us that three factors contribute to cheating. The potential cheats must first have a willingness to abandon the principle of integrity in the matter at hand. Second, they must regard the potential payoff as sufficiently significant to warrant the sacrifice of integrity. Finally, such people must assess their likelihood of being caught as low. Only then will they succumb. These three principles provide the fundamental connections to ethics in sports.

Psychological variables complicate the mix, as each individual has biases or perspectives that may cause him or her to interpret the demands of a situation differently and allow rationalization and self-justification of behaviors along scales of gray. When the individual in question is also a psychologist, the situation becomes more interesting as we consider their professional and personal roles across the range of continua that characterize the world of athletic accomplishment and competition. What roles are we willing to play when our clients stray from the straight and narrow path?

If a psychotherapy client tells me of illegal or unethical behavior, I have the obligation to treat that information confidentially within the limits set by law. Many contexts in which the sport psychologist operates may put a special twist on the issue, particularly when the psychologist's services come under team, agency, or other third-party auspices. Even when all multiple-role relationships are fully disclosed and consented to, the potential for error can be greater than expected.

In *Ethical Issues in Sport, Exercise, and Performance Psychology,* Edward F. Etzel and Jack C. Watson II have collected a fascinating set of ethical analyses and guidelines accompanied by rich examples to illustrate the challenges of practicing ethically in sport psychology. The outstanding contributors present fleshed-out ethical challenges and dilemmas in exquisite detail across a range of populations, settings, and modes of service delivery. They have truly done a service to sport psychologists, students, and coaches, and their work will open wide the eyes of many who had never fully considered these issues.

Gerald P. Koocher, PhD, ABPP
Professor of Psychology and Dean
College of Science and Health
DePaul University
Chicago, IL

ETHICAL PRACTICE

CHAPTER 1

SOME IMPRESSIONS ON ETHICS IN SPORT AND EXERCISE PSYCHOLOGY

Edward F. Etzel

"Between 'yes sir' and 'certainly not!' How much difference is there? . . . How confusing, there is no end to it all!"
Lao Tzu, Tao Te Ching, XX

INTRODUCTION

Some time ago, I tried my hand at learning the nitty-gritty of growing a garden from a duo of octogenarian West Virginians. They graciously passed on all manner of practical knowledge— even to a transplanted Yankee! While highly motivated, I confessed to my cantankerous neighbors that I knew basically nothing about "tillin' the land" and had rather limited confidence in doing so. In response, ol' "Pap" Osborn exclaimed, "Well, ya can learn, can't ya?" I thought so, and amazingly, with the help of some regular patient consultation, TLC, and Mother Nature's random acts of kindness, much of what they taught me about the right way to garden (to include the use of lots of potent pesticides and fertilizers) actually worked. Nice veggies and flowers emerged from the riverside soil over time in abundance—despite my confessed ignorance and inexperience. Nevertheless, I have thought over time that while they may have taught me what they had learned to be "right gardening" in their minds, it may not have been using the most healthy and environmentally sound approaches to doing a good thing.

What does this have to do with ethics? Well, in a sense, we are all in the business of growing our professional gardens. Ethics helps us do "right gardening" by developing a sense of conscience, which CBS and PBS's sage Fred Friendly suggested is loosely akin to "that little voice that tells you to brush your teeth at night—or to tell the truth, or to not hit your sister."(McLean, 2011). Collectively, sport and exercise psychology (SEP) professionals and our students are encouraged to develop a sense of specialized conscience by our ethics codes, coursework, and supervision/consultation, aspiring to take the two high roads of: (1) helping those with whom we work, study, teach, and serve (i.e., "beneficence"), and (2) doing so without harming others (i.e., non-malfeasance) (Bennett et al., 2006). Unfortunately, the line between what to do and what to avoid doing—the difference between "yes" and "no" and possibly right and wrong in our professional gardens—can be quite unclear and confusing at times, as suggested a very long time ago by Lao Tzu.

ETHICS IN SPORT AND EXERCISE PSYCHOLOGY OVER THE YEARS

Psychology—its diverse faces and forms, is grounded in ethics. Fromm (1990) observed that "the great ethical thinkers of the past . . . were philosophers and psychologists; they believed that the understanding of man's nature and the understanding of values and norms for his life were interdependent" (p. viii). In recent times, a great deal has been written about values in various corners of western society (e.g., business, law, politics, science, the family, sport, etc.). While an extensive amount of ethics-related literature has been published in professional psychology and allied fields such as counseling, social work, and medicine, comparatively little can be found on this and related topics in the sport and exercise psychology (SEP) literature (Andersen, Van Raalte, & Brewer, 2000; Andersen, Van Raalte, & Brewer, 2001; Aoyagi & Portenga, 2011; Etzel & Watson, 2006, 2011; Gardner & Moore, 2006; Moore, 2006; Oliver, 2011; Whelan, Meyers, & Elkins, 2002). One would suppose, given the uniqueness of aspects of our field of study and practice, and the ways the worlds of academic, applied and clinical sport psychology sometimes "collide" (Brown & Cogan, 2006), that much more would have been said on this topic. Oddly, just one book largely devoted to ethics has been published in SEP in over three decades (Nideffer, 1981). An examination of the field's major journals reveals only relatively few papers focused on ethics, with one journal special issue having examined selected aspects of this broad topic (Etzel & Watson, 2006). Ethics-related SEP conference presentations appear to be characteristically under-attended. For example, fewer than fifty people showed up to listen to the 2010 president of the American Psychological Association—an expert and prolific author on ethics—speak about her views on ethics in SEP at a recent international conference. How do we understand these phenomena in our unique corner of psychology?

ETHICS EDUCATION

While it is somewhat risky to speculate, it may be safe to say that the perceived loose state of ethics in SEP today has to do, at least in part, with inconsistent educational requirements in a field that has been challenging to define (American Psychological Association, Division 47, n.d). Although ethics is an important topic that both frames and shapes our best professional practices (Hays & Brown, 2004), perhaps the word is really not getting out in the classroom.

Unlike professional psychology and counseling graduate programs, there appears to be no current standardized curriculum (or accreditation) in SEP undergraduate or graduate programs. There is not a clear training model yet in our field (Division 47, n.d.). Ethics and professional education has been the norm in curricula for years in professional psychology. This requirement appears not to have been a "must" in SEP (Watson, Zizzi, & Etzel, 2006). Professional students in SEP have historically been exposed to ethical matters in different ways, seemingly as part of a mixture of course work and training. Furthermore, with few exceptions, (e.g., Haranhan & Andersen, 2011; Morris & Terry, 2011; Tennenbaum, Eklund, & Kamata, 2012) popular SEP textbooks tend to have little or no content on this topic. This can be seen quickly, merely by scanning the indexes of the various "sport psych" textbooks on the market today.

What does this possibly reflect? Are we disinterested, ambivalent, or assumed by everyone to be somehow ethical all the time in our work? Attention-grabbing or not, ethical challenges to SEP work issues are ever present and will not vanish or fade away; rather, they will probably become more frequent and complex as the years pass (e.g., tele-health consultation). In whatever the real world is, ethically thorny matters emerge repeatedly. Students need to be well versed in the values of our field so as to be well prepared to recognize and meet these challenges.

What are some of those challenges? One need only occasionally briefly peek at our listservs to be able to select from an assortment of recent topics of an ethical nature: professional self-representation, public criticism and verbal attacks on peer character, the proliferation of innovative computer-based performance enhancement technology, self-care, deception in research, Internet use and service provision, mis/use of the listserv to market businesses, and deception in research. Abundant examples of controversial, if not unethical, and/or possibly illegal practices appear to be common in our field. However, an encouraging trend has been seen: The importance of having such educational experiences is emphasized more in SEP education. For example, the Association for Applied Sport Psychology (AASP) is now requiring at least two graduate level courses in sport and exercise psychology to be eligible for certification as a Certified Consultant, or CC-AASP (AASP, n.d.). Greater consistency, needed within our emergent field, may come from such developments.

For example, views and expectations concerning the confidentiality of communication regarding an athlete who has sought consultation may vary greatly from one SEP psychologist to another, from a professional in our field to a head coach, athletic trainer, personal trainer, or athlete. Similarly, revelations to the media of one's work with identifiable athletes or organizations, the public identification of past clients, and perhaps discussing their challenges and issues during conference presentations (if not voluntarily consented to by those service recipients) are problematic. How one markets oneself (Heil, Sagal, & Nideffer, 1997) or allows oneself to be professionally portrayed (i.e., as a "sports psychologist") on a website or in the media can be tricky. Practicing what state and/or provincial laws often describe as the practice of psychology or counseling without a license is unethical and illegal—yet it seems to happen all the time. Posting unauthorized or solicited testimonial lists on business websites seems to be a rather common practice. Providing consultation either in person or via sophisticated technology across state or provincial lines seems widespread. While some readers might find one or more of the foregoing activities appalling, others would not think so or would merely write them off as unique aspects of practice in the field. Perhaps these examples can help us begin to appreciate the inconsistent application of ethics in our unique corner of psychology and the need to consider our professional behavior.

As one might imagine, ethical concerns are not unique to SEP; they are prevalent in all of the helping professions. Other general, ethically challenging issues with clear relevance to SEP professionals and students have merited American Psychological Association (APA) Ethics Committee attention and action for many years. These issues repeatedly include various forms of non-sexual and sexual dual or multiple relationships (Pope & Vasquez, 2010). Competence limits, billing for services, test data release, working in relatively new professional settings (e.g., military, life/personal coaching), addressing perceived ethical violations of peers, and social networking (Plugging In to Social Networks, 2009) also appear to be controversial ethical/legal topics of concern for others over time (APA, 2012).

WORKING IN THE GRAY ZONE

Clearly, the realm of ethics, like morality, is not a simple, uncomplicated area of study; its daily application from our professional thinking to behavior can be quite puzzling. SEP professionals and students sometimes find themselves having to function in a "gray" work zone in which what is acceptable or unacceptable behavior is sometimes rather difficult to determine (e.g., considering initiating a conversation with a past client in a public place) or can be at odds with others' views of what is and is not ethical (e.g., responding to a manager's demand for test data vs. a summary from team evaluation). Morgan (2007) observed that "part of the complexity of [ethics] is owed to the diverse ways in which the field is conceptualized—that is, to the many different ideas . . . regarding just what counts as an ethical consideration" (p.xiii).

Most of our SEP-linked ethical beliefs, assumptions, and practices seem generally grounded in those of professional psychology (i.e., the original then-AASP Ethics Code is based on the 1992 APA Ethics Code) and other allied professions There are at times disconnects between aspects of SEP ethics and aspects of psychology/counseling ethics—what is perceived to be ethical and what is not. For example, the use of the protected title "psychologist" is often used by professionals in SEP who are not psychologists. Some SEP and psychology/counseling professionals may apply interventions that may or may not be appropriate for them to teach or be part of their work given their training and what the law and ethics codes say about the limitations of practice. What counts as an ethical matter and how one apparently should normally go about business varies in our field—and in certain instances quite a bit. Why might this be so? Perhaps many professional behaviors in SEP seem inconsistent because the roots of SEP have evolved from kinesiology, physical education, coaching, and various corners of sport, athletics, and exercise. One should not forget the influence of the different cultures on our work (Hanrahan & Schinke, 2011). So, as members of the greater world of sport and exercise, we may be tempted to adopt some of the values and ethics of those who work and perform around us. Owen and Lee (1987) encouraged caution in this lure since our ethics could become "submerged" in demands of the world of sport.

Maybe the distinctive, domain-specific ethical practices of some SEP professionals have created some gray zones given the wide-ranging mix of beliefs, assumptions, and practices of SEP professionals tillin' their own fields over time. This might also reflect the challenges of "diversified" practice in performance psychology (Hays, 2006). Among AASP members, some evidence suggests that there has been, and likely remains, considerable variation in ethical beliefs and behaviors of male and female, students and professionals, Certified Consultants (CCs) and non-CCs, to include respondents' views from psychology and sport science/kinesiology backgrounds (Etzel, Zizzi, & Watson, 2004; Petitpas et al., 1994). SEP professionals' views of what is ethical or unethical may have been muddied too by the multiple roles and "mixed agencies" in which many SEP professionals often function (Johnson & Koocher, 2011; Watson & Clement, 2008). Then too, a recurring gripe in the field is that unethical behaviors are not challenged or consequated much, despite the fact that our codes encourage members of professional organizations to self-regulate their professional behavior and to encourage the ethical behavior of colleagues, students, and others with whom they work (AASP, n.d.; APA 2002).

CORE GUIDANCE: ETHICAL CODES

Like my distant gardening edification, the sense of what are the "right" professional assumptions and practices in our rapidly growing field usually spring from what we learn from others and acquire in our own gardens of experience both in and, perhaps more importantly, outside of the classroom in the real world of consulting, teaching, and research. Our ethics codes are excellent resources in this area of education and endeavor. They are grounded in the core organizational values of the professions of which many readers are members (e.g., Association for Applied Sport Psychology [AASP], American Counseling Association [ACA], American Psychological Association [APA], Canadian Psychological Association [CPA]). These guidelines communicate a condensed view of general principles and specific practice standards to help professionals and students do caring, effective work for others.

The ethics codes of the organizations to which SEP professionals belong provide the foundation for how we think and act in the various and sometimes non-traditional realms of SEP teaching, consultation, and research. While these values-based codes can certainly be very helpful resources, they are not intended to and do not necessarily provide black and white solutions to often gray work-related problems. Merely having rapid access to one or more codes is not a panacea for ethical dilemmas; however, these codes are go-to assets in the face of risky ethical challenges. Countless risky conditions make us vulnerable to ethical challenges. Some consist of those situations that are: (1) completely unexpected, (2) inadequately expected, (3) inescapable, (4) ambiguous, (5) caused by insufficient guidance, and/or (6) differing loyalties to clients and others (Koocher & Keith-Spiegel, 2008, p. 17). You may not know when you will encounter one until you do—but you will encounter them time and again in your working life. This fact speaks to the usefulness of understanding what guidance the codes afford.

From a precautionary perspective, ethics codes are valuable tools that can facilitate anticipation and avoidance of problematic situations. They offer information we need to be aware of that can help us "keep our ethical antennae up." There is definitely no guarantee that knowledge of the principles and standards and their application will somehow make us immune to ethically challenging dilemmas, nor will having such knowledge "guarantee a particular outcome in an ethically complex situation" (Nagy, 2005, p.5). In their book, *What Therapists Don't Talk About and Why. . .*, Pope, Sonne, and Greene (2006) offer wise perspectives to learning about difficult professional issues by encouraging a "mindful awareness of the complex, messy situations that occur in real life, how we respond to them, and . . . the need for openness, honesty, courage, and constant questioning" (p. 4). Perhaps this mindful approach, combined with a solid grasp of code content, is a constructive path to take.

What is in the balance of ethics as related to purpose and function? A healthy mix of so-called "principle" ethics (i.e., the application of codes' content when confronted by crises) and "virtue ethics" (i.e., internalized ways of thinking and behaving that reflect one's positive personal values, qualities, and character) seems to be the most effective path toward appropriate ethical decision making and action (Johnson & Koocher, 2011). Aoyagi and Portenga (2010) emphasized the usefulness of applying a proactive approach to ethical practice that builds on the regular development of one's self and character in addition to risk management. This perspective appears to be consistent with aspects of positive psychology and many of the values associated with the field of SEP (i.e., fostering potential, self-care, performing at one's best in the moment).

Beyond codes and textbooks, careful ethical awareness leading to prudent judgment and action can be obtained from other sources—sometimes life and good ol' know-how and common sense. Will Rogers observed that "good judgment comes from experience, and a lot of that comes from bad judgment" (Rogers, n.d.). One "must have" involves the availability and use of timely professional consultation. Each one of us needs to have at least one well-informed, experienced SEP colleague with good judgment to help us navigate through choppy ethical waters. Students need to develop a sense of when to seek supervision in a timely manner from their supervisors. Some are less insightful and inclined to wait to touch base or avoid bringing up issues to save face or avoid blame. Heaven forbid, but one might even entertain the notion of contacting members of ethics committees like AASP's or state/provincial professional ethics boards for guidance in perplexing times! Finally, continued education in ethics issues is also seen as a key to competence maintenance. Regular continuing education in ethics for psychology and counseling is typically required for license continuance.

SLIPS, SLIDES, AND FALLS: PRACTICING ETHICALLY IN SEP

Who is susceptible to ethical error, poor judgment, and unethical behavior? As mentioned above *everyone is*. Who then may be more vulnerable than another? There seems to be some insight into this question. Perhaps those more at risk are likely to be young and relatively inexperienced persons who want to "do it all," relatively new professionals who are exceptionally enthusiastic and want to engage in work that stretches or possibly exceeds their competence levels. Others who are vulnerable are those who have rather loose professional boundaries, who may be inclined to enter into multiple relationships (e.g., teacher-practitioners) that may be both beneficial and harmful to self and others (Watson & Clement, 2008; Watson, Clement,

Harris, Leffingwell, & Hurst, 2006). And then there are those grizzled veterans in the field who perhaps have grown sloppy or have a touch of omnipotence. Also, those who were not ethically well trained to begin with, and those who may not know differently may be at greatest risk (Koocher & Keith-Speigel, 2008).

Understandably, one cannot foresee many ethical pitfalls that are part of our multifaceted world of work. Ethical mistakes are usually unintentionally made and ordinary. Loosely adapted from the world of addiction treatment, we all are susceptible to such "slips" as well as "slides" and "falls." Slip possibilities are nearly endless: you can:

- leave your door open when speaking on the phone about a confidential matter;
- leave a file on your desk you should have put away;
- forget to write that note because someone else came by or called in an emergency;
- hear about a colleague's possibly unprincipled behavior and decide to do nothing;
- hit 'Send' and blast an email to the world on a sensitive topic;
- take on a client or other professional responsibility you are maybe not qualified to do;
- give the wrong grades to students;
- learn that one of your supervisees is dating a recent client and minimize your feedback to her/him;
- forget to cite a source or use the wrong source in a paper;
- go to work when you are feeling poorly for some reason(s) and you should not do so;
- have your credentials or title inaccurately portrayed by a reporter in the media and make no effort to seek a correction;
- spontaneously say hello to an ex-client at the check-out line who does not want you to be identified, and so on.

When mistakes are unclear, the professional is encouraged to seek consultation, or if the errors actually have been made by the professional or others he/she is responsible for, the ethical professional attempts to rectify them if possible (see Standard 25, AASP, n.d.; see Section H, ACA; Standard 8, APA, 2002).

Regrettably, the picture gets more troublesome when our work slides in quality and competence, and we fall down the slope of repeated mistakes and errors in judgment that may cause harm to others or ourselves. Selected examples of this worrisome path are often associated with impairment (e.g., very challenging life events, burnout, depression, addiction, greatly reduced or lost competence; see Anderson et al., 2000). Failing to attend to these challenges seems common; we sometimes do not even know they are happening to us or we are not together enough to do much about them. The potential of impairment speaks to the ethical responsibility of self-care in the face of the stressful demands of our work and life so that we can do our work effectively over time (Barnett, Baker, Elman, & Schoener, 2007). Instances in which professional behavior actually falls below so-called reasonable standards of care that results in harm enters the chilling realm of malpractice liability (Shapiro & Smith, 2011). Make certain you have a good attorney in these cases.

SUMMARY

Perhaps it has become rather cliché to suggest that we all need to know our "whys" in life. Despite its possible overuse, we nevertheless *really* do need to know our ethical whys—the purposefulness of our ideals and the numerous ways they become manifested into our work in SEP. After having read what follows in this book (you need not do so in any order), hopefully you will be more clear on your work-oriented values as well as why and how ethics has particular relevance to your daily work life. The meaningfulness of ethics in your professional life, in your teaching, consulting, research, and miscellaneous interactions in professional settings, are connected to what you do and do not do, and how you are seen by those you serve, your peers, and the public. Whether you are an established professional or student, ethics will likely influence the growth of much of what goes into and emerges from your professional garden, day to day and over the years. Your values-based ethical thinking, acquired in the classroom (but more often than not out of it), communicates your values—who you are, and what you individually stand for as a professional or student. Our professional culture, collective identity as a discipline, and trust in our emerging field is shaped by our ethics too. Future practice in established and emergent settings, with new clientele, requiring new competencies will present novel challenges emphasizing the significance of ethics for SEP professionals.

REFERENCES

AASP. (n.d.) Become a certified consultant. *Association for Applied Sport Psychology*. Retrieved from https://www.appliedsportpsych.org/Consultants/become-certified

American Counseling Association (2005). Code of ethics. Retrieved from http://www.counseling.org/Resources/CodeOfEthics/TP/Home/CT2.aspx

American Psychological Association (2002). Principles of psychologists and code of conduct. Retrieved from http://www.apa.org/ethics/code/index.aspx.

American Psychological Association (2012). Ethics committee annual report. Retrieved American Psychological Association, Division 47 (n.d.). Defining the practice of sport and performance psychology. Retrieved from http://www.apadivisions.org/division-47/about/resources/defining.pdf

Andersen, M., Van Raalte, J., & Brewer, B. (2001). Sport psychology delivery: Staying ethical while keeping loose. *Professional Psychology: Research and Practice, 32*(1), 12–18.

Andersen, M., Van Raalte, J., & Brewer, B. (2000). When sport psychology consultants and graduate students are impaired: Ethical and legal issues in training and supervision. *Journal of Applied Sport Psychology, 12*(2), 134–150.

Aoyagi, M., & Portenga, S. (2010). The role of positive ethics and virtues in the context of sport and performance psychology service delivery. *Professional Psychology: Research and Practice, 41*, 253–259.

Association of Applied Sport Psychology (n.d.). Ethics code: AASP principles and standards. Retrieved from http://www.appliedsportpsych.org/about/ethics/code

Barnett, J., Baker, E., Elman, N., & Schoener, G. (2007). In pursuit of wellness: The self-care imperative. *Professional Psychology: Research and Practice, 38*(6), 603–612.

Bennett, B., Bricklin, P., Harris, E., Knapp, S., Vandecreek, L, & Younggren, J. (2006). *Assessing and managing risk in psychological practice: An individualized approach*. Rockville, MD: The Trust.

Brown, J., & Cogan, K. (2006). Ethical clinical practice and sport psychology: When two worlds collide. *Ethics and Behavior, 16*(1), 15–23.

Canadian Psychological Association (2000). Code of ethics for psychologists. Retrieved from http://www.cpa.ca/aboutcpa/committees/ethics/codeofethics/

Etzel, E. (2011). A near fall. In W. B. Johnson & G. P. Koocher (Eds.), *Ethical conundrums, quandaries, and predicaments in mental health practice: A casebook from the files of experts* (pp. 241–248). New York, NY: Oxford University Press.

Etzel, E., & Watson, J. (2011). Ethics. In T. Morris & P. Terry (Eds.), *The new sport and exercise psychology companion* (pp. 424–440). Morgantown, WV: Fitness Information Technology.

Etzel, E., Zizzi, S., & Watson, J. (2004). A Web-based survey of AAASP members' ethical beliefs and behaviors in the new millennium. *Journal of Applied Sport Psychology, 16*(3), 236–250.

Gardner, F. & Moore, Z. (2006). Ethics in clinical sport psychology. In F. Gardner & Z. Moore (Eds.), *Clinical sport psychology* (pp. 199–220). Champaign, IL: Human Kinetics.

Fromm, E. (1990). Man for himself: An inquiry into the psychology of ethics. New York, NY: Henry Holt and Company.

Hanrahan, S., & Andersen, M. (Eds.) (2001). *Routledge handbook of applied sport psychology: A comprehensive guide for students and practitioners.* London, UK & New York, NY: Routledge.

Hanrahan, S., & Schinke, R. (2011). Culture in sport psychology. In T. Morris & P. Terry (Eds.), *The new sport and exercise psychology companion* (pp. 553–566). Morgantown, WV: Fitness Information Technology.

Hays, K. (2006). Being fit: The ethics of practice diversification in performance psychology. *Professional Psychology: Research and Practice, 37*(3), 223–232.

Hays, K., & Brown, C. (2004). A good fit: Training, competence, and ethical practice. In K. F. Hays & C. H. Brown (Eds.), *You're on!: Consulting for peak performance* (pp. 249–280). Washington, DC: American Psychological Association.

Heil, J., Sagal, M., & Nideffer, R. (1997). The business of sport psychology consulting. *Journal of Applied Sport Psychology, 9,* 109.

Johnson, W. B., & Koocher, G. (Eds.). (2011). *Ethical conundrums, quandaries and predicaments in mental health practice: A casebook from the files of experts.* New York, NY: Oxford University Press.

Lao Tzu. (1990). *Tao te ching: The classic book of integrity and the Way.* Translated by Victor H. Mair. New York, NY: Quality Paperback Book Club.

McLean, M. (2011). A case of conscientious refusal: Rights and responsibilities. Retrieved from http://www.scu.edu/ethics/practicing/focusareas/medical/conscientious-refusals.html

Moore, Z. (2003). Ethical dilemmas in sport psychology: Discussion and recommendations for practice. *Professional Psychology: Research and Practice, 34*(6), 601–610.

Morris, T., & Terry, P. (Eds.) (2011). *The new sport and exercise psychology companion.* Morgantown, WV: Fitness Information Technology.

Nagy, T. (2005). *Ethics in plain English: An illustrative casebook for psychologists* (2nd ed.). Washington, DC: American Psychological Association.

Oliver, J. (2010). Ethical practice in sport psychology: Challenges for the real world. In S. Hanrahan & M. Andersen (Eds.), *Routledge handbook of applied sport psychology: A comprehensive guide for students and practitioners* (pp. 60–68). London, UK & New York, NY: Routledge.

Owen, N., & Lee, C. (1987). Current status of sport psychology. *Australian Psychologist, 22*(1), 63–76.

Petitpas, A., Brewer, B., Rivera, P., & Van Raalte, J. (1994). Ethical beliefs and behaviors in applied sport psychology. *Journal of Applied Sport Psychology, 6*(2), 135–151.

Plugging in to social networks. (2009, spring/summer). *In Good practice* (pp. 8–12). Washington, DC: American Psychological Association.

Pope, K., Sonne, J., & Greene, B. (2006). What therapists don't talk about and why: Understanding taboos that hurt us and our clients. Washington, DC: American Psychological Association.

Pope, K., & Vasquez, M. (2010). *Ethics in psychotherapy and counseling: A practical guide* (4th ed.). New York, NY: Wiley.

Rogers. W. (n.d.). Miscellaneous. *The Official Website of Will Rogers.* Retrieved from http://www.cmgww.com/historic/rogers/about/miscellaneous.html

Sachs, M. (1993). Professional ethics in sport psychology. In R. N. Singer, M. Murphy, & L. K. Tennant (Eds.), *Handbook of research on sport psychology* (pp. 921–932). New York, NY: MacMillan.

Tennenbaum, G., Eklund, R., & Kamata, A. (Eds.). (2012). *Measurement in sport and exercise psychology.* Champaign, IL: Human Kinetics Publishers.

Watson, J., & Clement, D. (2008). Ethical and practical issues related to multiple role relationships in sport psychology. *Athletic Insight, 10,* 1–13.

Watson, J. C., Zizzi, S., & Etzel, E. F. (2006). Ethical training in sport psychology programs: Current training standards. *Ethics & Behavior, 16*(1), 5–14.

Watson, J., Clement, D., Harris, B., Leffingwell, T., & Hurst, J. (2006). Teacher-practitioner multiple-role issues in sport psychology. *Ethics and Behavior, 16*(1), 41–59.

Whelan, J., Meyers, A., & Elkins, T. (2002). Ethics in sport and exercise psychology. In J. Van Raalte, B. Brewer (Eds.), *Exploring sport and exercise psychology* (2nd ed.; pp. 503–523). Washington, DC: American Psychological Association.

CHAPTER 2

THE LAW AND SPORT PSYCHOLOGY: WHEN DOING WHAT IS RIGHT AND DOING WHAT IS LEGAL MAY NOT BE THE SAME THING[1]

Patrick H. F. Baillie

For Bill, as the consulting sport and exercise psychologist for the college's football team, weekend road games provided an opportunity to travel with the team, to spend time with the athletes on the bus and at the hotel, and generally to do good work without the usual distractions of being on campus. This weekend, the team was one state away from home, arriving late on Thursday night in anticipation of a grudge match on Saturday evening. However, when two of the key players missed the Friday night curfew, the new head coach decided team discipline was more important in the long run than putting forward the best set of players in this weekend's game. On Saturday morning, the two players were told they would stay at the hotel when the rest of the team rode to the stadium for warm ups.

Bill worked with the two players during the day and could clearly see how upset they were. Their emotions ranged from apologetic for their tardiness to outright anger at the coach's response to what they saw as being a minor infraction. On the drive to the stadium, Bill received an email from one of the players, speaking on behalf of both of them, suggesting that they were considering quitting the team. Bill wrote back, using the Reply All option so that each player would see his answer, and he commented that the coach, being new, wanted everyone to know he was in charge. Noting that the two players had not been drinking and had missed the curfew by just ten minutes, Bill added a comment that the coach was "a bit reactive, but that's his style. He's a little full of himself." Ordinarily, Bill would never write such a thing, but in the pre-game rush, self-editing was limiting.

What Bill did not know was that the original email had been sent to him and, on a blind carbon copy of the email, to the team captain. The Reply All function meant Bill's comments also went to the captain, who showed them to the coach.

Perhaps this was not the most eventful weekend, but, by his actions over the course of just a few hours, Bill found his job in jeopardy, placed himself in line for a complaint about unlicensed practice in his neighboring state, and became at risk for being sued for defamation. His limited malpractice insurance would be of no assistance in any of those three problems.

INTRODUCTION

Conducting oneself in an ethical, professional manner is a core principle to psychological practice, as much in the realm of work with athletes as in broader clinical practice. Sometimes, despite good intentions and a fervent commitment to engaging in best practices, being ethical isn't enough. Legal limits—whether derived from case law or from relevant statutes across various states, provinces, or countries—often encroach on practice, exposing psychologists to consequences that go far beyond what any professional regulatory body might impose.[2]

For many practicing psychologists, the fear of being sued usually revolves around the notion of malpractice. According to an older declaration from the American Psychological Association Insurance Trust, even that risk is very low, falling at less than one-half of one percent (Bennett, Bryant, VandenBos, & Greenwood, 1990). However, more recent publications have disputed that view, stating, for example, that the result of an international review of case law "reveals that claims against psychologists are increasing both in number and nature" (Trustcott, 2004, p. 33). While the potential exists for various non-malpractice claims to be brought (e.g., defamation, unlicensed practice, personal injury, or other torts), fear of legal consequences should not be so great as to impinge upon responsive professional conduct. Thankfully, most psychologists will never need to consult a lawyer over anything more serious than how to complete the task of making one's private practice into a corporation. But knowing some of the possible legal perils is likely to assist in reducing the potential for needing to defend oneself in a civil or even criminal complaint.

MALPRACTICE

Professional negligence, also known as malpractice, is an example of the historical tort of negligence, the elements of which have long been established. First, there must be some sort of relationship between the parties, such that one (e.g., the professional) owes to the other (e.g., the client) a *duty of care*. The duty of care arises when someone engages in an activity for which negative consequences are reasonably foreseeable.[3] For example, a psychologist working with a suicidal teenage athlete could reasonably foresee that substandard care might result in a disastrously negative outcome. In a claim for malpractice with respect to psychological services, the plaintiff (i.e., the person making the claim) has to show that a professional relationship existed between the psychologist and the plaintiff (likely creating a duty of care), that the psychologist failed to meet the level of care that is customary or standard within the profession (i.e., standard of care), that the client suffered some negative consequence, and that the psychologist's failure to meet the standard of care was the proximate cause of the harm experienced by the client.

In short, what a plaintiff has to show is that he or she suffered some loss as a result of having been provided with substandard care. Some jurisdictions will require the plaintiff to prove actual losses (e.g., salary lost by being off work, additional charges for extended therapy), though others may still award nominal damages once the poor level of care has been established. For example, where a plaintiff sues for breach of confidentiality, claiming that the psychologist erred in disclosing the client's personal information, the plaintiff may have considerable difficulty quantifying the value of any consequences that flowed from the breach of the standard of care. Embarrassment, poor sleep, heightened anxiety, and anger may be predictable short-term responses to the alleged breach, but putting a price on such consequences is difficult. Instead, once a court is satisfied that the breach occurred, damages in the order of a few thousand dollars may be provided. Of course, for the defendant, the emotional and financial costs of such litigation are likely to greatly outweigh the amount paid for the nominal damages.

STANDARD OF CARE

While claims of malpractice may fail on any of the four required elements (i.e., duty of care, breach of the standard of care, damages, and proximate cause), defining the standard of care and showing that the psychologist breached that standard can be particularly difficult. The test likely to be used by a court in attempting to determine whether the psychologist's actions were flawed becomes: What is the accepted practice within the profession? In order to answer that question, a court will ask: What is the usual practice that reflects the appropriate application of professional skill and that protects the interests of the client or a third party? Behaving in compliance with regulatory standards of practice and with codes of ethics will likely assist the defendant psychologist in showing that his or her conduct was consistent with a benchmark, but does not preclude a claim for negligence.

But which "profession" are we referring to—applied clinical psychology or applied sport psychology? There are important differences between the usual practices of these two groups.

For example, almost all clinical psychologists, by practice and in compliance with statute, keep notes of therapy sessions. Compared to this large group of clinicians, a reasonable psychologist would likely follow the pack and keep decent notes. However, a sport and exercise psychologist, working with an entire university football team, might opt not to keep notes of the various conversations and even furtive gestures that are part of the professional's attendance at a team practice or participation on a road trip. If many sport and exercise psychologists shared a similar habit, then deciding which standard applies—that of the general clinicians or that of the specialized group of sport and exercise psychologists—would become more challenging. Similarly, while many clinical psychology practitioners go to significant lengths to avoid the breach of confidentiality that may occur if clients who know each other then bump into one another in the waiting room, sport and exercise psychology is sometimes conducted on the field, in the training room, and at the side of the rink, where other observers (and even television cameras) are free to monitor at least the duration of the consultation. Is such conduct by a sport and exercise psychologist a breach of confidentiality and, therefore, of the standard of care or simply part of how sport and exercise psychology services are usually delivered?

However, although it may be difficult to determine which standard will be used to establish the appropriate standard of care, ultimately, a court will make that determination. If the plaintiff is a sympathetic local hero whose athletic career was impaired as a result of the actions of a sport and exercise professional, a court—which, undoubtedly, can be result-oriented—may be more likely to set a high threshold for the appropriate standard of care, and then find that the professional failed to meet that standard. Put simply, practitioners should take no comfort from the notion that a standard of care may be difficult to establish. Instead, anyone working in sport and exercise psychology should attempt to adhere to the highest standards of practice.

Clearer examples of failure to meet the standard of care exist when a psychologist attempts to provide services that are outside of his or her scope of practice or expertise, or when a psychologist misrepresents his or her credentials. One's expertise/competence is garnered by coursework, personal reading, practicum experiences, supervision, and ongoing professional collaboration (American Psychological Association, 2010). Except in situations of emergency, when a psychologist chooses to act outside of the scope of his or her expertise/competence (e.g., providing counseling for an athlete's eating disorder when the psychologist has had limited or no training and supervision in work with eating disorders), the psychologist is very likely to be found to have breached the standard of care. This outcome may occur even if the counseling itself was not obviously flawed, as, in the absence of verbatim records of the therapy session or sessions, a court is likely to find that the psychologist should not have been providing the service in the first place and breached certain ethical principles (i.e., just because you can do something doesn't mean you *should* do it).

Similarly, when the label of "psychologist" or "doctor" is applied to a person lacking the necessary credentials for such a designation, potential clients may be misled and the defending practitioner is likely to struggle to show that such a lack of clarity is the standard within the profession. If a client who was induced to receive services by the practitioner's wrongful identification suffers harm, then, assuming the issue of proximate cause can be determined, a claim for malpractice is likely to be upheld.

One final note regarding standard of care deserves attention. The standard under consideration is the standard within the profession, not the standard of someone with a comparable level of training or experience. Put another way, the standard of care assumes that all members of the profession have equal skills and abilities and there is no allowance either for a rookie member to say "I did not know" or for an experienced practitioner to argue "That's the way I have always done it." In that sense, the test under standard of care is objective, not influenced by the particular circumstances of the defendant psychologist.

LIABILITY TO THIRD PARTIES

While most people are able to understand the notion that a psychologist should be careful not to cause harm to a client—or else the psychologist risks incurring liability for that harm—that is not the limit of such liability. With a psychologist involved in team selection, for example, the client is the team, but any player harmed by the psychologist's actions could also make a claim of malpractice, as harm to that player was a reasonably foreseeable outcome. Misinterpreting a test result, offering an unsubstantiated diagnostic opinion, or failing to disclose any sources of bias in the psychologist's opinion could form the basis of professional negligence. Each of those three errors would also constitute a failure to meet the standard of care used by others in the profession.

No discussion of liability to third parties would be complete without some mention of the Supreme Court of California's decision in Tarasoff v. Regents of the University of California.[4] Surprisingly, given that case's significance to psychology, the decision is often misunderstood or even misrepresented. While a 1974 version of the Court's decision indeed found that mental health professionals have a "duty to warn," the Court agreed to rehear the case and accepted submissions from various parties, including the American Psychiatric Association, and rescinded the notion that only a warning was reasonable. The majority of the Court, in its 1976 decision, spoke instead of a "duty to exercise reasonable care to protect," suggesting that a mental health professional had to do something to reduce the risk, though not necessarily breaching confidentiality by warning the potential victim. Specifically, the Court wrote:

> In our view, however, once a therapist does in fact determine, or under applicable professional standards reasonably should have determined, that a patient poses a serious danger of violence to others, he bears a duty to exercise reasonable care to protect the foreseeable victim of that danger. While the discharge of this duty of due care will necessarily vary with the facts of each case, in each instance the adequacy of the therapist's conduct must be measured against the traditional negligence standard of the rendition of reasonable care under the circumstances. [5]

Put simply, once a psychologist has determined (or should have determined) that a client presents a risk to others, the psychologist has a *duty to do something,* with a view toward protecting the potential target. The traditional Hippocratic notion of "do no harm" is often interpreted as having a focus solely on actions directed toward the patient, but that interpretation should be broadened to, in effect, "permit no harm to anyone."

CREDENTIALS: TITLE USE AND SCOPE OF PRACTICE

Whereas Shakespeare, in *Romeo and Juliet,* wrote "A rose by any other word would smell as sweet," Gertrude Stein offered, "A rose is a rose is a rose." Whatever name is used to designate a mental health professional, the term "psychologist" is typically restricted to regulated members of a state or provincial professional body.[6] The regulatory body—usually itself the product of legislation—may restrict the use of title, the scope of practice, or both. For example, in Ontario, only a member of the College of Ontario Psychologists may use the title "psychologist" and only certain health professionals are allowed to engage in the act of communicating a diagnosis. In another example, a person in the state of Georgia who is not licensed under the Georgia Board of Psychology is barred from engaging in the practice of psychology[7] as described in state law, prohibited from using the title "psychologist," and forbidden from implying that he or she is a psychologist.

But what if the implication that a certain professional is a "sport and exercise psychologist" comes from someone other than the professional? A media report could describe a student or other practitioner as a "psychologist" even if that title was inaccurate. While the APA Ethical Principles of Psychologists and Code of Conduct (American Psychological Association, 2010) is now silent on requiring a correction to be made when erroneous information is presented about a member, a court may find—especially if the error resulted in a benefit for the practitioner—that a failure to act to fix the mistake was, in itself, negligent.

For sport and exercise psychologists who travel with teams, the issue of practicing across jurisdictions may become important. Even for those sport and exercise psychologists who use email, telephone, or online communication with athletes and those athletes travel out of state, the issue surfaces of where services are actually being provided.

Using Georgia as an example, state laws permit an individual licensed to practice psychology at the doctoral level in another jurisdiction to practice psychology in Georgia as long as, in addition to other requirements, at least five days before the intended practice, the individual submits appropriate documentation to the Georgia Board of Psychology. While certain exceptions exist (e.g., for services rendered in cooperation with the American Red Cross or other organizations responding to disasters), nothing in the rules allows an individual to practice psychology in that state simply on the basis that the client and the psychologist traveled there together. Sport and exercise psychologists must be acutely aware of the limitations on practice as included in state and provincial law.

Apart from reminding its members that the Ethical Principles apply to psychologists regardless of jurisdictional issues, APA acknowledges that the current code of conduct does not specifically address Internet activities (e.g., online therapy, voice-over-Internet protocol (VoIP) calls, Facebook "friending" of clients). In a recent interview, APA Ethics Director Stephen Behnke suggested that the next revision of the code will certainly address social media and the use of Internet communications (Martin, 2010).

At this time, there are no clear, generally-accepted rules regarding interstate communication via online video- or telephone-conferencing, by email, or through instant messaging, with the psychologist in one state and the client in another (Ohio Psychological Association, 2010). While the psychologist is likely to argue that the "service" is being provided in the state where the psychologist is located, since ethical codes are designed primarily to protect the consumer, the geographic location of the client may actually be the key factor in determining which state's laws govern the therapeutic exchange. Additionally, psychologists using online communication with clients must be aware of the limited confidentiality that may exist with certain electronic connections, with the use of encryption technology likely being the norm for file transfers or other sharing of client-specific information (see Chapter 13).

PUBLICATION LITIGATION

In one of the more unusual interactions between the courts and the profession of psychology, reports have surfaced regarding the efforts of one very prominent researcher to block publication of a peer-reviewed study that provided a critique of the researcher's widely used scale (Carey, 2010). Carey commented that while some argue that the attempt to block publication of scholarly work amounts to censorship of academic debate, the researcher's position was that the paper "misrepresented my views by distorting things I said." In part, the researcher's argument is that his critics may have been engaged in defamation, knowingly publishing information that is, in most cases, false and that detrimentally affects someone's reputation.

DEFAMATION

Broadly, defamation comes in two forms: (1) libel, involving communication that is written, published, or broadcast; and (2) slander, involving communication that is only spoken. In most jurisdictions, for defamation to be found, the communication must create a negative image of the person (or corporation) being defamed and must be made to a person other than the person defamed. The statement *does not* have to be false, though a finding that the statement was true does provide an absolute defense. Apart from the defense that the statement was true, other defenses that may be available (depending on where the claim is made) in a claim for defamation include that the statements were made in good faith with a reasonable belief that they were true and that the statements were merely an expression of an opinion (which cannot be shown to be true or false) about a public figure (i.e., "fair comment"). Still, though, where the opinion offers information that the speaker knows to be false (e.g., accuses a professional colleague of some impossible act), the defense of opinion is likely unavailable. In some jurisdictions, the defense of opinion is unavailable in any circumstance.

For a psychologist writing notes about a therapy session, the issue of defamation may arise in two general ways. First, the psychologist may offer an opinion about the client, with that opinion having the potential to harm the client's reputation. A particular colleague of mine had the unfortunate habit of scribbling his thoughts in the margin of a medical record in which he kept notes from therapy sessions. One entry described the client as a "disgusting, despicable, detestable human being." Arguably, that communication is not being made to the client—even though the therapy record does belong to the client. In any event, if the therapy record was disclosed to another psychologist, the usual conditions for defamation would be met. Second, the psychologist may write about things said by the client *about another person* without clarifying, in the notes, that this is, indeed, what the client said (and not merely the psychologist's opinion about the other person). For example, the client may *report* that he or she was sexually abused by his or her father or that his or her mother was "an alcoholic." The psychologist should clearly document that these are utterances from the client and that their inclusion in a therapy record does not comment on their truth.

In light of concerns about defamation, within the sometimes competitive realm of marketing sport and exercise psychology services, sport and exercise psychologists should be careful not to disparage other practitioners. Describing one's own years of experience, areas of special clinical skill, and past contracts (when confidentiality limits can be met and other provisions allow so) are each acceptable self-promotion techniques; questioning the skills of another psychologist, undermining their expertise, or perpetuating rumors are not.

INSURANCE

If the contents of this chapter have caused an increase in your anxiety, then one possible source of relief for that could be a decision to acquire sufficient insurance. "Sufficient" refers to the dollar amount of coverage provided by the policy, but also to the breadth of the coverage. Understandably, insurance companies generate profits by taking in premiums that outweigh the amount being paid in claims. Customers may be attracted by lower premiums than those offered elsewhere, but should remain mindful of obtaining insurance that addresses their likeliest needs. For example, in some cases, malpractice insurance covers only a very limited scope of professional activity, not including defamation, harm to third parties, or the injury suffered by a client who trips on the loose office carpet. Multiple types of insurance may be needed in order to obtain all of the insurance necessary for safely operating a private practice (e.g., malpractice, office liability, office contents, guaranteed income—i.e., for disability of the psychologist—and health).

Holders of professional practice insurance need to be aware of the difference between policies that cover the date of occurrence and those that cover the date of *claim*. For date-of-claim coverage, insurance must be maintained after the psychologist has retired from active practice as these policies depend on when the plaintiff files a claim, not on when the alleged malpractice occurred. Thankfully, most jurisdictions have limitation periods that restrict the timeframe in which a legal claim may be filed, preventing liability that could otherwise exist in perpetuity.

For psychologists who believe that they are covered by their employer (or the employer's insurance), such coverage is likely to apply only when the psychologist is functioning within his or her scope of employment.[8] Failing to keep up-to-date progress notes, for example, may be both a violation of a regulatory code of conduct and be outside the scope of employment, leaving the employee/psychologist on the hook for expenses incurred in defending the disciplinary complaint.

Conversely, sport and exercise psychologists also need to maintain insurance coverage for their employees and supervisees. As the psychologist will maintain ultimate responsibility for the actions of the people working for him or her or under his or her supervision, having proper coverage is as much protection for the psychologist as it is for the psychologists' secretary, psychometrist, research associate, or supervisee.

In addition to having coverage sufficiently broad to cover a range of possible claims, it is strongly recommended that all psychologists ensure coverage for expenses related to obtaining competent legal advice. In one Canadian case, while the mental health professional was ultimately exonerated, the legal bills he incurred may have amounted to more than $100,000.

Coverage is also available for legal costs related to responding to and defending against any complaints made to a disciplinary body.

SUMMARY

Returning to the story of Bill's weekend with the football team, we see that even a well-intentioned sport and exercise psychologist may make decisions that risk incurring significant legal liability. While predicting the outcome of any legal case is unwise, depending on the applicable case law and statutes, Bill may find himself guilty of professional misconduct for having practiced in a jurisdiction in which he was not licensed to practice and liable for defamation. While his "full of himself" comment about the head coach may be nothing more than a terse opinion, a court may find that the words were published in the email and damaged the reputation of the coach, with no defence of fair comment being available if the coach is deemed to not be a public figure. At the very least, the relationship between the coach and Bill may be strained. Even Bill's use of email may draw criticism as he (inadvertently) breached confidentiality when the email was also sent to the team captain. That breach may also expose him to a claim for malpractice.

As noted, malpractice claims against psychologists are rare, though they may be increasing. Malpractice exists when the practitioner has a duty of care toward the client or a third party, when the practitioner fails to meet the standard of care that is the accepted practice within the profession, when the other party suffers harm, and when there is sufficient connection between the practitioner's breach and the harm suffered by the client or third party. Undoubtedly, disputes will arise regarding what is accepted practice within the profession, even to the extent of whether the profession is applied clinical psychology or applied sport psychology.

Regardless, the costs of litigation can be massive, even for a successful litigant. Comprehensive insurance may provide a means of reducing the anxiety experienced by a sport and exercise psychologist who is doing nothing but looking out for the best interests of his or her clients. Sometimes, though, doing what's right and doing what's legal may not result in the same outcome.

REFERENCES

American Psychological Association. (2010). American Psychological Association ethical principles of psychologists and code of conduct. APA. Retrieved from http://www.apa.org/ethics/code/index.aspx

Carey, B. (2010, June 11). Academic battle delays publication by 3 years. *The New York Times*. Retrieved from http://www.nytimes.com/2010/06/12/health/12psych.html

Bennett, B. E., Bryant, B. K., VandenBos, G. R., & Greenwood, A. (1990). *Professional liability and risk management*. Washington, DC: American Psychological Association.

Martin, S. (2010). The Internet's ethical challenges. *Monitor on Psychology, 41*(7), 32.

Ohio Psychological Association Communications and Technology Committee. (2010). Telepsychology guidelines. Retrieved from http://www.ohpsych.org/resources/1/files/Comm%20Tech%20Committee/OPATelepsychology-Guidelines41710.pdf

Truscott, D., & Crook, K. H. (2004). *Ethics for the practice of psychology in Canada*. Edmonton, Alberta: University of Alberta Press.

END NOTES

1) In no way is the information and opinion presented in this chapter to be construed as legal advice. Differences in statute and case law across jurisdictions make the giving of any advice clearly unwise without having a full knowledge of the facts of a given case and of the relevant legal standards. Anyone accepting broad, generic commentary as specific legal advice incurs the significant risk of being completely misinformed.

   While much of the information presented in this Chapter is of particular relevance to psychologists licensed to practice in a given state or province—and thereby bound by some type of legally enforceable code of ethics or code of conduct—issues related to negligence, defamation, and the presentation of one's credentials are applicable to all practitioners in sport and exercise psychology, so the commentary may still have broad appeal.

2) Case law refers to the decisions made by various courts, establishing precedents for the interpretation and application of legal concepts (e.g., malpractice). Statutes, in contrast, are the laws passed by different levels of government, establishing rights and limits (including limits on courts).

3) As a simple example, all users of the road (e.g., car drivers) have a duty of care to ensure that no one—whether pedestrian, passenger, another driver, homeowner, or the corporation that owns the newspaper box—suffers harm as a result of the driver's behavior. Statute, however, may override the potential liability, when, for example, laws stipulate that a person cannot be held liable for injuries caused to a passing neighbor who slips on the snow-covered sidewalk in front of the person's residence.

4) 17 Cal.3d 425 (1976). For a discussion of Tarasoff, its current status, and resulting statute, see, for example, Ewing, C.P. (2005). Tarasoff reconsidered. Monitor on Psychology, American Psychological Association, July/August 2005, p. 112.

5) Ibid, p. 439.

6) In some jurisdictions, university professors teaching in a department of psychology may use the title "psychologist" without being licensed. However, in other jurisdictions, the title "Professor of Psychology" must be used. In still other jurisdictions, though, there is no special exemption for university faculty and traditional registration requirements must be met.

7) Title 43, Chapter 39, Section 1(3) of the Georgia Code states:

   "To practice psychology" means to render or offer to render to individuals, groups, organizations, or the public for a fee or any remuneration, monetary or otherwise, any service involving the application of recognized principles, methods, and procedures of the science and profession of psychology, such as, but not limited to, diagnosing and treating mental and nervous disorders and illnesses, rendering opinions concerning diagnoses of mental disorders, including organic brain disorders and brain damage, engaging in neuropsychology, engaging in psychotherapy, interviewing, administering, and interpreting tests of mental abilities, aptitudes, interests, and personality characteristics for such purposes as psychological classification or evaluation, or for education or vocational placement, or for such purposes as psychological counseling, guidance, or readjustment.

8) The sport psychologist employed by the Athletics Department may, for example, be covered by the University's insurance.

SPECIFIC POPULATIONS

CHAPTER 3

ETHICAL ISSUES IN YOUTH SPORT CONSULTING

Lindsey C. Blom, Amanda J. Visek, and Brandonn S. Harris

INTRODUCTION

The term "youth" is generally used to describe participants in the early periods of development, with respect to their physical, psychological, social, and emotional maturity. Within sport, *youth sport* largely encompasses physical activity and sport participation by persons under the age of 18 years. It has been estimated that more than 60 million boys and girls participate in organized sport throughout the United States (National Council of Youth Sports, 2008), making this special population the largest sport population across the lifespan. The sport opportunities available to youth are vast and vary by degree of involvement, skill level, competitiveness, and financial commitment. Youth sport ranges from the fundamental and recreational level of participation to the most select and elite levels of participation, and these opportunities exist in both schools and in local communities.

With respect to the provision of youth sport consulting services, the age and competitive level of the athletes will dictate: a) the role of the sport, exercise, and performance (SEP) psychology practitioner and the scope of practice; b) the potential risks involved in the provision of services; c) the standards of practice; and d) moral, ethical, and legal obligations. An SEP psychology practitioner's basic skill set may be similar when working with an adult or a youth client; however, there are additional competencies and ethical considerations needed in developmental, theoretical, technical, and assessment areas when working with children. Thus, the purpose of this chapter is to facilitate an understanding of how working with children and adolescents in the unique context of sport psychology influences ethical decision making. This chapter is written in a manner to foster the use of a positive ethics approach (see Aoyagi &

Portenga, 2010, for a full discussion of positive ethics) to ethically and responsibly serve youth clients. By incorporating this proactive approach to ethics, SEP psychology practitioners can determine their underlying character and ethical habits, which then helps them use a more proactive rather than a reactive method for handling ethical dilemmas (Aoyagi & Portenga, 2010). While the American Psychological Association (APA), the American Counseling Association (ACA), and the Association for Applied Sport Psychology (AASP) do not have specific ethical codes of conduct that focus on work with children, their codes do include guidelines about respecting the rights and dignity of all individuals and recognizing that demographic differences significantly affect best practices (see Standard 3: *Human Differences* in AASP Ethical Code, n.d.). In order to help practitioners clarify the ethical issues surrounding the provision of services with youth sport participants, this chapter provides best practices for: a) determining practitioner competence; b) fostering a sound ethical relationship through defining roles, establishing boundaries, and conducting informed consent and assent; c) identifying unique issues in group versus individual services; d) terminating the relationship appropriately, and e) using marketing and technology ethically.

COMPETENCE

Practitioner competence is largely determined by one's education, training, supervised experiences, and professional experiences (AASP, n.d.; APA, 2002), as well as by careful assessment of personal and professional strengths and challenges with regard to expertise in select populations and appropriate licensing and certification(s). Two organizations have been at the forefront of developing proficiencies and a certification review process to ensure the moral, ethical, and legal standards of practice: the APA Division 47: Exercise and Sport Psychology developed the sport psychology proficiency (APA, 2003), and the AASP has a certification process. The AASP certifies consultants (Certified Consultant-Association of Applied Sport Psychology; CC-AASP) who have completed a minimum standard of appropriate coursework in both exercise science and psychology, including mentored and supervised applied training with clients. CC-AASP professionals agree to abide by the AASP Ethics Code (n.d.), which is largely based on the APA's 1992 Ethical Principles of Psychologists and Code of Conduct. Both organizations have specific elements of their ethical codes that discuss the boundaries of competence and understanding human differences that influence one's consulting approach (AASP, n.d.; APA, 2002).

When working with a youth sport population, it is important for practitioners to not only take stock of their competencies and applied skill sets, but also their creativity and patience. The effective provision of youth consulting services requires creativity and patience given the inherent variability of clients' physical, social, and emotional development. For example, practitioners should consider the following within the developmental structure of youth sport age group divisions:

- Which age strata do I understand developmentally?
- Which age strata do I build rapport with easily?
- Which age strata am I most comfortable interacting with?

It is essential that practitioners reflect on these questions and carefully consider their responses because the responses will guide the parameters for their consulting practices. Services that are performance enhancement or life skills related are the two more common psychoeducational intervention approaches provided by CC-AASP professionals in youth sport. Clinical sport psychology services require a mental health scope of competency and carry considerably more risk—both to the client and the practitioner. These services should only be provided by licensed mental health professionals such as counselors, social workers, and psychologists, and psychiatrists who may also be a CC-AASP. Further, as previously discussed, youth clients are a unique population requiring a particular skill set for effective work. A CC-AASP professional who does not have supervised experience working with this population, or who has limited experience, should seek mentoring or consultation from another CC-AASP professional with youth sport experience.

Lastly, competence should be viewed as an ongoing process and not an end product (Stapleton et al., 2010). It is for this reason that many professional organizations require continuing education, which is true of both the AASP and the APA. Continuing education can be viewed as practicing positive ethics; that is, a practitioner's focus on reaching her or his fullest potential to better assist those they serve (Knapp & VandeCreek, 2006). The AASP and the APA do provide opportunities for continuing education through conference attendance and workshop participation at their annual conventions; however, continuing education specifically focused on youth in sport is not always abundant. Thus, the ethical youth sport practitioner must seek continuing education from other organizations (e.g., North American Society for Psychology of Sport and Physical Activity, National Alliance for Youth Sports, American College of Sports Medicine) and through other disciplines (e.g., sociology, public health). Practicing positive ethics is, by nature, congruent with the types of services sport psychology practitioners are providing by enhancing the performance of their clients. However, practicing positive ethics requires that practitioners excel in their ability to assist those they serve (Aoyagi & Portenga, 2010), which can be achieved, to a certain extent, through continuing education.

ESTABLISHING THE RELATIONSHIP

Children rarely refer themselves to a sport psychology practitioner; rather, the request comes from a third party (e.g., parent or coach). In cases like this and because of children's status as minors, multiple parties must be involved in the establishment of the provision of consultative services (Blom, Visek, & Harris, 2013). According to the AASP Ethical Code (n.d.), in this situation, practitioners must clarify the nature of the relationship to all parties involved which includes the child-client, the parent/guardian, and sometimes the coach. (The term *parent* will be used subsequently to represent the legal guardian or primary caregiver.) Thus, in following these recommendations in conjunction with the general ethical principle of integrity, it is imperative that in the initial meeting with the client and parent(s), the practitioner determines and defines the role expectations of each party, the boundaries of the relationship, confidentiality limits, and consent and assent.

Role Expectations

The role that a practitioner assumes directly influences all ethical issues (Aoyagi & Portenga, 2010). Therefore, it is crucial for practitioners to identify and establish their role as well as share their consulting approach and philosophy with both the child and parent very early in the relationship (Belitz & Bailey, 2009), which should be done in the first meeting involving all three parties. Providing details that define the what, why, how, when, and where of the consulting relationship can provide a vivid picture of what the client can expect (Moore, 2003). While the specific details of the role expectations of the practitioner will vary in each situation, the ethical practitioner will want to consider the roles of serving as a liaison, mediator, and advocate for the youth client (Kaczmarek, 2002).

Boundaries

When providing sport psychology services to children in youth sport, situations may arise in which the boundaries of the consultative relationship may become challenging to manage. These may include, but are not limited to: (1) the inclination or desire to coach/instruct a client while consulting; (2) being asked to provide both group services and individual athlete services for members with a team; (3) providing consultative services for the coaching staff and/or parents of team; and (4) providing services within the same organization in which the practitioner may have his or her own children enrolled as sport participants. Boundary issues and multiple relationships are inherent in on-site applied work such as sport and are likely to occur to some extent when working with children. The key is to manage multiple relationships by distinguishing between boundary crossing and boundary violation (Aoyagi & Portenga, 2010; Gutheil & Gabbard, 1998).

Boundary crossing involves departures from typical practitioner-client interaction, which can occur frequently in sport psychology, but does not cause harm to the client. In fact, boundary crossing behaviors may be helpful and constructive at times (Aoyagi & Portenga, 2010). An ethical challenge arises when boundary violations occur, which are deviations in the professional relationship that are harmful and exploitative. The APA, ACA, and the AASP Ethics Codes include guidelines discouraging multiple relationships where the secondary relationship undermines the responsibilities of the primary relationship and recommending practices that avoid harm to the client. In other words, practitioners are encouraged to guard against being in another relationship with a client at the same time or serving in a relationship with a person closely associated with or related to the client. These overlapping relationships could "impair judgment or be exploitative" (AASP, n.d., 9d.).

Confidentiality

Confidentiality is the act of keeping information shared by the client accessible to only those who are authorized to have access to it, and it is already challenging in SEP psychology environments because of the common practice of informal meetings and open communication with clients, and the added challenge of distinguishing between information discussed in confidence versus public (Aoyagi & Portenga, 2010). Moreover, this challenge is even greater with youth clients because of the practitioner's responsibility to balance the child-client's rights to confidentiality and the parents' need to fulfill parental responsibilities and legal right to access information. However, confidentiality is the foundation of the therapeutic relationship (Belitz & Bailey, 2009). Therefore, mutual trust must be established between the practitioner, child-client, and parent, which often hinges on the confidentiality of sensitive information. Thus, it is critical to identify the level of parental disclosure that will be involved in the relationship, which can be completed through the process of informed consent.

Informed Consent

This agreement between a client and practitioner is critical to the success and welfare of the helping relationship and has been noted to be at the foundation of ethical care among mental health professions as it addresses the ethical principle of respecting clients' rights and dignity (Belitz & Bailey, 2009). Research in ethics from the mental health professions has identified specific content that should be communicated to clients during the informed consent process (Braaten, Otto, & Handelsman, 1993; Fisher & Oransky, 2008). For example, Welfel (2006) and Moore (2003) outlined the following elements as being important to address during this process:

- The goals, procedures, parameters, risks, and positive outcomes of services
- Fees for service
- Confidentiality and its exceptions or limitations
- The practitioner's training and credentials
- Client's access to their records
- Client's right to be active in treatment planning
- Client's right to refuse consultation
- Alternatives to consultation and how to address grievances should those arise
- Client's right to pose additional questions regarding the consultation and having those questions answered in a comprehensible manner

This information is necessary to convey to prospective clients because it ensures that the decision to participate in consultation is made voluntarily by the client and with an understanding of the information addressed in the process of informed consent (Welfel, 2006). However, because working with youth sport participants will likely involve a clientele legally recognized as minors, youth athletes may not have the decisional capacity or competence to agree to sport psychology consultation without the consent of their legal guardian (Belitz & Bailey, 2009; Hall & Lin, 1995; Koocher, 2008). Therefore, except in extreme cases, a parent or guardian will traditionally provide consent for consultation with a youth athlete. However, for consultations to be effective and to uphold the dignity and autonomy of youth athletes while also adhering to the varied legal and ethical obligations pertaining to working with minor clients, it is recommended that practitioners seek assent from their youth athletes as well.

It is important to note that the youth assent process is not intended to replace, but rather supplement the informed consent provided by the child's parent (Welfel, 2006), while ensuring that the elements of informed consent topics are conveyed to children in a manner that is understood given their developmental stage (Belitz & Bailey, 2009). Although assent does not carry the same legal and ethical implications that the consent process does with adults, it does reinforce and honor the rights of all parties involved, while also encouraging the participation and decision-making of youth athletes (Gustafson & McNamara, 1987; Peterson, 2004; Welfel, 2006).

It is also crucial to dedicate time during consent and assent discussions to confidentiality limitations: abuse/neglect and duty-to-warn statutes (ACA, 2005; APA, 2002). These mandatory legal and ethical statutes require practitioners to report to the parents (and other relevant individuals as appropriate) if the child is engaging in or plans to engage in behaviors that are a danger to her/himself or others, or if there is suspicion of neglect or abuse. With this responsibility, practitioners should realize that they do not have to be able to prove neglect/abuse; suspicion is enough to warrant action. In fact, subtle forms of non-traditional abuse, such as parental or coach pressures regarding weight, overtraining, and injury recovery may be particularly relevant in the sport setting (Moore, 2003) and are issues that the youth sport practitioner must be willing to address, should they arise.

Delivering Services

There are a variety of sport psychology services that practitioners can offer clients, from psycho-educational group sessions to individual clinical sessions, and from team and group work on relational dynamics to individual sessions on mental skills and developmental transitions. While ethical guidelines should be considered throughout the process of developing a consulting relationship for all types of services (AASP, n.d.; APA, 2002), this section will focus on specific ethical challenges in group work and individual work with children. For a comprehensive model on youth sport consulting, see Visek, Harris, and Blom's (2009) Youth Sport Consulting Model.

Group Consulting

When consulting with a group of children or adolescents, the "best practice" guidelines published by the Association of Specialists in Group Work (ASGW, 1998) may be helpful in conjunction with the ethics codes of the APA, ACA, and AASP. Based on the ASGW guidelines and other researchers (e.g., Shechtman, 2007; Smead, 1995), the following seven topics are specifically relevant for sport psychology practitioners who are consulting with children in a group (i.e., team) setting: a) Orientation; b) Confidentiality; c) Voluntary Participation; d) Coercion and Pressure; e) Imposing Practitioner Values; f) Equitable Treatment; and g) Termination.

Orientation. It is crucial that practitioners clearly explain the purpose and goals of the consulting sessions to youth participants in developmentally appropriate language. It may be helpful to have parents, coaches, and athletes all involved in this discussion (Visek et al., 2009). This would allow for consent and assent to be obtained simultaneously and for the ground rules for the provision of services to be agreed upon. However, it is recommended that the practitioner follow up with the children to answer additional questions or concerns they may have after the adults have left.

Confidentiality. While the ethical responsibility of confidentiality from the practitioner's standpoint does not change when working with teams, it is important to let children know that confidentiality by other group members cannot be guaranteed (Orton, 1997; see 10.03 of APA Ethics Code). However, ground rules can be set during the orientation to encourage all participants to keep what is said during a team session within the team (Van Velsor, 2004). The duty to warn and suspicion of abuse/neglect mandates should also be discussed with the parents, coaches, and athletes.

Voluntary participation. Oftentimes, when coaches and parents ask children to complete an activity, they do so without realizing that they have rights or options. In this situation, practitioners should clearly highlight that members may leave the group at any time and can "pass" from participation in a specific activity (Smead, 1995). The orientation may be a good time to discuss this option.

Coercion and pressure. Peer pressure and group conformity readily occur in the sport environment and may spill over to team sport psychology consultations. Practitioners have an obligation to protect participants against this kind of peer behavior during sessions. "Friendly" banter among members can sometimes escalate into larger more intentional problems (Smead, 1995). It is recommended that practitioners work to create an environment that promotes respectful interactions between members and set clear standards of behavior (Doel, 2006). "Timeouts in sport psychology" (Visek et al., 2009, p. 282) may be an option for repeated inappropriate behavior. If a practitioner plans to use this approach, this should be discussed when setting and agreeing upon ground rules, and appropriate and inappropriate behaviors should be clearly identified and shared with parents and coaches. With this responsibility, practitioners want to proceed cautiously and clearly in an attempt to minimize role confusion and frustration.

Imposing practitioner values. Because practitioners must be more active when leading group sessions with youth athletes (Shechtman, 2007), there are two potential challenges that can arise due to this involvement: (1) identifying and respecting individual differences among the children and the values of their families of origin (Smead, 1995); and (2) staying focused on their role as a practitioner (not as a coach or parent). In these situations, practitioners may choose to offer "other sides" for clients to consider or may offer information about potential consequences of certain approaches, but must be careful not to impose their values or philosophy.

Equitable treatment. Humanistically, practitioners may naturally connect with or be more drawn to certain children in the group; however, they must be aware of potential favoritism or biases. Additionally, in following this guideline, practitioners want to be careful of their treatment of high self-disclosers or monopolizers in the group so they do not interfere with the experience and needs of the other members (Doel, 2006; Smead, 1995). By checking in with group members on a regular basis, practitioners can gather information to assess the environment and identify group perceptions.

Termination. While consultations may end unexpectedly for a variety of reasons (e.g., change in team goals, coaching change, youth athlete moves to a new team or city), practitioners want to attempt to offer as much information as early as possible regarding the projected timeline of services. It is recommended that practitioners plan an official last session in order to provide appropriate closure for all parties involved in the services (Orton, 1997). See the following section on *Termination of Consultations and Referrals* for more details on termination within group and individual sessions.

Individual Consulting

The ethical codes of the APA, ACA, and AASP pertain to individual consulting as they do to group consulting; the *Establishing the Relationship* section at the beginning of this chapter is particularly relevant when consulting with an individual client. In addition to these topics, there are several other points that should be noted when providing one-on-one consultations, in particular. For example, one of the first sessions might involve the client and the parent(s), with subsequent sessions involving just the client. To promote positive client-parent interactions regarding the consultation, youths can be encouraged to provide their parents with periodic progress reports or with reports at the end of each session. An alternative option would be for the youth athletes to invite their parents into the session at the end for 5-10 minutes so all three parties can work together to support the athlete. Furthermore, practitioners should provide their clients regular feedback on their progress throughout the working relationship (Orton, 1997). Individual sessions can be geared specifically to the child's needs and interests. Therefore, growth and development may occur at a faster rate than in a group session. If a practitioner is hired to work with a group or team, it is important to discuss at the onset how individual sessions will be handled.

TERMINATION OF CONSULTATIONS AND REFERRALS

An inevitable component to the sport psychology consultation experience involves the termination of services. While this process can be either anticipated or occur suddenly due to unforeseen circumstances, the appropriate termination of services has been described as the culmination of the consultation experience by fostering independence and enabling clients to use the skills learned without the continued guidance of the practitioner (Vasquez, Bingham, & Barnett, 2008). The anticipated or unanticipated circumstances surrounding consultation termination may influence how the process is handled. However, sport psychology practitioners have an ethical obligation to address this process both at the onset of consultation and prior to the end of service provision to protect the welfare of the athlete (Moore, 2003; Visek et al., 2009; Welfel, 2006). This also helps prevent client abandonment, which can occur from the premature or inappropriate termination of consultation (Vasquez et al., 2008). Just as various events may lead youth athletes to seek out sport psychology consultation, services may also be discontinued for a variety of reasons relating to personal, family, or team-based issues (e.g., discontinuation of sport in general, a change in team membership, a change in sport goals).

As the end of the sport season and consultation approaches, it is important to begin bringing closure to the youth athletes' sport psychology experiences (Visek et al., 2009). Children can quickly attach to adults who have effectively established a rapport with them (Corey & Corey, 2002) and may require additional time to prepare for the end of consultation. Additionally, a very important issue for practitioners to discuss during this time is continuity of care (Moore, 2003). Thus, practitioners should provide appropriate referrals for alternative practitioners should the youth athlete(s) desire to seek additional consultation from another professional to address their unique needs (Peterson, 2004; Vasquez et al., 2008).

OTHER ETHICAL CONSIDERATIONS

While the primary ethical issues for practitioners to consider when consulting with youth athletes have been addressed above, some less prominent issues will be discussed in the following section. Specifically, issues related to advertising and the use of technology will be briefly discussed.

Marketing and Gaining Entry

Advertising, community outreach, and building strong public relations within one's local youth sport community are necessary for the successful practitioner. Youth sport involves minors and therefore marketing practices and gaining entry to youth sport organizations requires sound ethical practices (see Standard 5: *Advertising and Other Public Statements* in the APA Ethics Code). Visek et al. (2009) advocate for practitioners to utilize an organizational "top-down" approach, whereby marketing and access entry is targeted first at the highest level of the organization (e.g., board of directors). For moral, ethical, and legal obligations, it is these adults within the organizational and family structures that are ultimately the gatekeepers and must first grant consent to provide services, followed by participant assent.

Although testimonials (with appropriate permissions) are sometimes used in marketing services in an adult population, the use of youth testimonials could be considered morally, ethically, and legally inappropriate. Both the APA (2002) and the AASP (n.d.) Codes of Ethics are clear regarding exploitation and harassment. Specifically, testimonials should not be solicited from those who are vulnerable to undue influence. Children and adolescents are particularly vulnerable to influence by helping adults and those that they may perceive to be in a position of authority or power (e.g., the practitioner). In sum, when attempting to gain entry to the youth sport community, more conservative principle, positive, and virtue ethics are recommended as best practices in marketing.

The Use of Technology

Sport and exercise psychology professionals have started to address the ethical issues surrounding the incorporation of technology with adult-aged athletes (see Chapter 12 of this book for a comprehensive review). However, over the past several years, the use of technology has become an increasingly popular element among youth culture and has changed the way in which people interact with one another (Dombrowski, LeMasney, Ahia, & Dickson, 2004; Patchin & Hinduja, 2010; Windham, 2008). For example, research indicates that the use of text messaging and online social networking sites have become the preferred methods of communication by youth (Windham, 2008). This is becoming particularly salient in youth sport psychology consulting. As such, it appears imperative that sport psychology professionals address the use of these forms of technology when working with youth sport participants. For example, sport psychology consultants might consider the following questions when considering how and when to incorporate the use of technology in their consultations:

- What types of communication and technology am I comfortable using in consultations, and which forms do I prefer to exclude?
- How might I use this technology to enhance the consultation experience of the athletes with whom I work?
- What, if anything, do the ethical codes of my professional affiliations say about technology use in consultation?
- What ethical implications might be associated with the use of this technology?

After considering responses to these considerations, practitioners are encouraged to discuss with the youth athletes and their parents the preference and guidelines for communication throughout the consultation experience (e.g., phone, email, text messaging, instant messaging, and video conferencing) and should clearly delineate those methods which are acceptable and those which will or should not be utilized. This information should be included in the informed consent and assent process so that all parties understand the parameters for communication.

CONCLUSION

The majority of practitioners involved with youth sport have the athletes' best interests in mind. Unfortunately, an awareness of the ethical guidelines and a desire to "do good" is not enough to protect the rights of young clients. Delivering sound ethical youth sport psychology services requires practitioners to realize the idiosyncratic needs of this clientele. Practitioners must be willing to exercise positive ethics and in doing so be willing to seek continuing education in working with youth populations. Furthermore, they must be aware of the importance and be willing to seek consultation from other competent youth sport psychology practitioners when ethical dilemmas arise and must be managed.

REFERENCES

American Counseling Association [ACA]. (2005). *Code of ethics.* Alexandria, VA: Author.

American Psychological Association [APA]. (2002). Ethical principles of psychologists and code of conduct. *American Psychologist, 57,* 1060–1073.

American Psychological Association [APA]. (2003). *APA sport psychology proficiency.* Retrieved from http://www.apa47.org/pracExSpPsych.php

Association for Specialists in Group Work [ASGW]. (1998). ASGW best practice guidelines. Retrieved from http://www.asgw.org/PDF/Best_Practices.pdf

Association of Applied Sport Psychology [AASP]. (n.d.). *Ethics code: AASP ethical principles and standards.* Retrieved from http://appliedsportpsych.org/about/ethics/code

Aoyagi, M., & Portenga, S. T. (2010). The role of positive ethics and virtues in the context of sport and performance psychology service delivery. *Professional Psychology: Research and Practice, 41*(3), 253–259.

Belitz, J., & Bailey, R. A. (2009). Clinical ethics for the treatment of children and adolescents: A guide for general psychiatrists. *The Psychiatric Clinics of North America, 32,* 243–257.

Braaten, E. B., Otto, S., & Handelsman, M. M. (1993). What do people want to know about psychotherapy? *Psycho-*

therapy, 30, 565–570.

Corey, M. S., & Corey, G. (2002).*Groups process and practice.* Pacific Grove, CA: Brooks/Cole.

Doel, M. (2006). Difficult behavior in groups. *Social Work with Groups, 28,* 3–22.

Dombrowski, S. C., LeMasney, J. W., Ahia, C. E., & Dickson, S. A. (2004). Protecting children from online sexual predators: Technological, psychoeducational, and legal considerations. *Professional Psychology: Research and Practice, 35,* 65-73.

Fisher, C. B., & Oransky, M. (2008). Informed consent to psychotherapy: Protecting the dignity and respecting the autonomy of patients. *Journal of Clinical Psychology: In Session, 64,* 576–588.

Gustafson, K. E., & McNamara, J. R. (1987). Confidentiality with minor clients: Issues and guidelines for therapists. *Professional Psychology: Research and Practice, 18,* 503–508.

Gutheil, T. G., & Gabbard, G. O. (1998). Misuses and misunderstandings of boundary theory in clinical and regulatory settings. *American Journal of Psychiatry, 155,* 409–414.

Hall, A. S., & Lin, M. J. (1995). Theory and practice of children's rights: Implications for mental health counselors. *Journal of Mental Health Counseling, 17,* 63–81.

Kaczmarek, P. (2002). The ethical and legal context of adolescent counseling. In J. Carlson & J. Lewis (Eds.), *Counseling the adolescent: Individual, family, and school interventions, 4th ed.* (pp. 17–38). Denver, CO: Love Publishing.

Knapp, S. J., & VandeCreek, L. D. (2006). *Practical ethics for psychologists: A positive approach.* Washington, DC: American Psychological Association.

Koocher, G. P. (2008). Ethical challenges in mental health services to children and families. *Journal of Clinical Psychology: In Session, 64,* 601–612.

Moore, Z. E. (2003). Ethical dilemmas in sport psychology: Discussion and recommendations for practice. *Professional Psychology: Research and Practice, 34,* 601–610.

National Council of Youth Sports. (2008). *Report on trends and participation in organized youth sport.* Stuart, FL: Author.

Orton, G. L. (1997). *Strategies for counseling children and their parents.* Pacific Grove, CA: Brooks/Cole.

Patchin, J. W., & Hinduja, S. H. (2010). Trends in online social networking: Adolescent use of MySpace over time. *New Media & Society, 12,* 197–216.

Peterson, J. (2004). The individual counseling process. In A. Vernon (Ed.), *Counseling children and adolescents* (pp. 35–74). Denver, CO: Love Publishing Company.

Shechtman, Z. (2007). How does group process research inform leaders of counseling and psychotherapy groups? *Group Dynamics: Theory, Research, and Practice, 11,* 293–304.

Smead, R. (1995). *Skills and techniques for group work with children and adolescents.* Champaign, IL: Research Press.

Stapleton, A. B., Hankes, D. M., Hays, K. F., & Parham, W. D. (2010). Ethical dilemmas in sport psychology: A dialogue on the unique aspects impacting practice. *Professional Psychology: Research and Practice, 41*(2), 143–152.

Van Velsor, P. (2004). Training for successful group work with children: What and how to teach. *The Journal for Specialists in Group Work, 29*(1), 137–146.

Vasquez, M. J. T., Bingham, R. P., & Barnett, J. E. (2008). Psychotherapy termination: Clinical and ethical responsibilities. *Journal of Clinical Psychology: In Session, 64,* 653–655.

Visek, A. J., Harris, B. S., & Blom, L. C. (2009). Doing sport psychology: A youth sport consulting model for practitioners. *The Sport Psychologist, 23,* 271–291.

Welfel, E. R. (2006). *Ethics in counseling and psychotherapy: Standards, research, & emerging issues.* Belmont, CA: Brooks/Cole Publishing Company.

Windham, R. C. (2008). The changing landscape of adolescent Internet communication and its relationship to psychosocial adjustment and academic performance. *Dissertation Abstracts International: Section B: The Sciences and Engineering, 68,* 8449.

CHAPTER 4

ETHICAL ISSUES IN WORK WITH COLLEGIATE STUDENT-ATHLETES

Mary Jo Loughran, Edward F. Etzel, and Doug Hankes

INTRODUCTION

Providing psychological services to a collegiate student-athlete population can be a challenging and rewarding experience. It may be very gratifying to provide consultation and teach skills that help the student-athlete flourish on the field, in the classroom, and in life. These skills may be taught in the context of therapy to address clinical issues (e.g., depression, anxiety, eating disorders, substance abuse, etc.) experienced by the student-athlete, while focusing on psychological skills training (e.g., arousal regulation, confidence, goal-setting, motivation, focus, etc.) specific to performance enhancement and improving athletic performance, or sometimes both in some unique combination. Frequently, the results of one's interventions are tangible and immediate, such as a slump that ends, a grade that improves, or notification of admission into law school or graduate school. The fruits of other work may evolve over time (e.g., change in mood, nature of relationships with others, or ascendency into a team leadership role). Further, student-athletes who seek consultation tend to make great use of psychological interventions. As a group, they are highly motivated for change, are solicitous of suggestions for improvement, and have demonstrated "coach-ability," which typically results in an increased openness to feedback and a willingness to try out new behaviors.

Like their non-athlete peers, student-athletes face considerable changing social, developmental, and academic challenges as they navigate the path through their collegiate experience (Etzel, 2009; Petrie, Hankes, & Denson, 2010). In addition, though, the student-athlete must negotiate the unique demands inherent to the competitive intercollegiate athletic environment (Andersen, 2007). Without question, the unique demands and stressors placed upon student-athletes are increasing, especially at large Division I universities. Intercollegiate athletics is big business in many places, and student-athletes, for better or worse, are part of that commercial system. Without highly functioning student-athletes, the business of intercollegiate athletics suffers. These cultural and systemic underpinnings make it challenging for both the student-athlete and sport psychology consultant to engage in the process of assisting the student-athlete effectively and ethically. In some respects, working within a college athletic department can be like swimming in murky water. Psychologists who work with collegiate student-athletes must remain vigilant in their efforts to become aware of the many unknown issues that present unique challenges to their ability to be effective (Etzel & Watson, 2007). High on the list of prerequisites for adequate preparation in this specialty area of practice is a clear understanding of the ethical dilemmas that will arise—some on a very regular basis.

COMPETENCE

The ethical codes of both the Association for Applied Sport Psychology (AASP) and the American Psychological Association (APA) are clear in conveying the expectation that professionals practice only within the limits of their competence (APA, 2002). While individuals may interpret licensure and certification to be indications of competence, it would be a mistake for practitioners to make this same mistake and believe that they have free reign to work with all clients. Licensure is a credential recognized by state governments to convey to the public that a psychologist has demonstrated a certain grasp of knowledge and experience sufficient to warrant independent practice. Likewise, AASP conveys the "certified consultant" credential to indicate to the public a minimum amount of preparation and experience in sport science and psychology. These credentials, however valuable, provide scant protection from individuals that practice beyond their levels of training or skill level.

To work ethically and effectively with any college student, the psychologist should have a thorough understanding of the developmental issues that are pertinent in the lives of this age group (Grayson & Meilman, 2006). In addition to this general body of knowledge, the psychologist should also have a strong working knowledge of the unique issues facing the collegiate student-athlete, particularly in comparison to his or her non-athlete peers (Etzel, 2009).

The following example illustrates the necessity for consultants to stay within the bounds of their training in their work:

As an undergraduate, Dr. Speedy competed on the cross-country team and now as a licensed psychologist has continued to participate in road races of distances ranging from 5k to half marathons. In an effort to grow her private practice, Dr. Speedy added "Sport Psychologist" to her business cards and distributed them to coaches at a local collegiate track meet.

STANDARD 2.01 (A) COMPETENCE

Psychologists provide services, teach, and conduct research with populations and in areas only within the boundaries of their competence, based on their education, training, supervised experience, consultation, study, or professional experience (APA, 2002).

In the example above, Dr. Speedy's past and current experience as an athlete are not sufficient to warrant her portrayal of herself as a sport psychologist. Should she wish to expand her practice to include work with competitive runners, Dr. Speedy would be advised to pursue additional training in sport psychology, possibly including coursework and supervised practice.

Although *psychologist* is a protected term that cannot be used in the U.S. by professionals without a state-issued license for independent practice, few protections exist to prohibit any psychologist from inserting "sport" as a modifier, much to the potential peril of an unsuspecting public. Hack (2005) has emphasized that putting the word "sport" in front of "psychologist" clearly indicates that the professional has mindfully obtained specialized education, training, and/or supervised experience in sport psychology. Since 2003, APA Division 47 (Exercise and Sport Psychology) has recognized sport psychology as an area of proficiency (American Psychological Association, 2007). First, licensed psychologists who describe themselves as sport psychologists must have supervised experience in applying psychological principles in sport settings and also must understand the specific needs of this special population. Second, they must have expert knowledge in the extensive sport psychology research literature. The APA proficiency recognizes sport psychology as primarily a post-graduate, post-doctoral specialization that requires additional training and knowledge. It should be noted that graduate programs do exist in counseling and clinical psychology departments that allow doctoral students to meet the proficiency criteria, and in some cases, the Certified Consultant-AASP requirements as well. Despite the existence of these competency standards, psychologists are left primarily to police themselves. For those professionals who have taken the extra, time-consuming steps to acquire the proper training, it can be frustrating to see practitioners usurping the title. In addition, psychologists must compete with individuals from a variety of training backgrounds outside of psychology who offer similar services without the constraints of an ethics code or state law applying to their scope of practice. Athletic department personnel and student-athletes are often not aware of (or do not know the differences between) licenses, credentials, titles, or training backgrounds of individuals who want to provide services. Coaches, in particular, may be more interested in results and the promises of guaranteed performance improvements from "mental training gurus" than they are about ethics codes and state law. Dr. Speedy has placed herself in a tenuous ethical position by using "sport" in her title; however, there may be nothing other than the ethical codes of APA and AASP to stop practitioners such as Dr. Speedy from simply usurping this title.

Even psychologists who undergo appropriate training and supervised experience to work with athletes must be careful about expanding the bounds of their practice without taking the proper steps.

Dr. Mesmer attended a weekend-long continuing education workshop on the topic of hypnosis and enhanced performance and decides that members of the gymnastics team would benefit from this technique. Dr. Mesmer begins using hypnotic suggestions during subsequent sessions with gymnasts.

Regardless of Dr. Mesmer's academic training and professional credentials, it would seem that any incorporation of new techniques into practice must be added only with considerable preparation and oversight. Unfortunately, the ethical codes are somewhat vague about what constitutes appropriate training when considering the expansion of one's claimed expertise. It is therefore incumbent upon the psychologist to err on the side of caution when incorporating new areas into one's professional practice. In the above example, Dr. Mesmer should seek continuing education, supervision, and ongoing consultation from a hypnosis expert when beginning to incorporate these techniques into professional practice.

CONFIDENTIALITY

As is the case in all psychology practice, confidentiality is the cornerstone of the therapeutic relationship in work with the student-athlete (Koocher & Keith-Spiegel, 2008). The culture of collegiate athletics is one that requires the student-athlete to surrender much of his or her right to privacy. For example, as a condition of eligibility, the student-athlete agrees to undergo random drug testing. Further, coaches and athletic trainers routinely have access to the athlete's complete medical history, including doctor's visits and prescription medications. Access to normally private academic records is also typically signed away in pre-participation waivers. This may set up the expectation that the consulting psychologist will share all information about work with the student-athlete, which can be a barrier for an athlete seeking consultation.

Standard 4.01, Maintaining Confidentiality
Psychologists have a primary obligation and take reasonable precautions to protect confidential information obtained through or stored in any medium, recognizing that the extent and limits of confidentiality may be regulated by law, established institutional rules, or professional or scientific relationship (APA, 2002).

Dr. Young is a psychologist in the counseling center of a Division I university, where Tom is a standout football player with a probable future in the NFL. Tom confides to Dr. Young that he has been experiencing blurred vision, headaches, and dizziness since he sustained a head blow during a preseason scrimmage. Tom refuses Dr. Young's recommendation that he report his symptoms to his trainer or doctor because "my draft status will suffer if it gets out that I'm not 100%." Further, he insists that Dr. Young not reveal this information to anybody.

Standard 4.02 (b)
Unless it is not feasible or is contraindicated, the discussion of confidentiality occurs at the outset of the relationship and thereafter as new circumstances may warrant. The above scenario illustrates the importance of clarifying in advance the parameters of the relationship between the psychologist, the student-athlete, and the athletic department. Such information may include what information, if any, can be shared and under what circumstances.

Issues involving confidentiality can arise even when the student-athlete consents via signed releases of information. It is critical for the psychologist to approach informed consent as a process and not simply a dry recitation of facts given at the beginning of the therapeutic relationship. Exceptions to confidentiality should be explained carefully, and the student-athlete not be allowed to quickly sign a form stating that they understand informed consent and confidentiality. Student-athletes are asked to sign many documents by the athletic department, and they may be in the habit of doing so without reading them, or simply trusting the individual who has asked them to sign. The process should be interactive, with the psychologist encouraging questions and a sense of curiosity from the student-athlete. As new information becomes available, the entire explanation of confidentiality should be revisited with the student-athlete.

In some situations, the student-athlete may give permission for information to be shared with his or her coach or athletic trainer. However, the psychologist must give careful consideration when making the decision about what information to share, taking into account the potential relevance of the disclosure as well as what consequences making a particular disclosure might have for the client.

Janet, a women's lacrosse player, reveals during a counseling session that Sam, the head coach, regularly calls his players by crude euphemisms for female body parts and engages in other behaviors that could be considered demeaning and sexist. Janet refuses the recommendation that she report her coach's behavior to the administration for fear that it would negatively affect her playing time.

The psychologist in this situation is presented with a challenging, yet not uncommon situation. Although he or she might feel strongly about the usefulness of reporting the coach's abusive behavior, the psychologist must be respectful of the student-athlete's refusal to do so even if doing so does not appear to be in the client's best interest.

PROFESSIONAL RELATIONSHIPS

In addition to confidentiality, another potential ethical issue with particular relevance to collegiate athletics work involves the necessity of clarifying precisely who the client is. Indeed, it is common for psychologists to be caught in the bind of determining who they are serving.

Dr. Taylor, a private practice psychologist, provides psychological consulting to the athletic department of University AAA, a Division II institution. The athletic director has asked Dr. Taylor for a monthly summary of each student-athlete's counseling attendance and progress, stating that, "after all, we're paying for this service, so we need to know what we're getting for our money."

Standard 4.02 (a)
Psychologists discuss with persons (including, to the extent feasible, persons who are legally incapable of giving informed consent and their legal representatives) and organizations with whom they establish a scientific or professional relationship: (1) the relevant limits of confidentiality, and (2) the foreseeable uses of the information generated through their psychological activities (APA, 2002).

Psychologists who provide services for student-athletes typically work in one of three different service delivery venues: (1) as a staff member of the college or university counseling center, (2) as a consultant in private practice, or (3) as an employee of the institution's athletic department. Regardless of the business or financial arrangement, it is incumbent upon the psychologist to clarify that the focus of treatment must remain on the student-athlete. It should be made explicit in these situations that the client is the student-athlete, not the athletic department or any other entity within the college or university. Trying to serve two masters may put the client at risk for harm.

Anita, a member of the women's tennis team, has been receiving counseling from Dr. Phillips at the university counseling center for support following a surgical repair of a shoulder injury. Mr. and Mrs. Jones, Anita's parents, contacted Dr. Phillips to report their intention to sue the university for damages because of their contention that poor coaching and overtraining were responsible for Anita's injury. They request a copy of Dr. Phillips' records to support their claim of damage to their daughter's psychological health.

In this case example, Dr. Phillips may experience conflict between the wishes or demands of his client (the student-athlete), her parents, and the university. Would the situation be different if Dr. Phillips worked in the athletic department, or in private practice? Likewise, if Anita's parents are paying the fees for counseling, either out of pocket or through their health insurance, do they have any more of a right to the requested records? In this and similar situations, the psychologist needs to consult with the client as to his or her wishes. This case also speaks to the necessity of clarifying who owns information about the client (i.e., the client) at the onset of the consultation during the informed consent process. Dr. Phillips may release the treatment records to any party, including Mr. and Mrs. Jones, provided that the client has provided her written consent.

BOUNDARY ISSUES

For the psychologist working in a collegiate setting, providing effective psychological interventions to student-athletes sometimes involves venturing outside the traditional parameters of practice (Andersen, Van Raalte, & Brewer, 2001; Etzel & Watson, 2007; Stapleton, Hankes, Hays, & Parham, 2010). Flexibility may be required in terms of scheduling, location, session length, and other aspects of practice in which psychologists interact with clients outside the typical 50-minute hour in the office. Because of the unique demands of working with the student-athlete population, the potential for boundary violations or crossings is increased (e.g., brief interactions in hallways, at practices, at games, or in other settings). Psychologists who are both clinicians and academics may occasionally have former clients or current clients enroll in their classes, perhaps because they have a positive pre-existing relationship with the professional. These situations should be avoided, and if avoidance is not possible, boundaries need to be discussed given the power differential that exists (Watson, Clement, Harris, Leffingwell, & Hurst, 2006).

Historically, it was assumed that as the frequency of boundary crossings increased, so did the likelihood of a boundary violation—the proverbial "slippery slope" (Gutheil & Gabbard,

1993). It should be emphasized, however, that boundary crossings in and of themselves are not unethical. In fact, others have strongly argued that boundary crossings can actually be therapeutic, and that not engaging in them can cause situational harm to clients (e.g., Lazurus & Zur, 2002; Zur, 2007). Gottlieb and Younggren (2009) have recently revisited this issue and concluded that while boundary issues are complex, they should not be automatically avoided or fixed by rigid rules. Instead, boundary issues should be approached thoughtfully, and the decision-making process as to how to proceed should be focused on what most benefits the client. To avoid misunderstandings, the psychologist working with the athlete should be attuned to the complexities of maintaining appropriate boundaries in situations that may be quite conducive to blurring or pushing of limits.

CONFLICTS OF INTEREST

Standard 3.06, Conflict of Interest
Psychologists refrain from taking on a professional role when personal, scientific, professional, legal, financial, or other interests or relationships could reasonably be expected to: (1) impair their objectivity, competence, or effectiveness in performing their functions as psychologists, or (2) expose the person or organization with whom the professional relationship exists to harm or exploitation (APA, 2002).

Jason is the starting goalkeeper of the national champion Ace University men's ice hockey team. Following the press coverage after the championship game, Jason has become somewhat of a celebrity on campus. Jason asked his psychologist at the university counseling center if he could schedule his appointments after hours so that he could avoid being seen by other students in the waiting room.

The psychologist in this example must weigh the consequences on the therapeutic relationship of granting Jason's request. By agreeing to meet with Jason after hours, the psychologist demonstrates sensitivity to the vulnerability Jason experiences as a campus personality. On the other hand, granting Jason's request for special treatment may increase his sense of entitlement and may prove to be counterproductive to his progress in counseling. The psychologist in this case would be well served to explore the issue thoroughly with Jason prior to making any adjustments to the schedule. This example also allows an opportunity to address the importance of peer consultation and/or supervision. As previously emphasized, the practice of psychology in intercollegiate athletics settings is ripe for ethical dilemmas. Behnke (2008) has noted that the pit of one's stomach can be as good an indicator of an ethical dilemma as one's frontal lobe. Psychologists working in athletic departments will want to pay special attention to these feelings. When in doubt, consult as soon as possible with a trusted colleague.

Standard 4.02 (c)
Paul, a member of the university's diving team, has made great progress in managing his performance anxiety due in large part to his work with Dr. Rivera. Paul will be traveling to compete over the coming summer and has expressed a desire to continue his work with Dr. Rivera via text messaging and the Internet.

For the student-athlete, the reality of participation in intercollegiate athletics involves a grueling schedule of training and competition, including significant travel away from campus, even during periods of peak academic demands of the semester. This performance-based lifestyle may present a challenge to the boundaries of the counseling relationship that must be anticipated and dealt with by the psychologist. Psychologists who offer services, products, or information via electronic transmission inform clients/patients of the risks to privacy and limits of confidentiality (APA, 2002).

Much has been written about the ethical issues pertinent to Internet counseling (Watson, Lubker, & Zakrajsek, 2006), most frequently regarding the threats to confidentiality that accompany electronic communication (see chapter 13 of this book). Although clients are very comfortable with electronic communication and Facebook postings, psychologists need to be extremely careful about consultation at a distance. Dr. Rivera would be wise to take into consideration the pros and cons of providing and not continuing to provide services to Paul during his travels. Ideally, Dr. Rivera and Paul would explore this situation well in advance of Paul's departure to allow for a solution that both preserves the student-athlete's privacy and confidentiality but also avoids any potential of his feeling abandoned. Also unclear in the above example is the ethicality/legality of practicing at a distance (e.g., in other states than where one is licensed) through electronic means (Dielman et al., 2009). A thorough exploration of practice guidelines crafted by the Ohio Psychological Association for electronic psychological services can be found on the association's website (Ohio Psychological Association, 2011)

OTHER BOUNDARY ISSUES

Another boundary issue that may arise in this area of practice involves travel with a team by the consulting psychologist.

Dr. Xu has provided team building and goal setting training to the university's tennis team. After a significantly improved season, the team has qualified to participate in a conference tournament in a distant city. The university's athletic director invites Dr. Xu to travel, all expenses paid, to the tournament to ensure that the team is mentally prepared for the big competition.

It is not unusual for members of the sports medicine team to attend away competitions. The argument could be made that a consulting psychologist should be part of such a team. Certainly, the potential impact of an on-the-spot intervention either immediately before or after competition could dwarf what might be attainable days or even weeks later in the consulting office. Despite these potential benefits, there are some potential sticky ethical issues that should be considered before agreeing to travel with a collegiate team. This is clearly a boundary crossing. The first and foremost concern is related to the comfort and privacy of each individual student-athlete who might be jeopardized by having his or her psychologist along on a road trip. The student-athlete must be in control of who knows about his or her status as a client.

In this situation, it would behoove the psychologist to discuss the potential impact of traveling with the team to this event. What would be the role of the psychologist at the tournament? Is the psychologist attending the tournament and associated activities to work or play? The psychologist would want to clarify with any of the tennis players who he is working with individually what his or her role will be on the trip. Perhaps more importantly, how will the student-athlete and psychologist interact with one another during the week of the tournament? The psychologist would also want to be cognizant that any communication he or she engages in within a public setting could be interpreted by others as an indication that the student-athlete is a client.

An additional boundary issue that pertains to this situation involves the financial arrangement for the trip. The administrator who invites the psychologist along for the trip may view the invitation as a bonus or reward for a job well done rather than as compensation for professional services, which may result in further miscommunication by either or both parties. This should be clarified when the invitation is extended. This again speaks to the importance of clarifying the purpose of the trip. Is the sport psychologist working or enjoying the rewards for the work he did with the team earlier in the season? The Standard 3.07, Third-Party Requests for Services should also be consulted in addressing this ethical dilemma.

MULTIPLE RELATIONSHIPS

Even on a very large university campus, the world of collegiate athletics can be a small world. Psychologists who work in this setting can be vulnerable to entering into multiple relationships, often unavoidably or without prior knowledge.

Dr. Sherman is providing personal counseling to two members from the same women's field hockey team. Janie reveals during one session that she has been the victim of bullying by her teammates, including incidents involving physical hazing and verbal abuse. Janie identifies one of her tormenters as Linda. Unbeknownst to Janie, Linda is also one of Dr. Sherman's clients. Linda has been receiving counseling to work on relationship issues.

Standard 3.05 (a)
A multiple relationship occurs when a psychologist is in a professional role with a person and (1) at the same time is in another role with the same person, (2) at the same time is in a relationship with a person closely associated with or related to the person with whom the psychologist has the professional relationship, or (3) promises to enter into another relationship in the future with the person or a person closely associated with or related to the person.

A psychologist refrains from entering into a multiple relationship if the multiple relationship could reasonably be expected to impair the psychologist's objectivity, competence, or effectiveness in performing his or her functions as a psychologist, or otherwise risks exploitation or harm to the person with whom the professional relationship exists (APA, 2002).

Multiple relationships that would not reasonably be expected to cause impairment or risk exploitation or harm are not unethical. It could be argued that Dr. Sherman should have considered the possibility that working with several members from the same team could be risky for this very reason and should have referred one of the women to a colleague. However, this is not always possible, particularly in "one-person departments," as psychologists would be limited in the number of clients they see by the number of teams on campus. Sport psychologists working within athletic departments have been compared to psychologists practicing in rural or military settings where multiple demands exist and frequent contact outside the traditional therapy offices is common, expected, or even viewed as positive (Gardner & Moore, 2006). Dr. Carter must work to maintain the best interests of both of his clients, even when those interests may seem to be in conflict with one another. APA (2002) Standard 3.06: Conflict of Interest might also be considered in dealing with this ethical dilemma.

Standard 3.05 (b)
Multiple relationships may be at risk for occurring when the psychologist wears more than one hat in an institution.

Dr. DeSoto has a dual appointment at State University as a psychologist in the athletic department and a faculty member in the psychology department, where she teaches an undergraduate course in Sport and Exercise Psychology. On the first day of the semester, Dr. DeSoto discovers that one of the members of the class had been a counseling client for performance anxiety during the previous academic year.

If a psychologist finds that, due to unforeseen factors, a potentially harmful relationship has arisen, the psychologist takes reasonable steps to resolve it with due regard for the best interests of the affected person and maximal compliance with the ethics code (APA, 2002).

Is Dr. DeSoto guilty of engaging in a multiple relationship by having a former client as a student? Does the presenting issue (performance anxiety) of the former client versus another more complicated or severe clinical issue affect the decision-making of the psychologist in this situation? Even if both the professor and the student are in agreement that their former counseling relationship is over, there remain potentially troubling consequences that might ensue. What if, for example, the student requests extended time on exams due to the previously disclosed performance anxiety? For a more comprehensive overview of this situation and the potential ramifications methods for moving forward, please see Watson, Clement, Harris, Leffingwell, and Hurst (2006). The ideal solution to Dr. DeSoto's dilemma may well depend upon the discussions that should take place as part of the informed consent process at the outset of the treating relationship.

Even when the psychologist is clearly defined in only one role on a university campus, multiple relationships may still be difficult to avoid.

Over the years, Dr. Walker has worked successfully with several men's tennis players from Main University and, as a result, has developed a good working relationship with the team's coaching staff. One day Dr. Walker receives a telephone call from the team's assistant coach, who requests an appointment to discuss recent marital difficulties. When Dr. Walker attempts to refer the coach to a colleague, the coach tells him that he would not feel comfortable working with anyone else.

Dr. Walker may feel torn about how to handle this situation. On the one hand, there is the reality that in the world of collegiate athletics, trust is a precious commodity. Dr. Walker has built trust with the tennis coaching staff through years of hard work. On the other hand, should Dr. Walker agree to treat this coach, the potential for further blurring of lines would increase. Should Dr. Walker remain adamant about not entering into a treatment relationship with the coach, the risk is that this coach will forego counseling altogether. This scenario points to the importance of psychologists who work in intercollegiate athletics being clear about who they are obliged to serve. In this instance, perhaps a brief conversation with the coach for the purpose of making a timely referral would be useful.

SELF-CARE

Any discussion of ethics should include the topic of self-care. Psychologists who neglect their own wellbeing do so at the peril of their effectiveness with their clients (Pope & Vasquez, 2005). Despite its many rewards, work with a collegiate athlete population can be rife with stress and pressure, mirroring the environment of the athletic department. Often, the psychologist in this environment works in relative isolation and is the only professional in the department or counseling center who is solely responsible for the emotional health of the student-athletes.

Dr. Katz is the university counseling center's liaison to the athletic department and is the designated psychologist to work with student-athletes. Due to the busy schedule at the counseling center, Dr. Katz's colleagues have suggested that he curtail his work with athletes and focus on students with "real problems." Dr. Katz has recently begun to experience migraine headaches and during his most recent physical exam was found to have elevated blood pressure. Dr. Katz's physician suggested that stress might be contributing to these health problems.

As a psychologist who specializes in work with athletes, Dr. Katz faces many of the same stereotypes faced by collegiate student-athletes, namely that they are overindulged, immature college students. Without taking steps to seek out support and collaborative relationships, Dr. Katz risks isolation and burnout. Further, involvement in national professional associations such as AASP and APA Division 47 (Exercise and Sport Psychology) can also provide critical affiliation to professionals working in relative isolation. Dr. Katz would be wise to cultivate a local network of supportive peers to further decrease the loneliness of the work as a psychologist within the collegiate athletic culture.

Dr. Williams is the athletics department psychologist. Recently, the department has been asked to trim its budget, and Dr. Williams is concerned that his position might be eliminated. In an effort to increase his job security, Dr. Williams has been working long hours, often conducting counseling sessions and attending practices and competitions early mornings, late evenings, and weekends. Dr. Williams has been feeling tired and anxious much of the time.

Despite the plethora of research studies that have documented the effectiveness of mental training and other psychological interventions to enhance the health and welfare of collegiate student-athletes, sport psychological services can be considered a "luxury item," particularly in this age of fiscal belt-tightening. In an effort to prove oneself as invaluable, psychologists working in this environment must be careful not to sacrifice their own emotional balance in the service of the work. Consultation with trusted and competent colleagues with whom they can openly share their professional fears, doubts, and concerns is a critical element of psychologists' self-care (Bennett, Bricklin, & Harris et al., 2006). Stress and burnout can be dealt with prophylactically when a commitment to personal and professional self-disclosure within a consultative relationship is made.

CONCLUSION

This chapter has presented a brief overview of selected ethical issues that often arise in the consulting psychologist's work with collegiate student-athletes. Commonly occurring ethical dilemmas involving informed consent, confidentiality, boundary issues, multiple relationships, and professional competence were examined within the framework of the unique environment of collegiate athletics. It is incumbent upon the psychologist working with collegiate athletes to have a firm grounding of education and training in sport psychology in order to provide effective psychological services to this population. This includes being thoroughly familiar with the ethical codes of both the American Psychological Association and the Association of Applied Sport Psychology in order to anticipate, prevent, and quickly resolve difficulties that may surface due to the high-stress world of this area of practice. Finally, as in any area of professional practice, psychologists working in the world of collegiate athletics are encouraged to develop a strong network of knowledgeable colleagues with whom to consult and seek needed support.

REFERENCES

American Psychological Association. (2002). Ethical principles of psychologists and code of conduct. *American Psychologist, 57*(12), 1060–1073.

Andersen, M. B. (2000). Beginnings: Intakes and the initiation of relationships. In. M. B. Andersen (Ed.), *Doing sport psychology* (pp. 3–16). Champaign, IL: Human Kinetics.

Andersen, M. B., Van Raalte, J. L., & Brewer, B. W. (2001). Sport psychology service delivery: Staying ethical while keeping loose. *Professional Psychology: Research & Practice, 32,* 12–18.

Association for Applied Sport Psychology. (n.d.). *Governing documents-Ethics code.* Retrieved from http://applied-sportpsych.org/about/ethics/code

Dielman, M., Drude, K., Ellenwood, A. E., Heinlen, K. T., Imar, T., Lichstein, M., & Asch, P. S. (2009). Telepsychology guidelines. *Ohio Psychological Association.* Retrieved from http://www.ohpsych.org/psychologists/files/2011/06/OPATelepsychologyGuidelines41710.pdf

Etzel, E. F. (Ed.). (2009). *Counseling and psychological services for college student-athletes.* Morgantown, WV: Fitness Information Technology.

Etzel, E. F., & Watson. J. C. (2007). Ethical challenges for psychological consultations in intercollegiate athletics. *Journal of Clinical Sport Psychology, 1,* 304–317.

Grayson, P. A., & Meilman, P. W. (Eds.). (2006). *College mental health practice.* New York, NY: Routledge/Taylor & Francis Group.

Koocher, G. P., & Keith-Spiegel, P. (2008). *Ethics in psychology and the mental health professions: Standards and cases* (3rd ed.). New York, NY: Oxford University Press.

Ohio Psychological Association. (2011). Telepsychology guidelines. Retrieved from http://www.ohpsych.org/psychologists/files/2011/06/OPATelepsychologyGuidelines41710.pdf

Petrie, T. A., Hankes, D. M., & Denson, E. L. (2010). *A student-athlete's guide to success: Peak performance in class and life.* Boston, MA: Wadsworth.

Stapleton, A. B., Hankes, D. M., Hays, K. F., & Parham, W. B. (2010). Ethical dilemmas in sport psychology: A dialogue on the unique aspects impacting practice. *Professional Psychology: Research & Practice, 41,* 143–152.

Watson II, J. C., Clement, D., Harris, B., Leffingwell, T. R., & Hurst, J. (2006). Teacher-practitioner multiple role issues in sport psychology. *Ethics and Behavior, 16,* 41–60.

Watson II, J. C., Lubker, J., & Zakrajsek, R. (2006, August). Ethical issues of Internet use in practice of sport psychology. Presented at the 2006 annual convention of the American Psychological Association, New Orleans, LA.

CHAPTER 5

ETHICAL ISSUES IN PROFESSIONAL SPORT
Leonard D. Zaichkowsky and Mark Stonkus

INTRODUCTION

Although the field of sport and performance psychology is a relatively new professional field, the issue of *ethics* has always been a concern. The Association for the Advancement of Applied Sport Psychology (AAASP), now known as AASP ("advancement" dropped), the largest professional sport psychology association in the world, adopted a code of ethics in 1994 that was modeled after the 1992 American Psychological Association (APA) Code of Ethics. However, journal articles and book chapters that discussed unique ethical issues in sport, performance and exercise contexts were slow to follow. A chapter published by Whelan, Meyers, and Elkins (2002) and a paper by Anderson, Van Raalte, and Brewer (2001), appear to be examples of early written text on the topic. Etzel and his colleagues at West Virginia University (Etzel, Watson, & Zizzi, 2004) have probably contributed the most to sensitizing practicing sport psychologists about ethics, both with their publications and conference presentations. In recent years, several outstanding papers have been written on ethics in the broad world of sport, performance, and exercise psychology (Aoyagi & Portenga, 2010; Brown & Cogan, 2006; Etzel & Watson, 2007; Haberl & Peterson, 2006; Moore, 2003). Yet, literature specifically targeting ethical issues in professional sport appear to be non-existent or in short supply. The Haberl and Peterson (2006) paper that dealt with psychological consulting in the Olympic Games comes close to portraying the many ethical issues present in professional sport. Lane (2009) recently published an excellent paper on the ethical issues surrounding work in the world of professional boxing. Nevertheless, ethical concerns in the sport of boxing are perhaps in a "league of their own," not only because of the long and rather tarnished history of the boxing culture but also because the end goal is to "do harm to your opponent." This latter issue prompted an excellent paper by Wildes (1995) entitled "Is Boxing Ethically Supportable?" As such, psychological consultants in this professional sport have numerous ethical dilemmas with which to contend.

In this chapter, the authors identify and discuss selected, central ethical issues for sport and exercise psychology consultants working in the arena of professional sport. The authors have a combined forty plus years of experience working with professional athletes and team personnel from the National Basketball Association, National Football League, Major League Baseball, National Hockey League, Major League Soccer, and World Cup of Soccer.

THE WORLD OF PROFESSIONAL SPORT

Professional sport is rather unique in that it involves not only sport, but is also big business: It is a form of popular entertainment. As such, there are those who would say, "There are no ethics in professional sport." It is understandable that such a statement might be made when one reads or hears about issues like cheating as exemplified by the New England Patriots' "spying" on opponents' defensive signals in 2007 and the more recent New Orleans Saints 2012 "bounty scandal," the use of performance enhancing drugs (e.g., baseball's Barry Bonds and Roger Clemens), and other unethical or illegal activities. However, our experience tells us that there are more ethical and moral athletes and professional organizations than not and that they take ethical issues concerning all their employees seriously. Indeed, there are numerous ethical concerns, issues, and dilemmas for psychologists and other sport psychology professionals working in the various areas of professional sport (e.g., personal counseling, mental skills training, team development, talent identification, substance abuse intervention).

Each chapter in this book suggests in some way that sport and performance psychology is somewhat different from traditional clinical and counseling psychology contexts—this is correct. Rather than being exclusively about DSM-IV diagnosis and therapeutic intervention, performance consulting often follows an educational and consulting model of which there is no "gold standard" or generally accepted model (Anderson, 2002). This is the case when working for a professional sport organization (PSO) either as a consultant or a full-time employee. Although there are instances when clinical issues arise and the athlete is in need of therapy, these instances are relatively rare in our combined decades of consulting in professional sport.

Haberl and Peterson (2006) and Werthner and Coleman (2009) described their experiences as sport psychology consultants for the United States and Canadian Olympians respectively. These authors specifically addressed some of the unique ethical issues that arise during international competition that appear to be quite similar to those encountered in the professional sport ranks. Like sport psychology professionals working with Olympic athletes, sport psychology consultants with professional sports teams regularly travel with the team, spend a considerable amount of time with athletes, coaches and support staff, so they often establish long-term, rather close relationships. Accordingly, traditional boundaries between sport psychology consultants and clients are sometimes difficult to maintain. While travelling, one is in close proximity to the athlete, either on the plane, bus, or hotel, eating meals, attending practices and games, facilitating meetings, as well as working with athletes and coaches. Consultation, rather than occurring in the office for the standard 50-minute hour, is typically brief and may take place in a restaurant, the weight room, on a practice field courtside, or on ice (see Giges & Petitpas, 2000 for a discussion of brief contact interventions).

THE IMPORTANT ETHICAL ISSUES FOR PSYCHOLOGISTS IN PROFESSIONAL SPORTS

Many ethical challenges exist in this realm of SEP practice. Hankes and Baillie (2010), in discussing ethical issues in the care of collegiate and elite athletes, correctly pointed out that the "holy trinity" of ethical issues in sport psychology is: (1) competence, (2) confidentiality, and (3) multiple relationships. This trinity has considerable applicability to ethical work in professional sport, and will be discussed along with some discussion of title use as related to sport psychology practice.

Competence and Title Use

The original American Psychological Association "Ethical Principles of Psychologists and Code of Conduct" (1952) and most recently updated code of conduct (2010) have two standards that are particularly germane to this discussion. Those sections of the code are:

> *2.01 Boundaries of Competence. (a) psychologists provide services, teach, and conduct research with populations and in areas only within the boundaries of their competence, based on their education, training, supervised experience, consultation, study, or professional experience. (b) In those emerging areas in which generally recognized standards for preparatory training do not yet exist, psychologists nevertheless take reasonable steps to ensure the competence of their work and to protect clients, students, supervisees, research participants, organizational clients and others from harm.*

> *2.03 Maintaining Competence. Psychologists undertake ongoing efforts to develop and maintain competence.*

Since the emergence of the field of sport psychology there has been concern and controversy regarding the use of the title sport "psychologist" and the boundaries of competence practice (Nideffer, 1981). The central issue appears to center around how sport psychologists are trained and the issue of what is minimum practice competence in our field. At this point in time, there is not a generally agreed upon model of training in the field linked to at least minimal professional competence. AASP's Certification and APA Division 47s Proficiency in sport psychology models offer some useful guidance in these matters. Two basic training models appear to exist. One model of training is in the field of sport and exercise science where individuals primarily focus on developing expertise in the psychological factors affecting sport performance. The second model is training in traditional counseling or clinical/counseling psychology programs and developing an expertise or specialization in working with an "athlete" population. Arguments have been made in support of both training models. However, in North America and in other countries around the world, the practice of psychology and competencies associated with graduate level training in psychology programs are restricted—typically by state and provincial law. The use of the term psychologist is restricted, generally meaning that only those persons who are "licensed" or "credentialed" by states and/or provinces as psychologists can legally use the term. The debate over title use and just who is a competent sport psychologist continues to be controversial today.

SOME PROFESSIONAL SPORT PRACTICE ISSUES AND EXAMPLES

There appear to have been many instances where PSOs have employed licensed [sport] psychology professionals to assist the organization with performance or hired such professionals to assist with needs like talent identification testing prior to professional drafts in the NBA, NHL, NFL, or MLB. However, in some cases the practitioners, although credentialed, were sometimes 'out of their league' in terms of professional sport related competence. In those instances, their consultative, therapeutic, or testing competence did not match well with the professional sport environment or the organization. They appeared to not understand the 'culture' of professional sport and/or the particular sport with which they were working. The greatest asset of these sport psychology professionals may have been marketing skills rather than the skills mentioned above to identify outstanding talent or teach performance enhancement skills. Often the professionals came with a "clinical" vocabulary and skill set and as such failed to connect in a PSO with the athletes and coaches.

There also appear to be many instances in which "non-credentialed" sport psychology consultants have marketed themselves as sport psychologists who began work with PSOs, and similarly practiced outside their areas of professional competence and perhaps outside of practice and title use laws. Although these professionals may have understood the culture of sport and professional sport, they perhaps did not have the essential skills required of a more clinically trained, licensed psychologist. In these cases, the individuals appear to have earned terminal degrees in sport psychology but were not license eligible. How were they able to work in PSOs? Management officials in PSOs likely were not aware of and did not appear to care about credentialing, and assumed the competence of these consultants. It may also be true that many individuals practicing as sport psychologists were not aware of the legal, competence-linked restrictions concerning practice behaviors (e.g., interventions employed) and the use of the word "psychologist" in their title.

Case 1. One of the early cases (1992) that highlighted these issues is the case of Dr. Jack Llewellyn. Llewellyn received some notoriety for his work with the Atlanta Braves baseball team and in particular, All-Star pitcher John Smoltz. But soon this work came to the attention of the Georgia Psychology Licensing Board and claims were made that Llewellyn was practicing as a psychologist without proper credentials. Writing in the Atlanta Constitution, Joe Strauss observed that Llewellyn believed that he should be exempt from psychology practice laws because he was practicing sport psychology and that he did not think he was doing anything wrong (Strauss, 1992). Llewellyn graduated from Florida State University in 1972 with a PhD in physical education. His concentration was sports science in sports psychology.

Decades later there are still persons who appear to have "no idea they are doing anything wrong" because they do not know that they cannot use the term psychologist (regardless of education, training and sport competence) unless they have a license to practice. This is true not only in Canada and the United States but also in numerous other countries around the world. Referring to oneself as a psychologist or sport psychologist without proper credentials remains a contentious ethical issue today which will probably continue for some time. Section 5.01 of The American Psychological Association Ethical Principles of Psychologists and Code of Conduct (2010) states that psychologists must not make fraudulent or deceptive statements concerning: (1) their training, (2) their degrees, (3) their credentials, (4) their affiliations, (5) their services, (6) their scientific or clinical success of their services, (7) their fees, and (8) their publications or research findings.

Case 2. The following situation is a more modern hypothetical illustration of the ethical issues associated with a recent area of popular sport and exercise psychology practice. This case involves the use of bio/neurofeedback in work with athletes in the professional sport realm.

According to their media guide and website, a PSO has a "consulting sport psychologist" on staff. Although this person has a terminal degree, the consultant is not licensed to practice psychology or any other allied mental health field (e.g., counseling, social work, psychiatry) in any U.S. state or Canadian province. The general manager of the PSO has just read several magazine articles on the use of biofeedback and EEG neurofeedback for performance enhancement of athletes in a number of sports. He asks the consulting sport psychologist if she could bring this "cutting edge" technology to the PSO. The PSO provides the funding to purchase the necessary technology. The consultant has apparently read these same magazine articles. Because she is somewhat familiar with the concepts and application of bio/neurofeedback, but without extensive formal training, she assures the general manager she would research the industry for appropriate equipment. Subsequently, the consulting sport psychology professional begins training the team's athletes for recovery training, stress management, and focus control. Some questions arise when one considers the foregoing situation, such as:

1. Is there possibly an ethical issue in this case with use of the "psychologist" title?

2. Is there possibly an ethical issue in this case with practicing beyond one's training and competence?

3. If these are in fact ethical concerns, how might the ethical issues be resolved and by whom?

Consultants working in PSOs need to continuously upgrade their knowledge base and clinical skills (e.g., in bio/neurofeedback) through continuing education workshops, coursework, supervision/mentoring, professional study, etc. This knowledge base is not only from the field of psychology but also from the applied sport sciences in general. In the world of professional sport, practitioners are arguably working with and for some of the "best in the world." This means that the practitioners also need to be the best they can be. The expertise literature makes it quite clear that regardless of domain, one needs to prepare for and deliberately practice skills to be proficient (Ericsson, 1996; Skovholt, Ronnestad, & Jennings, 1997). To be competent, one needs to understand the issues (knowledge of theory), be aware of the context (sport), demonstrate skill in application of this knowledge, and be able to effectively intervene to provide a desirable outcome for the athlete.

Confidentiality

As sport psychology professionals, confidentiality is often seen as the cornerstone of much of our work in the realms of teaching, research, and consulting (Oliver, 2012). However, it is a particularly constant challenge in the environment of professional sport. Physicians, physical therapists, athletic trainers, and psychologists regularly struggle with confidentiality and privacy issues in this milieu. The first author of this chapter has always tried to "fly below the radar" as a psychologist in a PSO. However, professional sport and its participants are under incredible media scrutiny. For example, nowhere is there more of a media "paparazzi" environment than in the World Cup of Soccer. But, it is also true that most professional team sports in North America have a "sensation seeking" and "investigative" media and as such it is nearly impossible for a sport psychologist not to be observed while in the work environment. When players are not able to play, league rules will often mandate explanations, and oftentimes it is easy to identify the individuals. In some cases, vague descriptions can be used, such as "lower body injury" or "upper body injury." PSOs regularly remind their health service providers about confidentiality issues, but these issues are always a challenge to maintain. Confidentiality within a professional club is also generally emphasized. However, different rules apply depending upon whether the health issue is physical (e.g., injured knee), or if there is a mental health or other psychological issue. Athletes who are injured physically enter the training or therapy room with teammates present and do not care that others see them receiving "therapy."

On the other hand, sport psychology consultants usually operate with very different ground rules. A player with performance psychology or other personal concerns would not likely consider talking to a sport psychologist in an open training room-like environment. Mental health issues are never referred to as "upper body injuries." Nor are mild traumatic brain injuries (i.e., concussions) referred to as an upper body injury. Even the teaching of "performance enhancement" skills is difficult in an open environment (such as the gymnasium, on the edge of the field or ice), in part because of the general perception of what psychologists do—deliver mental health services to rather crazy or somehow weak people.

Much like Olympic team sports, in professional team sports (Haberl & Peterson, 2006; Werthner & Coleman, 2009), performance consultants are constantly navigating confidentiality issues and challenges. As noted above, the helping environments are frequently dissimilar to those of traditional counseling and clinical psychology (i.e., consultation services delivered in a private office for the standard 50-minute hour). As such, the wonderful advice provided to "traditional" psychologists by authors such as Campbell, Vasquez, Behnke, and Kinscherff (2010), and Koocher and Keith-Spiegel (1998) serve only as general guidelines for sport psychology professionals in a professional sport milieu. In traditional counseling or clinical psychology, the issue of confidentiality is much less difficult to harness than it is in a PSO.

Consider some examples from PSO practice. Whenever entering into a consulting agreement or full-time position with a PSO, one must make it clear to management that the content of meetings with players must remain confidential and clarify why this is so important to effective work. Even if general management understands confidentiality, when they want answers to specific questions about athletes, confidentiality often has a different meaning for them. In other words, "tell me but I will not share this with anyone and for sure the athlete will not know the source of this information." Nevertheless, it is quite common for upper management or the coaching staff to inquire about how the meetings are going or how particular athletes are doing. Unlike the orthopedic surgeon who can be completely upfront with a diagnosis or a report on advances in recovery, a psychologist's response is often quite vague, followed with a reminder of the importance of keeping the trust of the player and team and not violating any confidential agreements. It is important, though, that as sport psychology professionals, we do not hide under the cloak of confidentiality whenever difficult situations arise. Again, reminding management of this issue and impressing upon them that saying too much about a player and certain issues not in the public domain truly can only damage and perhaps end the trusting relationship that took some time to establish in the first place. There are also times when it may be prudent to ask an athlete if it would be okay to discuss certain situations with coaches and upper management and why this may be useful to the person. If the athlete is amenable to such a discussion, it is prudent to have the client sign a release of information form, and to document this release of information.

A second example of confidentiality that could possibly go astray is when a consultant is working collaboratively with a full sport science team (i.e., strength and conditioning coach, dietician, skills coach, physician). Historically and professionally, these professionals feel comfortable sharing all kinds of information about a given athlete. This practice differs significantly from what sport psychology professionals believe and do. However, when psychological or mental health issues come to the surface and need to be discussed, quick decisions must be made about what, if anything, can or cannot be shared with these professional peers. Experience often allows one to navigate this difficult terrain by creatively diverting questions and protecting the private information one has concerning one's clients.

Before concluding this section on confidentiality, the authors present the reader with a hypothetical, but realistic confidentiality dilemma. The case involves a professional golfer and the use of performance enhancing drugs (PEDs).

A professional golfer sought the services of a sport psychology professional as a means of optimizing his golf performance. During one of their sessions, the golfer revealed that he has been using a performance enhancing drug which is banned from use by the golf governing body. A PED is a substance that is considered to provide a competitive advantage to a golfer's play by increasing strength, speed, power, and recovery, while decreasing fatigue, anxiety/nervousness, and injury. As an aside, this example is particularly interesting because it involves a sport in which there are few if any referees or umpires during game play. Instead, golfers are essentially required to police themselves, and often find themselves challenged to report rule violations on themselves during their rounds. The consequence for breaking a rule in a given round can be as simple as a one-stroke penalty. However, PED use, if detected, carries penalties ranging from disqualification to single-year, multi-year, and even lifetime bans from the sport for repeat offenders. Golfers are subject to random drug testing during and outside of tournament play at any given time, without warning or advanced notice. Given the extent of such consequences on a golfer's career, as well as the collateral damage of loss of earnings, credentials/ranking, and reputation, it becomes clear that the risk of using a PED is severe.

The golfer in this example did not test positive; rather, he chose to self-report his PED use to his sport psychology consultant As a result, the onus of the dilemma now fell on the psychologist to ensure an ethical course of action. Even though the golfer sought services for improved sport performance, his revelation brought this case to an entirely different level. The consultant had to continue with the focus of the sessions in assisting the golfer with the mental training skills to improve his performance, but he then had to also consider and address the use of PEDs.

One option for the psychologist at that time would have been the temptation to consider this revelation as worthy of remaining confidential, by rationalizing it as being non-threatening to the golfer and to others. The psychologist may fear losing this high-profile client, or also be afraid that future clients may avoid his/her services if this generates the reputation of him/her being a "whistle-blower." In such a circumstance, the psychologist is thinking more about his/her benefit than that of the client. And if the decision is made to not do anything additional with this information, the psychologist is willfully risking the golfer's welfare by dismissing him to an environment that will indeed punish him if his use is detected. This type of risk should never be assumed, regardless of the potential loss for the consulting psychologist. As the reader will agree, this is a challenging situation.

The American Psychological Association (2010) mandates that all psychologists adhere to a strict ethical code of conduct, one which stipulates that the first guiding principle of all psychologists is "beneficence and nonmaleficence" ("Principle A"): to strive to maximize benefit and minimize harm to a client. In this case, the sport psychology consultant is not only faced with the task of providing benefit to the golfer via mental skills training for optimal performance, but now must also assess and perhaps minimize harm resulting from the client's PED use. To do this, the sport psychology consultant must assess the potential levels of harm associated with such use; and such harm is not merely related to the possible sanctions from the golf organization if the golfer tests positive. There are also many substantial known and undetermined health complications associated with many of the substances banned from competition, and as a result, the golfer may also be threatened by significant health risks.

This is where the issue of competence once again comes into play. If the practitioner is experienced working with substance/drug use and abuse cases, then he may be able to provide counseling services to the golfer to promote the abstinence and healthy recovery from PED use. If the sport psychology consultant has been practicing mostly as a performance sport psychology consultant with limited or no clinical expertise, then he has the ethical obligation to consult with a competent colleague and likely refer the golfer to a more qualified specialist in treating drug use. The golfer may be reluctant to seek this type of clinical evaluation and intervention; however, the fact that he disclosed his PED use requires that the consulting sport psychology consultant take necessary measures to protect the client from harm. This must be explained to the golfer in detail, and may actually be received better than one might think, as the golfer could use this opportunity to receive clinical consultation as a means of resolving his use of performance enhancing drugs, while avoiding the risks of testing positive and incurring the resulting consequences. It may require a hiatus from competition to allow for the course of treatment, and to cleanse his body and mind from such behaviors. However, his return to golf may be far more productive than it was prior to the intervention, as the removal of a guilty conscience may actually result in increased performance, which was the goal for his seeking the support from a sport psychologist in the first place.

Multiple Relationships and Boundary Issues in Professional Sport

As mentioned earlier in this chapter, working full-time as a sport psychology consultant often results in professional boundary issues. Practitioners in this setting constantly interact with athletes, professional staff members, coaches, and management both at home and on the road. Consultants and these individuals travel together, eat together, and sometimes may room together. This environment allows one to truly understand the dynamics of the PSO, and how to optimally intervene when necessary. However, at the same time, potential ethical dilemmas exist regarding professional boundaries.

Multiple relationship issues as defined in traditional counseling settings are commonplace in professional sport. The athlete is your client but perhaps not your only client. For example, the consultant who has become "one of the team" over time may be tempted or become somewhat of a friend to athletes and staff. Others you serve in a PSO may include management, coaches, sports science staff, and professional scouts—perhaps even the ownership group and their family. Boundaries indeed get blurry, so one must always be on guard. Consultants need to choose words carefully when discussing not only individual athletes, but also professional staff members and perhaps others noted above. It is also important that one not damage the trusting relationship of athletes, and it is equally important that one not lose the trust and respect of professional colleagues such as physicians, trainers and others in the PSO.

Years of consulting in elite and professional sport have enabled the first author to witness questionable handling of matters considered to be boundary issues that have been a challenge. Questions posed by consultants include:

1) Am I placing myself in a position of perceived "power?"

2) Is anyone susceptible to "exploitation?"

3) Am I losing my sense of objectivity?

4) Am I less competent because of how I deal with this situation?

5) Is there potential for harm?

Fortunately, the answer is frequently "no." However when a "yes" comes up, it is essential to quickly try to change the situation so that one does not lose the crucial aspect of organizational trust.

FINAL COMMENTS ON ETHICS AND THE MATTER OF INTEGRITY

Working in the arena of professional sport necessarily brings questions about competence, confidentiality, and boundary issues. However, what truly matters is having clear professional core values and integrity that translate into ethically sound professional behavior. Barbara Kiplinger (2010), in a wonderful treatise on what integrity is, writes this: "integrity is a personal choice that is an uncompromising and predictably consistent commitment to honor moral, ethical, spiritual values and principles" (p. 12). Kiplinger further writes that living with integrity requires us to be aware of and incorporate the values of empathy, sympathy, compassion, and honesty into our daily work habits. If we listen, understand and share the feelings of others (empathy); if we can begin to have not only feelings toward others but a true regard and concern for them (sympathy); if we have the burning desire to help others (compassion); and if we are sincere, morally upright, and virtuous (honesty), we will have succeeded as psychologists/sport scientists in a difficult sport environment—professional sport. The American Psychological Association lists "Integrity" as "Principle C" in its code of ethics (American Psychological Association, 2010). The importance of a sport psychologist/scientist to remain honest, accurate, and credible cannot be understated. If we are ever tempted to misrepresent ourselves to our constituents, we not only break the ethical code governing us, but we jeopardize the wellness of existing and future clients who depend on us to provide them with highly specialized and valuable support that is not easily found. If we do not respect our field and the safe transfer of our expertise, how will they?

We must be constantly vigilant or as Watson and Cowan (2009) stated, "develop ethical antennae" while working in a professional sport environment. Maturity of judgment typically develops with experience; however, it is crucial that we maintain a network of supervisors/professional colleagues that one can call on to discuss unique issues related to ethical behavior. Consult with your colleagues and document why certain actions were taken. Develop awareness of potential ethical issues, help your clients in the PSO, respect their dignity, do no harm, and be true to your core values. Professional sport organizations will only benefit from this form of integrity and professional behavior.

REFERENCES

Anderson, M. B., Van Raalte, J. L., & Brewer, B. W. (2001). Sport psychology service delivery: Staying ethical while keeping loose. *Professional Psychology: Research & Practice, 32,* 12–18.

American Psychological Association. (1952). *Ethical standards for psychologists.* Washington, DC: American Psychological Association.

American Psychological Association. (1992). Ethical principles of psychologists and code of conduct. *American Psychologist, 47,* 1597–1611.

American Psychological Association. (2002). Ethical principles of psychologists and code of conduct. *American Psychologist, 57,* 1060–1073.

American Psychological Association. (2010). *Ethical principles of psychologists and code of conduct.* Washington, DC: American Psychological Association.

Anderson, M. (2002). Comprehensive sport psychology services. In J. Van Raalte & B. Brewer (Eds.), *Exploring sport and exercise psychology, 2nd ed.* (pp. 13–24.) Washington, DC: American Psychological Association.

Aoyagi, M. W., & Portenga, S. T. (2010). The role of positive ethics and virtues in the context of sport and performance psychology service delivery. *Professional Psychology: Research and Practice, 41,* 253–259.

Association for Applied Sport Psychology. (1994). Ethics code: AASP ethical principles and standards. Retrieved from http://appliedsportpsych.org

Brown, J., & Cogan, K. (2006). Ethical clinical practice and sport psychology: When two worlds collide. *Ethics and Behavior, 16,* 15–24.

Campbell, L., Vasquez, M., Behnke, S., & Kinscherff, R. (2010). *APA ethics code commentary and case illustrations.* Washington, DC. American Psychological Association.

Ericsson, A. E. (Ed.). (1996). *The road to excellence: The acquisition of expert performance in the arts and sciences, sports, and games.* Mahwah, NJ: Erlbaum.

Etzel, E., Watson, J., & Zizzi, S. (2004). A Web-based survey of AAASP member ethical beliefs and behaviors in the new millennium. *Journal of Applied Sport Psychology, 16,* 236–251.

Etzel, E., & Watson, J. (2007). Ethical considerations for psychological consultations in intercollegiate athletics. *Journal of Clinical Sport Psychology, 1*, 304–317.

Giges, B., & Petitpas, A. (2000). Brief contact interventions in sport psychology. *The Sport Psychologist, 14*, 176–187.

Haberl, P., & Peterson, K. (2006). Olympic-size ethical dilemmas: Issues and challenges for sport psychology consultants on the road and at the Olympic Games. *Ethics & Behavior, 16*, 25–40.

Hankes, D., & Baillie, P. (2010). Fear and loathing in Big Sky: Ethical issues in the care of collegiate and elite athletes. Paper presented at the annual meeting of the Big Sky Sport Psychology Counseling Group. Big Sky, Montana.

Kiplinger, B. (2010). *Integrity: Doing the right thing for the right reason.* Montreal, Quebec: McGill-Queens University Press.

Koocher, G., & Keith-Spiegel, P. (1998). *Ethics in psychology: Professional standards and cases* (2nd ed.). New York, NY: Oxford University Press.

Lane, A. (2009). A profession of violence or a high contact sport? Ethical issues working in professional boxing. In R. Schinke (Ed.), *Contemporary sport psychology* (pp. 253–261). New York, NY: Nova Sciences Publishers, Inc.

Moore, Z. (2003). Ethical dilemmas in sport psychology: Discussion and recommendations for practice. *Professional Psychology: Research and Practice, 34*(6), 601–610.

Nideffer, R. (1981). Ethical standards for sport psychologists. In R. M. Nideffer (Ed.), *The ethics and practice of applied sport psychology* (pp.9–16). Ithaca, NY: Movement Publications.

Oliver, J. (2010). Ethical practice in sport psychology: Challenges for the real world. In S. Hanrahan & M. Andersen (Eds.), *Routledge handbook of applied sport psychology: A comprehensive guide for students and practitioners* (pp. 60–68). London, UK & New York, NY: Routledge.

Skovholt, T. M., Ronnestad, M. H., & Jennings, L. (1997). Searching for expertise in counseling, psychotherapy, and professional psychology. *Educational Psychology Review, 9*, 361–369.

Strauss, J. (1992, January 1). Llewellyn plans to meet with state authorities, continues work with Braves. *Atlanta Constitution.*

Watson II, J., & Cowan, M. (2009). The ethical issues involved with the care of collegiate and elite athletes – Decision making made easier. Presented at the 2009 Big Sky Sport Psychology Conference. Big Sky, MT.

Werthner, P., & Coleman, J. (2009). Sport psychology consulting with Canadian Olympic athletes and coaches: Values and ethical considerations. In R. Schinke (Ed.), *Contemporary sport: Contemporary psychology* (pp. 233–251). New York, NY: Nova Sciences Publishers, Inc.

Wildes, K. W. (1995). Is boxing ethically supportable? In R.C. Cantu (Ed.), *Boxing and medicine* (pp.117–128). Champaign, Illinois: Human Kinetics.

Zaichkowsky, L. D. (1975, October), Combating stress: What about relaxation training and biofeedback? *Movement,* 309–312.

Zaichkowsky, L. (2009). A case for a new sport psychology: Applied psychophysiology and fMRI neuroscience. In R. Schinke (Ed.), *Contemporary sport psychology* (pp. 21–32). New York, NY: Nova Sciences Publishers, Inc.

Zaichkowsky, L. D., & O'Neill, D. (2011). Biofeedback applications in sports medicine. In L. Micheli (Ed.), *Encyclopedia of sports medicine* (pp. 161–163). Thousand Oaks, CA: Sage Publications.

CHAPTER 6

FIVE RING FEVER: ETHICAL CONSIDERATIONS WHEN CONSULTING WITH OLYMPIC ATHLETES

Mark W. Aoyagi and Steven T. Portenga

INTRODUCTION

It is the largest stage in the world, in front of the biggest audience ever simultaneously watching. You have dedicated the prime years of your life to preparing for this moment that only happens once every four years. Although you have delivered your performance thousands of times leading up to the Olympics, everything surrounding your event is telling you this is something different, bigger, and more important than anything you have done prior. You recognize that your task is the same, and that giving in to the exaggerated narrative surrounding your performance will only hurt you. The challenge is to remain true to your training, your preparation, and your routine, while allowing for the necessary adaptations. Anyone who has consulted with Olympic athletes likely relates to this scenario, having assisted in preparing athletes to succeed in this environment. Yet, how many of these consultants have considered that the same pressures they are attempting to help athletes manage are also exerting their force on the consultant? Consultants must regulate themselves at an Olympics or working with Olympic athletes in many ways similar to how they help others manage the scenario above. If consultants do not properly cope with the pressure, they are likely to succumb to Five Ring Fever—an intense desire to be a part of the Olympics with symptoms including impaired judgment, over identification, self-interest, and self-aggrandizement. Our hope is that all consultants of Olympians answer in the affirmative to the question posed above, and have also engaged in self-reflection and peer consultation on the issues we will be addressing in this chapter: the context of consulting with Olympic athletes, multiple relationships and boundary issues, confidentiality, and self-regulation.

CONTEXT OF CONSULTING WITH OLYMPIC ATHLETES

In many ways, the context of consulting with Olympic athletes is similar to working with any other elite performer. And yet the differences are important enough to understand with respect to ethics. Ethical practice cannot be described devoid of the context within which the sport, exercise and performance practitioner is practicing (Fay, 2002). Behavior that may be evaluated as unethical practice in one context may not be so in another, to the extent that not engaging in this behavior may be considered withholding quality care. Advanced ethical practice requires the practitioner to go beyond a list of prescribed behaviors and integrate ethical principles into their clinical decision making (Aoyagi & Portenga, 2010; Knapp & VanDeCreek, 2006). Because working with Olympic athletes and at the Olympics represents a unique context, aspects of it that influence clinical and ethical decision making will be briefly shared here.

Understanding the context within which Olympic preparation takes place starts with an understanding of the multiple stakeholders present within this system. In addition to the usual suspects (i.e., athletes, coaches, support staff, and agents), you also have the National Governing Bodies (NGBs) and the United States Olympic Committee (USOC). Within both of these organizations there are an assortment of people with influence and varying levels of control over each Olympic sport. All of these people have their own personal reasons for being involved in their respective sport, many of which can run counter to ensuring the athletes' success. Imagine an NGB administrator giving his mistress a credential for the Olympic Village instead of the sports medicine team member to whom it was assigned! If sport or performance practitioners intend to work for an NGB directly, they must be aware of the stakeholders with the most influence and their agendas in order to avoid being caught in the middle (Fuqua, Newman, Simpson, & Choi, 2008). Such a situation can exert pressure on practitioners to make decisions that allow them to maintain their connection with the NGB, but these decisions may limit the effectiveness of the performance psychology services that are being delivered.

The ongoing training and competition environment of Olympic sports presents another unique aspect of the context. Olympic sports operate over a quadrennium (four-year cycle). NGBs and athletes must plan and wait for four years to reach the Olympic Games. This leads to long periods of build-up, interspersed with intense, high-pressure performances (e.g., World Championships, US Trials). Working over a quadrennium allows for a great deal of development to occur between Olympic Games. However, the delay between Olympics also creates a unique pressure in qualifying and competing at the Games (Vernacchia & Henschen, 2008). Once at the Games, McCann (2008) has described how any issue that creates stress or a distraction can have a negative impact on the athlete's performance.

Operating on a quadrennial cycle also influences the context in other ways. In many Olympic sports, the actual Olympic team is not decided until the sport's trials before the Games. In a sport like track and field, the trials may be held as close as three weeks prior to the Games. Thus, performance psychology services must target a large group of athletes to ensure that those who do make the team have had the necessary time to learn and develop. Waiting until the team is selected may not provide enough time to be of assistance. Another impact of the quadrennial cycle is that many NGBs do not have a permanent training site for their athletes. This results in a great deal of travel for the athletes, coaches, and sport psychology practitioners. This distance and travel influences the quality, quantity, and nature of the sport/performance psychology practitioner's work. In summary, sport/performance psychology practitioners must be aware of the pressure and expectations that derive from the politics, quadrennial preparation, pressure, and travel that come with preparing athletes for the Olympic Games.

COMMON ETHICAL ISSUES WHEN CONSULTING WITH OLYMPIC ATHLETES

In general, the uniqueness of consulting with Olympic athletes does not greatly differ from similarly elite athletes. The context of the Olympics is where uniqueness enters, and as detailed in the previous section, the differences are primarily due to intensity rather than a complete qualitative shift. The typical ethical issues can also become more challenging if one is hired by an NGB instead of an individual athlete. Therefore, the ethical issues common to consulting with Olympic athletes are similar to those experienced when consulting with other elite athletes; there is simply a greater intensity to them. The three selected areas of ethical challenge to be covered in this section are: 1) multiple relationships and boundary issues, 2) confidentiality, and 3) self-regulation.

Multiple Relationships and Boundary Issues
Although challenges related to multiple relationships have been identified in the sport psychology literature (e.g., Andersen, Van Raalte, & Brewer, 2001), this is a prime example of increasing the intensity of the challenge when working with Olympic athletes. Primarily, this is due to the significant amount of time a consultant will likely spend embedded with a team during training camps and international competitions including the Olympics. Because Olympic teams generally spend very little time together, they often attempt to accomplish a sense of team by holding periodic, intense times of team training and bonding. Frequently, Olympic teams hold these sessions in remote locations where the team will be forced to come together with limited outside distractions. Thus, when sport psychology practitioners travel on these trips, they are expected to be part of the team. This means practitioners share rooms with other members of the support staff, attend practices and team meetings, participate in coaching and medical staff meetings, eat meals with the team, and socialize with the team (Haberl & Peterson, 2006). Multiple relationships and boundary crossings (APA Standard 3.05; APA, 2002) are not only inevitable, they are essential to effective work.

Clearly, the emphasis for consultants is on establishing, communicating, and maintaining appropriate boundaries. This suggestion is consistent with both APA Standard 3.05 (Multiple Relationships) and AASP Standard 9 (Multiple Relationships), which make clear that multiple relationships are not unethical when they cannot reasonably be expected to cause impairment or harm. Still, the language of both codes also emphasizes the increased risk, and thus increased awareness, a consultant must have in situations where boundary crossings exist. Therefore, it is necessary for consultants to recognize prior to entering into these situations what their boundary limits will be. While some aspects of this decision are individual and personal, it is clear from the codes that the needs of the clients are paramount. Ultimately, clients must be protected from harm and interacted with in such a way as to reasonably ensure the effectiveness of the consultant. Haberl and Peterson (2006) discussed their belief that talking about their personal lives was key in building trust and allowing them to be effective.

Personal interactions such as eating meals, hanging out in the sports medicine clinic, riding buses, and socializing with the team are examples of boundary crossings (Gutheil & Gabbard, 1998). Boundary crossings are instances where the practitioner-client relationship may be different from the traditional therapeutic relationship, but are helpful, constructive, and clearly not harmful. Boundary crossings are differentiated from boundary violations where deviations from the normal professional relationship are likely harmful or exploitative of clients (Gutheil & Gabbard, 1998). This distinction between boundary crossings and boundary violations is useful when working with Olympic athletes, as this distinction provides one way to assess how and where to set boundaries.

Furthermore, when boundary crossings are made ethically, with the best interests of the client as the foremost consideration, they may actually reduce the likelihood of harm and potential exploitation. This is because carefully considered boundary crossings allow clients to see their consultants as people, which reduces the power differential between clients and consultants (Zur & Lazarus, 2002). Power differentials are a common component of clients' being exploited (Kitchener, 2000), and therefore reducing power differentials is thought to make clients more likely to speak out against any impropriety and correspondingly less likely to be taken advantage of. Additionally, the ability of clients to see consultants as people within their same environment allows opportunities for role modeling of appropriate relationships and professional comportment in informal settings (Helbok, 2003).

A slightly different, yet closely related, feature of multiple relationships is conflict of interest (APA Standard 3.06; APA, 2002). A conflict of interest occurs when a pre-existing relationship (personal, professional, or otherwise) could reasonably be expected to impair the consultant's effectiveness or result in harm or exploitation of the client (APA, 2002). Due to the multilayered aspects of the professional relationship when working with Olympic athletes, conflicts of interest are a necessary consideration when working with this population. As outlined in the context section, consultants may be hired by the NGB, coach, or an individual athlete. Regardless of who hires the consultant, effective work will often require building relationships with all of these and other (e.g., sports medicine) constituents (Fuqua et al., 2008). This situation is common in the military where psychologists are employees of the Department of Defense and also serving units and troops, and they have coined the phrase "dual agency" to describe this situation (Hines, Ader, Chang, & Rundell, 1998).

Dual agency differs from multiple relationships in that both roles in which the consultant is engaged are professional roles. For example, the consultant may be hired by the NGB to support the team, and is involved in a situation where there is a conflict between what the coach desires and what an athlete desires. Obviously this scenario presents an entirely different, and conceivably more complex, set of challenges than when a consultant is balancing a professional role (sport psychology consultant) and personal role (member of the performance team at dinner with the team). In dual agency dilemmas, the common refrain of "Who is the client?" is not sufficient, as all parties involved are clients (Newman, Robinson-Kurpius, &

Fuqua, 2002). The military literature (Johnson & Wilson, 1993; Kennedy & Johnson, 2009) provides three common approaches psychologists have taken when confronted with dual agency, and they are very informative for our work. The first is called the military manual approach, in which psychologists see their foremost duty as being to the military and thus adhere strictly to military law, even when in conflict with ethical standards. The inverse is the stealth approach, where ethical standards are valued over military law in situations where there is not an imminent risk of harm. Lastly, the best interest approach is when a sincere attempt is made to account for the best interests of all clients and agencies involved.

Clearly, the best interest approach is the method of choice. However, this is typically more easily implemented on paper than in the real world. The best interest approach requires excellent communication between the consultant and all clients and agencies, and a correspondingly high degree of trust. Also, confidentiality (APA Standard 4.01) becomes a large part of this process, and will be covered extensively in the next section. Fortunately, dual agency dilemmas are commonplace amongst the support staff of Olympic athletes, so while there may be issues specific to consultants, the athletes and coaches are intimately familiar with the demands of multiple agencies. Therefore, they are generally appreciative of consultants who are willing to acknowledge dual agency demands and include them in the process of working to resolve the resulting challenges.

A final issue we will address under multiple relationships is one that has been particularly vexing for the field of sport psychology: clinical work and performance work. In many ways, the cauldron of the Olympics simplifies this discussion: "At the Olympics, everything is a performance issue" (McCann, 2008, p. 267). When athletes have invested years of their life into an opportunity to perform that occurs once every four years, and the difference between success and failure (as defined by athletes, coaches, significant others, etc.) is often measured in milliseconds and millimeters, anything that can take away from optimal performance is a performance issue. Therefore, it is critical to be able to competently address both clinical and performance issues when working with Olympic athletes. Ideally, this would be accomplished by an individual consultant, but whether it is individually or part of a team of consultants it must be accounted for. Practitioners working with Olympic athletes who are not competent to work with clinical issues must have immediate access to a referral network of practitioners with clinical competency. At any major competition, competent clinicians should be available on site.

Confidentiality

Performance practitioners working with Olympic athletes, especially at international competitions, are often embedded as part of a team. Whether a sports medicine, sports science or support staff team, open communication and collaboration within this team is necessary in order to be the most effective in assisting the athletes. Yet psychologists trained in individual therapy are taught that client confidentiality means all information must be protected at all times. Performance practitioners that desire to remain a part of such a high performance system must find an ethical balance between the two extremes. Standard 4: Privacy and Confidentiality of the APA (2002) Ethics Code explains that psychologists have a primary obligation to protect confidential information. Allowing clients the freedom to talk about their experiences, thoughts, and emotions without fear of disclosure is vital to the process of psychotherapy (Bennett et al., 2006), having even been acknowledged by the United States Supreme Court (*Jaffee v. Redmond,* 1996). Violations of confidentiality may lead to embarrassment, a loss of trust, and disruption of the therapeutic alliance (Welfel, 2006). The APA (2002) Ethics Code does take into account the fact that in some settings there may be limits to confidentiality. For instance, if an institution provides an employee access to a psychologist, they may request information from that psychologist. Any limits to confidentiality and any possible use of client information should be discussed with the individual client as part of the informed consent process (APA Standard 3.10, 3.11, 4.02a, APA, 2002). Thus, limits to confidentiality are acceptable as long as they are communicated to the client as services begin.

When working with an NGB, whatever the decisions regarding the nature of confidentiality, they must be discussed with NGB administration, coaches (personal and/or national team), sports medicine staff, and athletes ahead of time (Fuqua et al., 2008; Sharkin, 1995). Likewise, the performance practitioner should discuss the expectations of the NGB regarding confidentiality before agreeing to any working relationship (APA Standard 3.11a, 4.02a; APA, 2002). When working as part of a support team, obtaining the athletes' consent for limited disclosure should be a goal of the performance practitioner. If services are mandated as a part of the athlete's participation, the performance practitioner needs to make certain to clarify the nature of the work and any limits to confidentiality (APA Standard 3.10c, 3.11a; APA, 2002). The performance psychologist should discuss with athletes the possibility of the psychologist talking to others about the individual athlete based on public information, ensuring that they will not disclose information revealed within sessions (APA Standard 10.01a; APA, 2002). It is also advisable to share with athletes the possibility of working with a teammate, especially one with whom the athlete may be competing for a spot on the team. If an athlete finds this out from someone other than the practitioner, it may jeopardize the working alliance (Sharkin, 1995). Thus, addressing these issues preemptively during the informed consent process may prevent the need for the performance practitioner to address these issues and struggle to maintain confidentiality later on.

It should be emphasized that any disclosure of information relating to an athlete should be done with consent, in a respectful manner and in a way that minimizes the details that are shared. Quite often the performance practitioner can make a recommendation that does not require a discussion of the details that led to the recommendation. However, this requires the appropriate character and fitness (discussed below) to make appropriate disclosures in a respectful manner (Aoyagi & Portenga, 2010; Johnson & Campbell, 2002, 2004; Newman, 1993). We must highlight that the need for collaboration is not a call for full disclosure or the complete abandonment of confidentiality.

CONFIDENTIALITY WITHIN A SYSTEM

When working with Olympic athletes, performance practitioners often work with or for an NGB. Psychologists that work with organizations introduce a confounding variable into the confidentiality equation. No longer is the therapeutic relationship a dyad, but now consists of a triad between the client, organization, and practitioner (Davies, 2000). The nature of being an internal or embedded consultant is different from providing one-on-one clinical therapy (e.g., Frisch, 2001; Gould, Tammen, Murphy, & May, 1989; Johnson, Ralph, & Johnson, 2005; Poczwardowski, 2001; Portenga & Aoyagi, 2007; Sharkin, 1995; Thompson & Ravizza, 1998; Yukelson, 2001).

Scholarship regarding confidentiality when working in a system highlights some of the added challenges. Spiegel (1990) points out that in some contexts, rigidly adhering to confidence can create negative consequences for the current and future clients. For example, when working with Olympic athletes, it is rare to be able to meet in confidential settings. Performance practitioners often talk to athletes in the hotel lobby, the stands, or other visible areas. One author, while working with a team in Berlin, had to meet with athletes in a beer garden, as it was the only quiet place in the hotel. Because of this visibility and because of the close nature of teams, it is often the case that other athletes, coaches, and administrators know who is working with the performance practitioner. In such cases where a person knows one of the psychologist's clients, refusing to acknowledge the relationship can harm trust between that person and the practitioner due to the practitioner's engaging in deceit (Spiegel, 1990). Certainly the performance practitioner can, and should, continue to educate people about the professional nature of confidentiality, yet despite being "correct," the end result may well be a strain in relationships. Additionally, in a closed system, the continual denial of working relationships by the performance psychologist may help perpetuate the stigma that is usually associated with psychology (Sharkin, 1995).

When working in a system, performance psychologists will quite often get connected to individual athletes by way of referral. Most referral sources are genuinely interested in the athlete's well-being and want to know that the services that were suggested to the athlete are actually helping (which often includes knowing that the athlete actually showed up). Referral sources need to be informed about the limits of confidentiality in advance of the onset of work with a referred person to hopefully avoid negative reactions. By refusing to share information with referral sources, performance practitioners risk being perceived as uncooperative, unhelpful, and of no use (Sharkin, Scappaticci, & Birky, 1995). Research on the referral process on college campuses has found that refusing to provide any information to the referrer about the student elicited anger, confusion, disgust, and fewer feelings of appreciation (Birky, Sharkin, Marin, & Scappaticci, 1998). When the performance practitioner has to continue to work with these referrers and rely on them for continued referrals, and perhaps continued employment, these emotions are not conducive to prolonged effective work (Schank & Skovholt, 2006). Clearly, working within a system creates challenges that the performance practitioner needs to learn how to navigate. One must not abandon confidentiality, yet a strict, rigid adherence to confidentiality when working for NGBs may violate the principle of beneficence (APA, 2002).

It is very different for the performance practitioner to talk generally about an athlete compared to revealing what an athlete has disclosed in session. When the performance practitioner is embedded within the high performance system, they have access to information about that athlete, the same as any other member of that system. The performance practitioner can talk about an athlete based on this publicly available information without breaking confidentiality, as long as they do not disclose that something has been discussed in session. Many practitioners interpret confidentiality as an admonishment to avoid any discussion of their client at all costs. However, absolute secrecy is not a requirement of Standard 4.01: Maintaining

Confidentiality. The APA Ethics Code prohibits discussion of what happens in session. In small communities, a practitioner may learn much about a client from others in the community that may be called "public knowledge" (Barnett & Yutrzenka, 2002; Kertesz, 2002; Kessler & Waehler, 2005). For example, a practitioner may hear details about an athlete's lack of confidence from a sports medicine provider, training partner, personal coach, and/or the athlete's social media outlets (Twitter, blog, etc.) before the athlete ever talks to the practitioner about this issue. The practitioner does not have to refrain from talking about a client completely if they stick to a discussion of what is publicly known. Even if the client shares some of this information in session, it is acceptable to discuss it as long as it is not revealed that it was discussed in session. In many small communities it would be highly awkward, inappropriate, and damaging to trust for the practitioner not to engage in a general discussion (Sears, 1990). Choosing not to do so may make it clear to others that the person being discussed is a client. Keeping track of what information is public knowledge carries risks, and requires certain character and fitness to do so appropriately (Johnson & Campbell, 2002). Talking about a client should only occur with great attention to APA Principle A: Beneficence and Nonmaleficence (2002).

The USOC's Sport Performance Division has adopted the philosophy that high performance support services should be: (a) coach driven, (b) athlete centered, and (c) performance focused. The principle of *performance focused* includes the desire to have quantitative evaluation of the support services provided. This requires the sport scientists involved in elite athlete support to report on their services. Performance practitioners are not excluded from this need to report on their services and present evidence of effective service. At times, the NGB may require the performance practitioner to share confidential information as a part of the employment contract.

PREPARING FOR THE MEDIA
Talking to the media is another aspect of being in the Olympic setting. Journalists may seek out a performance practitioner if they know one is working with a team or NGB. Although this can be a great opportunity to promote the profession, any contact with the media must be done carefully (Haberl & Peterson, 2006). Because it may make a "better" story to personalize your work, anticipate that the media may try and connect what you do to a particular athlete. Performance psychologists must maintain vigilance in talking to the media to ensure that they don't imply having worked with an individual athlete.

Self-Regulation
As has been evident throughout this chapter, consulting with Olympic athletes can present some challenges. Perhaps the most difficult aspect of being an ethical practitioner in this environment is that the consultant is almost always the only person in the environment with an understanding of the ethics involved with the role (Haberl & Peterson, 2006). Therefore, the consultant often bears the responsibility of ethical practice in isolation (Haberl & Peterson, 2006; Watson, Zizzi, & Etzel, 2006). This is a major reason why we have called for a greater influence of virtue ethics on the training of sport psychology practitioners (Aoyagi & Portenga, 2010). Virtue ethics focus on the character of the practitioner, believing that ethical behaviors are dependent upon the practitioner (Newman et al., 2002). In contrast to ethical systems that

ask practitioners to consider, "What should I do?" virtue ethics would guide practitioners to consider, "Who shall I be?"

In attempting to answer this question, we would direct consultants to the Ethical Principles of Psychologists and Code of Conduct (APA, 2002). The aspirational General Principles (APA, 2002) provide an excellent guidepost for those seeking to answer the question of "Who shall I be?" Unfortunately, many professionals are trained to analyze ethical dilemmas with rationality and objectivity (Rogerson, Gottlieb, Handelsman, Knapp, & Younggren, 2011), which causes them to rely solely upon the Code of Conduct (i.e., Standards) and overlook the General Principles (Jordan & Meara, 1990). While the General Principles are not intended to provide clear examples of what we should do, they are what we should all be striving toward.

Consultants working with Olympic athletes must have a solid personal and professional foundation, grounded in the General Principles, in order to work effectively. While many consultants may believe they are immune to the allure and glamour of the Olympics, there is no known vaccine for "Five Ring Fever." We are all susceptible to it, and those who believe in immunity are likely more at risk to catch a case of the Fever at the most inopportune time. Therefore, vigilant self-awareness and frequent consultation are the best preventative medicine (Rogerson et al., 2011).

As with all threats to ethical practice, it helps to be proactive prior to entering the Olympic environment that is the catalyst for "Five Ring Fever." This is when character becomes critical, and is another reason why we favor the further proliferation of virtue ethics in sport psychology training. Johnson and Campbell (2002) define character primarily in relation to honesty, and we would also point again to the General Principles (APA, 2002): beneficence and non-maleficence (Principle A), fidelity and responsibility (Principle B), integrity (Principle C), justice (Principle D), and respect for people's rights and dignity (Principle E). Johnson and Campbell also introduce the idea of fitness into the psychological professions, and we view this as a needed addition to sport psychology as well (Aoyagi & Portenga, 2010). Fitness refers to competence to practice, and is evidenced by psychological stability, knowledge of the profession, and a well-adjusted personality, among other traits (Johnson & Campbell, 2002). While the field of sport psychology has not fully defined appropriate benchmarks of character and fitness to practice, let alone with Olympic athletes, it is incumbent upon consultants desiring to work with Olympic athletes that they establish a firm professional track record of such attributes.

CASE STUDY

It is the second week of the Olympic Games, and after three weeks of preparation in country, the track and field events are finally starting. As has been the case in previous Olympics, the relay selections have been stressful for the athletes, coaches, agents, and national office staff. Of the pool of ten or more athletes that could run each relay, only six get medals and only four get to run in the finals, thus having the chance to be photographed draped in the American flag. Finding the right combination of athletes based on ability to run a relay and based on health is always a challenge. As the consultant to the team, you have been talking to athletes in the pool, personal coaches, national team coaches, sports medicine staff, and national team staff since arrival. As the deadline for submitting the names of the relay team approaches, you notice that the stress of everyone involved increases dramatically, and the national team coaches responsible for the selection second- and third-guess their decisions.

Your roommates for the trip include the sprints/relays coach and the head coach. Having worked with you on previous teams, they trust your judgment, welcome any insights you can provide, but respect your need for confidentiality. However, you find that in casual conversation in the evenings they constantly try to pick your brain for information. The high performance director of the NGB has made it clear that they want to know from all staff members about concerns anyone has about relay pool athletes' ability to perform at their best. Despite knowing about confidentiality, the director has made it clear that he needs to know from you if you have any concerns as well. As the deadline looms, you indeed do.

You are aware that at least two athletes are in the last year of their shoe sponsorship contracts and are likely to be dropped if they do not run in the finals. Both of them have expressed some concerns about being at their best given that they have other events in which to compete before the relays. One has disclosed that she is struggling with a lingering injury of which she has not disclosed the full extent to the medical staff for fear of being left off the relay. Additionally, the national team coaches have expressed some worries regarding another athlete's confidence and readiness to compete. They are familiar with the athlete from previous teams and notice that her behavior is different and a bit aloof. You have been working with this athlete and know that her confidence is spot on. She has been struggling with a family situation back home that she does not want to share with anyone else on the team. She is embarrassed about the situation and worried that the coaches may think she is too distracted to compete. Despite keeping to herself more than usual, you know that she is still ready to compete at her best. Several questions appear salient to this dilemma:

- Are you fulfilling the principle of Beneficence for all members of the team if you do not disclose your concerns about the injury or that the aloof athlete is ready to perform?

- Is there a way to talk about the injured athlete without breaking confidence? Same for the confidence issue?

- How might you get the sports medicine staff to intervene on your behalf?

- Is it fair for an athlete to withhold an injury so they can compete in the finals?

- What is in the best interest of your client? Who is your client in this case? The NGB? The athletes individually? The national team coaching staff? The high performance director?

- As is often the case in a closed system, you suspect that news of the injury and your knowledge about it will get to the high performance director eventually, even if not until a year after the Olympics. If (and more likely when) the director hears about this, it is likely that you will be fired and the position eliminated. If the position is retained, the director will probably hire someone who is completely loyal to him over the athletes. When this happens, the athletes will no longer have access to needed performance psychology services. Knowing the possibilities for larger implications, how might this influence your process?

- What types of character and fitness attributes would help a consultant in this situation? What types might hinder a consultant?

SUMMARY AND CONCLUSIONS

By way of summary, we will share a few of our thoughts on how we might approach the case study. First, we would recognize all of the identified constituents as clients. We would attempt to serve the best interests of all clients by helping them to achieve their shared goal of gold medals. From this perspective, the major challenge is the injured athlete whose individual goal of gold may hinder the best chances of the team gold. While a direct recommendation of informing the coaches and sports medicine staff with this athlete would likely be futile, we might take an approach of protecting the athlete's long-term best interests by considering the ramifications of running while injured. Although the Olympics are the athletes' platform to gain sponsorship dollars, failure at the Olympics can have the opposite effect and thus consideration for ongoing success may be important to the athlete. Consulting with the sports medicine staff will give the athlete an honest assessment of the injury and also allow the trainers to provide the coaches an accurate assessment of the athlete's ability to perform (we would also ensure the athlete was aware of this ramification prior to making a decision to consult with sports medicine). In terms of the athlete with perceived confidence issues, we would encourage this athlete to seek out the coaches and demonstrate her confidence and readiness to perform to them. This could likely be done relatively easily without the athlete having to disclose anything about her personal life. Finally, we would view judgment and flexibility as important character and fitness attributes in this situation, while rigidity would be a large hindrance.

Performance psychologists have specific and unique knowledge, skills, and abilities that can help in the competitive development process (APA Division 47 Practice Committee, 2011). We make ourselves a valuable asset when we are perceived within the system as trusted advisors to the NGB, coaches, and sports medicine staff (Sheth & Sobel, 2000). Performance psychologists should be proactive in building relationships with coaches to develop trust and reinforce the limits of confidentiality (Sharkin, 1995). The benefits of collaboration are especially true at major international competitions (Blumenstein & Lidor, 2008; Haberl & Peterson, 2006; McCann, 2008; Vernacchia & Henschen, 2008; Vernacchia, Henschen, & Lidor, 2005).

REFERENCES

American Psychological Association. (2002). Ethical principles of psychologists and code of conduct. *American Psychologist, 57,* 1060–1073.

American Psychological Association Division 47 Practice Committee. (2011). Defining the practice of sport and performance psychology. Retrieved from http://www.apa47.org/pdfs/Defining%20the%20practice%20of%20 sport%20and%20 performance%20psychology-Final.pdf

Andersen, M. B., Van Raalte, J. L., & Brewer, B. W. (2001). Sport psychology service delivery: Staying ethical while keeping it loose. *Professional Psychology: Research and Practice, 32,* 12–18.

Aoyagi, M. W., & Portenga, S. T. (2010). The role of positive ethics and virtues in the context of sport and performance psychology service delivery. *Professional Psychology: Research and Practice, 41*(3), 253–259.

Association for Applied Sport Psychology. (1994). *Ethics code: AASP ethical principles and standards.* Retrieved from http://appliedsportpsych.org/about/ethics/code

Barnett, J. E., & Yutrzenka, B. A. (2002). Nonsexual dual relationships in professional practice, with special applications to rural and military communities. In A. A. Lazarus & O. Zur (Eds.), *Dual relationships and psychotherapy* (pp. 273–286). New York, NY: Springer Publishing Co.

Bennett, B. E., Bricklin, P. M., Harris, E., Knapp, S., VandeCreek, L., & Younggren, J. N. (2006). *Assessing and managing risk in psychological practice: An individualized approach.* Rockville, MD: The Trust.

Birky, I., Sharkin, B. S., Marin, J., & Scappaticci, A. (1998). Confidentiality after referral: A study of how restrictions on disclosure affect relationships between therapists and referral sources. *Professional Psychology: Research and Practice, 29*(2), 179–182.

Blumenstein, B., & Lidor, R. (2008). Psychological preparation in the Olympic village: A four-phase approach. *International Journal of Sport and Exercise Psychology, 6*(3), 287–300.

Davies, L. (2000). Private work in public places: Confidentiality and role tensions in a university counselling service. *Psychodynamic Counselling, 6*(1), 65–78.

Fay, A. (2002). The case against boundaries in psychotherapy. In A. A. Lazarus & O. Zur (Eds.), *Dual relationships and psychotherapy* (pp. 146–166). New York, NY: Springer Publishing Co.

Frisch, M. H. (2001). The emerging role of the internal coach. *Consulting Psychology Journal: Practice and Research, 53,* 240–250.

Fuqua, D. R., Newman, J. L., Simpson, D. B., & Choi, N. (2008). *Who is the client in organizational consultation?* Paper presented at the annual meeting of the American Psychological Association, Boston, MA.

Gould, D., Tammen, V., Murphy, S., & May, J. (1989). An examination of U.S. Olympic sport psychology consultants and the service they provide. *The Sport Psychologist, 3,* 300–312.

Gutheil, T. G., & Gabbard, G. O. (1998). Misuses and misunderstandings of boundary theory in clinical and regulatory settings. *American Journal of Psychiatry, 155,* 409–414.

Haberl, P., & Peterson, K. (2006). Olympic-size ethical dilemmas: Issues and challenges for sport psychology consultants on the road and at the Olympic Games. *Ethics & Behavior, 16,* 25–40.

Helbok, C. M. (2003). The practice of psychology in rural communities: Potential ethical dilemmas. *Ethics & Behavior, 13,* 367–384.

Hines, A. H., Ader, D. N., Chang, A. S., & Rundell, J. R. (1998). Dual agency, dual relationships, boundary crossings, and associated boundary violations: A survey of military and civilian psychiatrists. *Military Medicine, 163,* 826–833.

Jaffe v. Redmond. 135 L. Ed. 2d 337 (1996).

Johnson, W. B., & Campbell, C. D. (2002). Character and fitness requirements for professional psychologists: Are there any? *Professional Psychology: Research and Practice, 33,* 46–53.

Johnson, W. B., & Campbell, C. D. (2004). Character and fitness requirements for professional psychologists: Training directors' perspectives. *Professional Psychology: Research and Practice, 35,* 405–411.

Johnson, W. B., Ralph, J., & Johnson, S. J. (2005). Managing multiple roles in embedded environments: The case of aircraft carrier psychology. *Professional Psychology: Research and Practice, 36,* 73–81.

Johnson, W. B., & Wilson, K. (1993). The military internship: A retrospective analysis. *Professional Psychology: Research and Practice, 24,* 312–318.

Jordan, A. E., & Meara, N. M. (1990). Ethics and the professional practice of psychologists: The role of virtues and principles. *Professional Psychology: Research and Practice, 21,* 107–114.

Kennedy, C. H., & Johnson, W. B. (2009). Mixed agency in military psychology: Applying the American Psychological Association Ethics Code. *Psychological Services, 6,* 22–31.

Kertesz, R. (2002). Dual relationships in psychotherapy in Latin America. In A. A. Lazarus & O. Zur (Eds.), *Dual relationships and psychotherapy* (pp. 329–334). New York, NY: Springer Publishing Co.

Kessler, L. E., & Waehler, C. A. (2005). Addressing multiple relationships between clients and therapist in lesbian, gay, bisexual, and transgender communities. *Professional Psychology: Research and Practice, 36*(1), 66–72.

Kitchener, K. S. (2000). *Foundations of ethical practice, research, and teaching in psychology.* Mahwah, NJ: Erlbaum.

Knapp, S. J., & VanDeCreek, L. D. (2006). *Practical ethics for psychologists: A positive approach.* Washington, DC: American Psychological Association.

McCann, S. (2008). At the Olympics, everything is a performance issue. *International Journal of Sport and Exercise Psychology, 6,* 267–276.

Newman, J. L. (1993). Ethical issues in consultation. *Journal of Counseling & Development, 72,* 148–156.

Newman, J. L., Robinson-Kurpius, S. E., & Fuqua, D. R. (2002). Issues in the ethical practice of consulting psychology. In R. L. Lowman (Ed.), *The California School of Organizational Studies handbook of organizational consulting psychology: A comprehensive guide to theory, skills, and techniques* (pp. 733–758). San Francisco, CA: Jossey-Bass.

Poczwardowski, A. (2001, May 31). *Sport psychology service delivery model: A heuristic for systemizing and optimizing consulting practice.* Paper presented at the 10th World Congress of Sport Psychology, Skiathos, Greece.

Portenga, S. T., Aoyagi, M. W. (2007, October). *Ethical practice for consultants working directly for university athletic departments.* Symposium conducted at the Association of Applied Sport Psychology annual conference, Louisville, KY.

Rogerson, M. D., Gottlieb, M. C., Handelsman, M. M., Knapp, S., & Younggren, J. (2011). Nonrational processes in ethical decision making. *American Psychologist, 66*(7), 614–623. doi:10.1037/a0025215

Schank, J. A., & Skovholt, T. M. (2006). *Ethical practice in small communities: Challenges and rewards for psychologists.* Washington, DC: American Psychological Association.

Sears, V. L. (1990). Ethics in small minority communities. In H. Lerman, N. Porter, H. Lerman, & N. Porter (Eds.), *Feminist ethics in psychotherapy* (pp. 204–213). New York, NY: Springer Publishing Co.

Sharkin. B. S. (1995). Strains on confidentiality in college-student psychotherapy: Entangled therapeutic relationships, incidental encounters, and third-party inquiries. *Professional Psychology: Research and Practice, 26,* 184–189.

Sharkin, B. S., Scappaticci, A. G., & Birky, I. (1995). Access to confidential information in a university counseling center: A survey of referral sources. *Journal of College Student Development, 36,* 494–495.

Sheth, J. N., & Sobel, A. (2000). *Clients for life: Evolving from an expert for hire to an extraordinary advisor.* New York, NY: Fireside.

Spiegel, P. B. (1990). Confidentiality endangered under some circumstances without special management. *Psychotherapy: Theory, Research, Practice, Training, 27,* 636–643.

Thompson, M. A., & Ravizza, K. (1998). The value of failure. In M. A. Thompson, R. A. Vernacchia, & W. E. Moore (Eds.), *Case studies in sport psychology: An educational approach* (pp. 247–256). Dubque, IA: Kendall/Hunt.

Watson, J. C., Zizzi, S., & Etzel, E. F. (2006). Ethical training in sport psychology programs: Current training standards. *Ethics & Behavior, 16,* 5–14.

Welfel, E. R. (2006). *Ethics in counseling and psychotherapy: Standards, research, and emerging issues* (3rd ed.). Belmont, CA: Thomson Brooks/Cole Publishing Co.

Vernacchia, R. A., & Henschen, K. P. (2008). The challenge of consulting with track and field athletes at the Olympic games. *International Journal of Sport and Exercise Psychology, 6*(3), 254–266.

Vernacchia, R. A., Henschen, K. P., & Lidor, R. (2005). The road to the Olympic Games: Sport psychology services for the 2000 USA Olympic Track and Field Team. *New Studies in Athletics, 20*(1), 51–56.

Yukelson, D. (2001, May 31). *Immersion into the intercollegiate athletic department: Benefits, risks, and management.* Paper presented at the 10th World Congress of Sport Psychology, Skiathos, Greece.

Zur, O., & Lazarus, A. A. (2002). Six arguments against dual relationships and their rebuttals. In A. A. Lazarus & O. Zur (Eds.), *Dual relationships and psychotherapy* (pp. 3–24). New York, NY: Springer Publishing Co.

SPECIAL SETTINGS

CHAPTER 7

THE ETHICAL PRACTICE OF EXERCISE PSYCHOLOGY

Samuel J. Zizzi and Vanessa Shannon

INTRODUCTION

When many of us think about the field of sport, exercise, and performance (SEP) psychology, we tend to focus on sport performance psychology and the exciting opportunities it brings for us to work with athletes, teams, and coaches. Time spent reading the other chapters in this book will illustrate for the reader that there is an art to the effective and ethical practice of sport psychology. However, many SEP psychology professionals fail to recognize and use "performance psychology" to serve a much larger population—recreational exercisers. Yes, the "E" in SEP is often forgotten. While there has been a rapid growth over the last decade in the development of handbooks and other resources for the practicing sport psychology professional, unfortunately *applied exercise psychology* has been neglected. Currently, there are only two practitioner-oriented texts available, namely Anshel's (2006) *Applied Exercise Psychology* and Hays's (1999) *Working It Out: Using Exercise in Therapy,* both of which focus on helping mental health professionals integrate exercise into their clients' therapeutic experience. There are few additional sources for those in SEP to learn about how to ethically practice exercise psychology, particularly outside of the context of therapy.

This chapter will explore several key issues related to the non-clinical practice of exercise psychology, including scope of practice, competence, and multiple issues with coordinated health care. The current approach to exercise psychology will be grounded in performance psychology, exercise physiology, and behavior change theory rather than clinical or counseling psychology. Hopefully, this unique treatment of the topic will appeal to all SEP psychology professionals.

APPLIED EXERCISE PSYCHOLOGY: WHAT IS THE SCOPE OF PRACTICE?

The role of exercise psychology (EP) professionals is to help their clients adopt and maintain an active, healthy lifestyle with the goals of improving physical and mental health while preventing chronic disease. It is becoming common knowledge that a healthy lifestyle can be a major protective factor against chronic disease, and regardless of genetics, a particular set of controllable health behaviors plays a critical role in future health (Meyers et al., 2002; Vita, Terry, Hubert, & Fries, 1998). These health behaviors, including being active, consuming food and alcohol in moderation, and not smoking, are thought to prevent what authors Lees and Booth (2004) call "sedentary death syndrome" (p. 447).

Though this diagnosis sounds ominous, the good news is that there are plenty of people to help. The inactivity and obesity epidemics in the United States are well documented. Based on recent self-reported estimates, approximately 25-30% of the U.S. population would be considered obese based on a Body Mass Index of 30 or higher (Centers for Disease Control and Prevention [CDC], 2009a), less than 50% of the population would meet current physical activity guidelines based on self-report data (Macera et al., 2005), and approximately 25% of the population report no leisure-time physical activity (Centers for Disease Control and Prevention, 2009b). The second piece of good news is that behavior change programs work, and many sport psychology professionals have already been trained to use the necessary critical skills within a sporting context. After a systematic review of literature, a task force at the CDC has strongly recommended individual behavior change interventions that include goal setting and self monitoring, self-talk, relapse prevention, problem solving, time management, and social support (Guide to Preventative Services, 2001). These interventions that help clients navigate the process of behavior change are regularly practiced by a variety of health education professionals including certified fitness professionals, registered dieticians, public health department staff, and community health educators. With appropriate training, SEP psychology professionals are poised to help clients change and to help train students and allied health professionals to facilitate change.

ARE YOU FIT TO HELP OTHERS GET FIT?

Both the Association for Applied Sport Psychology (AASP, n.d.) and American Psychological Association (APA, 2010) Ethical Codes strongly emphasize competence (Principle A) as a key to effective practice. One question central to this chapter is: "Can sport psychology professionals competently practice exercise psychology?" The answer, as with most ethical dilemmas is, "it depends"—on the professional's education, knowledge, training, and experience. So, what education, knowledge, training, and experiences are necessary to be competent and maintain competence in exercise psychology or health performance consulting so that we "do no harm?" Previous work discussing the competencies needed to practice exercise psychology (Pauline, Pauline, Johnson, & Gamble, 2006) has suggested that interdisciplinary training is critical. Below is a table of suggested requirements for a professional to gain competence in applied exercise psychology, while contrasting this proposed skill set to the other more well-established paths in sport psychology (see Table 7.1).

Table 7.1. Training Background and Skills Needed to Practice Across Three Domains

Clinical or Counseling Psychology	Sport Performance Consulting	Health Performance Consulting
Core Training - PhD in Clinical or Counseling Psychology[1] - Approved 2000 hr internship - Meet licensure requirements in state of practice	Core Training - MS/MA or PhD blending training in Exercise Science and Psychology - coursework to meet AASP Certification criteria[2] - 400 hours of mentored practice	Core Training - MS/MA degree blending training in counseling, public health, and exercise science
Shared Psychological Skills Goal setting and self-monitoring Identifying and modifying self-talk Relapse prevention techniques Behavior modification techniques Confidence building strategies Time management & planning		
Clientele	Clientele	Clientele
Children, adults, and families across the lifespan	Athletes, teams, coaches, athletic trainers, and sport managers	Inactive/overweight/obese children and adults; adults with chronic disease
Additional Training or Skills	Additional Training or Skills	Additional Training or Skills

- Specialized training in assessment and treatment of common psychological disorders
- Individual and group counseling skills
- Use of imagery and relaxation techniques (general application)
	- Team building/team cohesion
	- Pre-performance routines
	- Sport attention/concentration control techniques
	- Training sciences (under or over-training) & effective coaching principles
	- Sport injury rehabilitation
	- Sport-adaptation for various imagery and relaxation techniques
	- Assessment and intake techniques targeting health behavior change
		- Background in health behavior change theories, including:
		  · Social ecological model
		  · Transtheoretical model
		  · Health belief model, theory of planned behavior
		- Psychoneuroimmunology
		- Basic understanding of exercise physiology and diet assessment and prescription process
		- Obesity, diet, and physical activity epidemiology
		- Assessment and intake techniques targeting health behavior change
		- Psychological effects of exercise
		- Familiarity with medical history process and common medications used to prevent/treat chronic disease

[1]For a full listing of APA Standards, visit www.apa.org/ed/accreditation/about/index.aspx
[2]For the AASP CC Standards visit www.appliedsportpsych.org/consultants/about-certified-consultants

Who Are Your Clients and How Can You Help?

Most people who seek help to change their health behaviors, for example to increase physical activity or improve their diet, are not elite athletes. The client population, therefore, is often dissimilar in appearance to sport clients. They might look more like clients that visit community mental health centers or a private psychologist's office. These clients are typically unfit, overweight or obese, have one or more recurring physical health issues, and are either already diagnosed with or are at risk for a chronic disease such as type 2 diabetes, heart disease, high blood pressure, or high cholesterol. Coming from a sport background, this entry into a "less healthy world" can be confusing and may be uncomfortable at first for some SEP professionals. Professionals may even hold biases towards these types of clients (e.g., that they are just lazy), which may impede work with clients and translate to a lack of respect from clients (Principle D: Respect for rights and dignity). Highly trained SEP professionals have a social responsibility (Principle F) to "make public" knowledge and training to those who can benefit most. Health performance consultations offer SEP professionals a great opportunity to make a significant impact on the health of their clients. If these services are extended to those who need it most (e.g., poor, less educated, less healthy), then the professional is truly upholding these aforementioned ethical principles in his/her practice.

Learning to build rapport and feel competent with these less-healthy, less-active clients comes with supervised or mentored experience in either exercise or mental health/counseling settings. Seeking out relevant information and experiences to prepare for ethical practice would confirm a professional and scientific responsibility (Principle C) to the profession. In particular, these supervised experiences would help SEP professionals understand and discuss some of the specific ethical issues that may emerge, including confidentiality and informed consent (Standards 17 & 18), fee structure and third-party billing (Standards 12 & 15), multiple relationships (Standard 9), and sharing of information among other health professionals (Standard 12). These issues will be addressed in greater depth in a subsequent section of this chapter.

Have You Read the Literature?

One of the greatest challenges when transitioning from sport psychology into exercise psychology is the sheer volume of research to consider. The organization *Active Living Research* (www.activelivingresearch.org) has estimated that since the year 2004, there have been approximately 200-300 articles published per year focusing on interpersonal, social, and built environment factors linked to active living or healthy eating. Therefore, it is a daunting task to maintain one's professional education in this field, and it is highly likely that professionals will need to attend meetings outside of AASP or APA. To support this assertion, a recent analysis of the 2009 AASP conference program revealed that only 11% of all abstracts fell under health or exercise topics and that few of these were applied in nature (Zizzi, 2009). The upside of this high volume of research and professional activity is that there are excellent resources and tools available for educating clients and professionals on active living and healthy eating. For a list of publicly accessible resources or organizations sponsoring training in this area, please see Table 7.2.

Table 7.2. Publicly Accessible Resources or Organizations Sponsoring Training in Physical Activity

Organization	Website	Description
Active Living Research	www.activelivingresearch.org	Provides resources and grant funding for physical activity as a means of preventing childhood obesity in special populations
Exercise is Medicine	www.exerciseismedicine.org	Promotes the role of physicians in making exercise a mechanism for prevention and treatment of disease
International Society for Physical Activity and Health	www.ispah.org	Provides resources, professional development, and an international forum for professionals in physical activity and health
International Society of Behavioral Nutrition and Physical Activity	www.isbnpa.org	Provides resources (e.g., journal, newsletter, annual conference) for research and policy in the area of behavioral nutrition and physical activity
National Society of Physical Activity Practitioners in Public Health	www.nspapph.org	Provides resources and organizes conferences and trainings regarding physical activity promotion
Physical Activity and Public Health Postgraduate Course on Research Directions & Strategies*	www.sph.sc.edu/paph/research.htm	Designed to help participants improve develop research skills related to physical activity and public health
Physical Activity and Public Health Practitioner's Course on Community Interventions*	www.sph.sc.edu/paph/practitioners.htm	Directed at individuals engaged or interested in community-based programming promoting physical activity
Society for Behavioral Medicine	www.sbm.org	Provides resources (e.g., journal, newsletter, annual conference) promoting the study of the interactions between biology, behavior, and the environment to improve health

*Sponsored by Centers for Disease Control and Prevention (CDC) and the University of South Carolina Prevention Research Center (PRC)

So what is missing from sport psychology training that might be useful when working in this context? First, as noted in Table 7.1, SEP professionals are encouraged to move outside of the comfort zones of sporting environments to working with non-athletes in non-sport settings such as fitness facilities, hospitals, or other community centers (e.g., churches, senior centers, YMCA/YWCA). If SEP professionals or students can find a supervisor or mentor to help guide these experiences, it is likely that these experiences will help the student or professional develop and appreciate the challenges others face, and foster respect and dignity for clients (Principle D) with these presenting health concerns. Standard 3 (Human Differences) also applies, which encourages professionals to recognize and respect individual differences and the needs of those they serve, as well as to not involve themselves in discriminatory practices. An ethical supervisor can be an excellent guide to help SEP professionals make the transition into health performance consulting. The value of this mentoring process between supervisor and supervisee has been well documented in sport psychology (Watson, Clement, Blom, & Grindley, 2009).

One of the next training steps that aspiring health performance consultants (HPCs) can take to build competence would be to become familiar with the research literature in obesity, physical activity, and behavior change. Being able to identify the demographic, interpersonal, and social factors related to obesity, and a person's likelihood of meeting dietary and physical activity guidelines will allow professionals to expand their range of competence (Principle A and Standard 2). Specifically, understanding the theory and applied research related to these health behaviors will help professionals to develop effective intake and assessment protocols which can be used to build effective interventions.

EXERCISE PSYCHOLOGY AS COORDINATED HEALTH CARE

The social ecological model (SEM) helps us better understand the complexity of improving individuals' attitudes toward physical activity and increasing physical activity behavior. According to the SEM, individuals are influenced by multiple levels of factors (McElroy et al., 1988). Although the way an individual thinks and feels about exercise has a direct effect on exercise attitudes and behavior, other extrinsic influences (e.g., social, work, family, physical environment) may have an equally powerful effect. As a result, behavior change becomes more complex and the individual may need to learn new skills or acquire additional support. From this perspective, exercise psychology can be viewed as part of a faceted system of co-ordinated healthcare.

ETHICAL ISSUES IN COORDINATED HEALTH CARE

Within this system, a number of professionals can assist clients to improve their health; specifi-cally, an HPC, an exercise/fitness professional, a nutritional professional, and a physician may be directly or indirectly involved in modifying unhealthy behaviors and increasing healthy behaviors. Ultimately, a coordinated care approach, where all providers share data related to their experiences with each client, provides the highest chance for client success (i.e., adoption and maintenance of new health behaviors). This model has been successfully integrated into the clinical care of athletes, particularly the management of concussions (National Athletic Trainers' Association, 2004) and eating disorders (Baer, Walker, & Grossman, 1995). Within this team approach to patient care, role clarity, role acceptance, and flow of information are incredibly important. Functional confidentiality, third-party requests for information (e.g., insurance agencies), and multiple relationships must be discussed and navigated carefully in this context. Standard 12 (Third-Party Requests for Services) of the AASP code states that "when an AASP member agrees to provide services to a person or entity at the request of a third party, the AASP member clarifies, at the outset of the service, the nature of the relationship with each party." This issue also links with Principle B (Integrity), which focuses on AASP members' outlining qualifications, services, and fees fairly and honestly without making false or misleading statements.

Ultimately, identifying who is the client at the onset of the process, and the specific role(s) of each provider in helping the client, will minimize risk for harm and maximize efficiency of service. This clarification will then, in part, help to establish the flow of information. What information you can share and with whom you can share it is governed by not only ethics, but health care laws as well. It is especially important that HPCs be familiar with the Health Insurance Portability and Accountability Act of 1996 (HIPAA) Privacy and Security Rules.

Are You Hip to HIPAA?

As part of this coordinated care system, the HPC is responsible for supporting the individual client or patient, and may be asked to provide secondary training to exercise and nutrition professionals and participate in or facilitate sharing of information between all involved parties. The Health Insurance Portability and Accountability Act of 1996 (HIPAA) provides legal protection for individuals' personal health information, and links closely with the ethical issue of third-party requests for service (Standard 12). The Privacy Rule defines rules and limitations regarding access to all forms of personal health information, whereas the Security Rule delimits electronic information. HIPAA defines who must follow laws regarding protected health information (PHI), who is exempt from the limitations of HIPAA, what information is protected, how the information is protected, who has access to PHI, and what rights individuals have with respect to their PHI. Typically, during an initial visit or consultation with a service provider (e.g., a medical doctor or psychologist), patients are asked to read and sign a waiver so information can be shared among all potential service providers. From a legal perspective, HIPAA allows the sharing of PHI within a coordinated healthcare system as long as the individual has given consent to all members of the coordinated care team. Standard 17 (Informed Consent to Practice) and Standard 18 (Maintaining Confidentiality) provide guidance on this process as well. However, laws do not govern ethical thinking, and do not always protect an individual from harm (Principle E, Concern for Others' Welfare). Therefore, critical thinking is still important when considering what information to share verbally or in written documentation.

In addition to the Privacy Rule, the HIPAA Security Rule adds some ethical complexity to coordinated healthcare. Consent from the individual, which addresses the Privacy Rule, is only one hurdle; the Security Rule serves to shelter the individual's information after access has been allowed. In order to clear this second hurdle, the healthcare team must find ways to protect confidentiality while PHI is being shared electronically between team members. The team members must also develop a system of recordkeeping that best serves the purpose of the team but also protects the individual's rights. There are several options for record keeping that are readily available, such as traditional hard copy files (securely stored at the exercise facility for easy access) or electronic medical records (see Richards, 2009) that provide access to participating professionals. Electronic medical records can be shared via internal systems (e.g., within a hospital) or a Web-based portal. One potential way of preventing ethical issues from arising when participating in a coordinated care setting is to have a discussion with all providers early on in the process to review HIPAA practices at the facility and documentation/information sharing procedures. Scheduling regular staff meetings that most professionals attend can provide an excellent opportunity for information sharing as well.

Two ways an HPC can become more familiar with these issues is to pursue online training through the CITI group (www.citiprogram.org) or to spend time exploring the continuing education resources on HIPAA at the APA's informative practice website (www.apapractice.org). The CITI training is used as a prerequisite for human subjects' research and clinical practice at many U.S. institutions and is a good place for students and young professionals to gain familiarity with the nuances of research and practice ethics.

In a field like sport and exercise psychology where individuals come from diverse backgrounds (e.g., sport sciences, counseling psychology), discussion of ethical issues often revolves around competence and "not knowing what we don't know." The problem is that we are usually unaware of exactly how much we know or don't know until a specific situation arises and tests our knowledge and understanding. The case below will provide you with an opportunity to test your ethical knowledge and critical thinking skills.

THINKING CRITICALLY: ETHICAL DECISION MAKING IN EXERCISE PSYCHOLOGY

A Case Study: Insurance Incentivized Weight Management

A health insurance company is offering a weight management program at approved sites throughout your state. Sites must be able to provide program participants with the support they need to complete the program—nutritional services, fitness testing, exercise training and prescription, and access to a fitness facility. The insurance company recognizes the financial toll of treatment for chronic and preventable disease and has determined that an incentivized weight management program that encourages individuals to make healthy behavior changes is a cost-effective alternative. Participants will pay a nominal copayment for the first year of the program, and in the second year the insurance company will pay half of the fitness facility membership. In addition to the on-site services provided, the insurance company provides individuals in the program with access to a health performance consultant (HPC). In this role, you will provide individuals within the program with health performance consulting via the telephone, as well as coordinate the efforts of on-site staff. In your most recent conversation with Sally, a first-year participant in the program who just moved to the town in which you live and whose site happens to be the fitness facility to which you belong, Sally tells you that she is having trouble adhering to her exercise program because she finds the routine boring. When you suggest several behavior changes (e.g., listening to music, an exercise partner), she asks you to be her exercise partner and help her modify her exercise program. Before you continue, take some time to consider the discussion questions presented below:

1) What ethical issues stand out to you in the scenario?

2) How would the ethical issues surrounding this case be different depending on the gender of the HPC?

3) How would you address these ethical issues or dilemmas?

Case Discussion

We will now present one interpretation of the ethical issues that could emerge in this case. Helping professionals often provide their clients with support. However, too much support can actually be *maleficent*. Eventually your client will no longer require your professional services, and if you have become the client's only source of social support then the termination of your relationship may in fact harm your client. This situation often occurs when a *multiple relationship* is developed between HPC and client—for example, working as Sally's HPC, as well as serving as her exercise partner. In this type of situation, the lines of ethical boundaries can blur. It is also important to note that the issue of physical attraction can further complicate this issue. Regardless of gender, there is the potential that Sally finds you physically attractive, and the issue may only be exacerbated by fitness attire or meeting in a less formal setting (Pauline et al., 2006). On one hand, it is your responsibility to be concerned for your client's welfare and act beneficently; Sally has just moved to town and doesn't have any other options for exercise partners. On the other hand, this type of multiple relationship could be unethical and ultimately harmful to Sally if it impairs your professional judgment or is not resolved quickly.

In addition, your interactions with Sally at the fitness facility could compromise *confidentiality* and Sally's right to privacy. As for any input regarding Sally's exercise program, if you do not have a background or educational foundation in exercise prescription, then providing input to Sally is outside the realm of your *competency*. If you do have an educational background or professional experience in exercise prescription, it is important to remind yourself of your role in the current situation. You are Sally's HPC and as part of the program, Sally has an on-site exercise professional who is responsible for her exercise training and prescription. As such, despite your competence, if you choose to assist Sally in modifying her exercise prescription, you again run the risk of creating a multiple relationship, thereby clouding your role and disrupting the coordinated care approach.

The solutions to many of these issues might involve a direct conversation with Sally, clarifying your role and increasing her awareness of the potential pitfalls that may emerge with multiple relationships. This conversation would likely lead into a discussion of other alternatives for finding additional support for her exercise goals. In sum, establishing proper consenting procedures and a secure means of sharing information will help minimize ethical issues at the beginning of many, but not all, of your consultations. The informal setting is likely to promote multiple relationships that may or may not lead to harm, and thus, professionals should be prepared to quickly address problems as they emerge.

CONCLUSIONS

Exercise and health behavior consultations provide a different context for the application of the same ethical principles as the other chapters in this textbook. "Do no harm" still applies, but the contextual variables that affect ethical practice differ substantially when working with less-healthy clients, particularly when practicing in an informal environment that may require working with a variety of allied health professionals. With the complexity of managed care, and systems of coordinated care expanding, many of these issues will not go away—they may actually become more common and increasingly difficult to manage. Sport and exercise psychology consultants serve their profession by engaging in continuing education and training to build their own competencies in "health performance," and they will have the potential to help many new clients navigate the path to health behavior change.

REFERENCES

American Psychological Association. (2010). Ethical principles of psychologists and code of conduct: 2010 amendments. Retrieved from http://www.apa.org/ethics/code/index.aspx

Anshel, M. (2006). *Applied exercise psychology: A practitioner's guide to improving client health and fitness.* New York, NY: Springer.

Association for the Advancement of Applied Sport Psychology. (n.d.). Ethics code: AASP ethical principles and standards. Retrieved from http://appliedsportpsych.org/about/ethics/code

Baer, J. T., Walker, W. F., & Grossman, J. M. (1995). A disordered eating response team's effect on nutrition practices in college athletes. *Journal of Athletic Training, 30*(4), 315–317.

Bandura, A. (1977). Self-efficacy: Toward a unifying theory of behavioral change. *Psychological Review, 84,* 191–215.

Brownell, K. D., & Battle-Horgen, K. (2004). *Food fight: The inside story of the food industry, America's obesity crisis, and what we can do about it.* Chicago, IL: McGraw-Hill.

Centers for Disease Control and Prevention. (2009a). US obesity trends, 1985-2009. Retrieved from http://www.cdc.gov/obesity/data/trends.html#State

Centers for Disease Control and Prevention. (2009b). Prevalence of no leisure time physical activity - behavioral risk factor surveillance system, 36 states, 1998-2008. Retrieved from http://www.cdc.gov/nccdphp/dnpa/physical/stats/leisure_time.htm

Guide to Community Preventive Services. (n.d.). Behavioral and social approaches to increase physical activity: Individually-adapted health behavior change programs. Retrieved from www.thecommunityguide.org/pa/behavioral-social/individuallyadapted.html

Lees, S. J., & Booth, F. W. (2004). Sedentary death syndrome. *Canadian Journal of Applied Physiology, 29*(4), 447–460.

Lox, C. L., Martin-Ginis, K. A., & Petruzzello, S. J. (2006). *The psychology of exercise: Integrating theory and practice* (2nd ed.). Scottsdale, AZ: Holcomb Hathaway.

Macera, C. A., Hootman, J. M., & Sniezek, J. E. (2003). Major public health benefits of physical activity. *Arthritis and Rheumatism, 49*(1), 122–128.

Macera, C. A., Ham, S. A., Yore, M. M., Jones, D. A., Ainsworth, B. E., Kimsey, C. D., & Kohl, H. W. (2005). Prevalence of physical activity in the United States: Behavioral risk factor surveillance system, 2001. *Preventing Chronic Disease, 2*(2), 1–10.

Myers, J., Prakash, M., Froelicher, V., Do, D., Partington, D., & Atwood, S. (2002). Exercise capacity and mortality among men referred for exercise testing. *New England Journal of Medicine, 346,* 793–801.

National Athletic Trainers' Association. (2004). Management of sport-related concussion. *Journal of Athletic Training, 39*(3), 280–297.

Pauline, J. S., Pauline, G. A., Johnson, S. R., & Gamble, K. M. (2006). Ethical issues in exercise psychology. *Ethics and Behavior, 16*(1), 61–78.

Prochaska, J. O., & DiClemente, C. C. (1992). The transtheoretical approach. In J. C. Norcross & M. R. Goldfried (Eds.), *Handbook of Psychotherapy Integration* (pp. 300–334). New York, NY: Basic Books.

Richards, M. M. (2009). Electronic medical records: Confidentiality issues in the time of HIPAA. *Professional Psychology: Research and Practice, 40*(6), 550–556.

Ryan, R. M., & Deci, E. L. (2000). Self-determination theory and the facilitation of intrinsic motivation, social development, and well-being. *American Psychologist, 55*(1), 68–78.

Vita, A. J., Terry, R. B., Hubert, H. B., & Fries, J. F. (1998). Aging, health risks, and cumulative disability. *New England Journal of Medicine, 338,* 1035–1041.

Watson II, J. C., Clement, D., Blom, L., & Grindley, E. (2009). Mentoring: Processes and perceptions of sport and exercise psychology graduate students. *Journal of Applied Sport Psychology, 21,* 231–246.

Zizzi, S. (2009). How training in health and exercise psychology can make you a better "athlete" in the job market. *AASP Newsletter,* 28–29.

CHAPTER 8

ETHICS IN PEAK PERFORMANCE BUSINESS COACHING

Doug Hirschhorn, Daniel Leidl, and Joe Frontiera

INTRODUCTION

Performance-based psychological training such as that practiced in sport and exercise psychology (SEP) provides a foundation for understanding key mindsets behind achievement, the dynamics of successful teams, and the tactics of driven and respected leaders. According to Meyers, Coleman, Whelan, and Mehlenbeck (2001), the field may be a niche discipline where applied work merely accounts for supplemental income. Over the past decade, however, it appears that this has changed somewhat, and those trained in performance psychology are uniquely prepared on a full-time employment basis to offer insights regarding the inter- and intra-personal dynamics pertinent for success in many fields, including business.

For those who choose to become practitioners outside of the sport and exercise worlds (such as administrators, financial executives, traders, CEOs, and other business professionals), understanding and conveying these dynamics can prove beneficial. Any individual or group who is focused on advancing themselves and/or a team toward the pursuit of a defined goal can greatly benefit from skills such as self-talk, stress management, and goal setting as well as broader conceptual processes such as team and leadership development. While the market to advance services built on the foundation of performance psychology is expansive, accessing potential markets can be difficult, time consuming, and oftentimes ethically precarious.

Warren Buffet captured the consequences of loose business ethics succinctly when he stated, "It takes 20 years to build a reputation and five minutes to ruin it." He continued with the obvious statement, "If you think about that, you'll do things differently" (Lowenstein, 1996). Unlike in the field of psychology, the business community has not gathered to create a universal code of ethics. But the field of business ethics attempts to provide ethical guidance to individuals engaged in, or part of, business. Business ethics extends beyond individual actions to encompass the actions of organizations and how they impact society (Brenkert, 2010).

Despite the absence of a universal code of ethics, consultants who have chosen to enter the world of business are well served to maintain a focus on ethics. By thinking about the challenges of practice in this domain and potential consequences of unethical behavior, professionals can avoid harming others and ruining reputations and relationships. But how many scenarios can one truly predict, plan to avoid, and work to prepare for? The reality is that mistakes happen, and at any moment, one can be blindsided by unforeseen events. Below, we will review two cases that illustrate potential ethical difficulties consultants may face when managing a business and managing relationships. We will begin by exploring the benefits of maintaining a network of trusted colleagues and advisors to whom one can turn with questions and concerns, and we will then look out into the landscape of professional relationships and business practices to identify some common ethical pitfalls.

A NETWORK OF TRUSTED COLLEAGUES

A background in performance or SEP can serve as a competitive advantage in the corporate world. When considering the pursuit of an advanced degree in industrial organizational psychology, consulting psychology, or SEP, the rationale for SEP is quickly apparent. Industrial, organizational, and consulting psychology degrees are valued in business coaching and consulting, but rarely seem to be considered an asset in athletics. In contrast, with a doctorate in performance or SEP, athletic organizations find the background valuable while corporations may see a value to the content as well. Not only does a background in performance and SEP afford options, it also offers a competitive distinction to a consultancy or coaching practice. Those trained in performance psychology can work with athletic teams or individual athletes, and their skill set may be seen as a refreshing change of pace to a high-performing business team or executive interested in learning more about peak performance mental skills.

While the positives to building a coaching or consulting career on the foundation of a performance or SEP degree are considerable, there are also some cautionary points of concern. First, a disconnect exists between theory and practice in performance psychology that is by no means new. Three decades ago, Martens (1987) made the claim that two different forms of sport psychology were developing: (1) academic and (2) practicing. Martens argued that this divide originated with the very nature of knowledge, whereas academics trusted only knowledge that arose from the scientific method, while those practicing sport psychology were more focused on experiential methods that demonstrated results.

Although Martens himself believed that he gained far more knowledge practicing sport psychology than applying the scientific method to the field, the academic side seems to maintain the upper hand. In fact, one of the few undergraduate SEP programs in existence suggests that its foremost mission is "to prepare students for further graduate studies in sport psychology" (WVU College of Physical Activity and Sport Sciences, 2011). Likewise, the majority of those who matriculate from graduate programs tend to find work in academia. Therefore, it is no stretch to assert that academic programs in SEP relying primarily on the scientific method often fail to truly prepare students for a consulting role in the field of SEP, let alone for applying the discipline to the corporate world. It is not that these academic programs are ill-equipped or incapable of training practitioners, but that they appear to rarely place a considerable focus on consulting and coaching because it is not consistent with their mandate or mission. While those graduating with advanced degrees in SEP are qualified to pursue a career in professional consulting or coaching, they are often at a disadvantage when compared to the many other qualified professionals who have more business experience or richer professional networks upon which to draw.

Second, because so few trained SEP consultants pursue careers outside of academia, the professional network for consulting and coaching practitioners with SEP credentials seems lean. Even though there are some academicians who have pursued vibrant consulting careers, barriers ranging from generational differences and professional focus to the perception of limited practitioner opportunities and self-interest sometimes inhibit the advancement of collegial networks and trusted mentor/mentee relationships. In short, professional support for practitioners with an SEP or performance psychology background may be minimal if it exists at all. With this said, how does one advance a consulting or coaching career with sport psychology credentials in an effective and ethical manner?

CASE STUDY #1: WHO DO YOU TRUST?

Background. Rita has a PhD in SEP, is an active member of the American Psychological Association, and has been working as a professional consultant in business for more than ten years. She works for a multinational, multimillion-dollar firm, and has recently spearheaded an initiative to advance management consulting principles within sport organizations. Combining her passions for consulting and sport, Rita is working alongside general managers, athletic directors, and coaches to explore the benefit of general management consulting techniques in developing athletic administrators and coaching staffs. Craig is an administrator at a major Division I athletic program who has expressed interest in Rita's program. After months of meetings and discussion, Craig agrees to sign Rita to implement a program that he sees as inventive and exciting. Unlike arrangements that are often drawn up for larger corporations and businesses, Craig asks Rita to keep their professional relationship a secret from competing schools unless she talks with him first. However, rather than have Rita sign a non-disclosure and confidentiality agreement before work begins, the agreement is made verbally, and Rita shakes on it. While these agreements typically state that Rita would be unable to disclose the names of the athletic department and individuals with whom she is working, prohibiting her from discussing or marketing the relationship using any medium, the collegial nature of athletics seems to warrant a handshake as opposed to a legal document.

About a year into Rita's engagement with Craig's department, she gets a phone call from the president of the university. She heard through the "grapevine" that Rita has been successfully working with Craig and his staff, and they are interested in bringing in a consultant to guide discussion about much-needed facility upgrades, and possibly even moderating a meeting with the board of directors, athletic department, and university cabinet. She has seen Craig's department improve dramatically throughout Rita's involvement, and wants to include Rita in larger university-wide projects.

When Rita hangs up the phone, she immediately seeks the counsel of her supervisor. Without hesitation, Rita's supervisor asks if a non-disclosure and/or confidentiality agreement was signed as a precursor to the consulting engagement. Rita explains how a handshake took the place of the standard legal documents, as it seemed more appropriate for the sporting environment. Additionally, she explains that working alongside the larger school could be a profitable revenue stream but may be wildly outside her area of competence and expertise. Rita's supervisor first laughs about the handshake, saying, "I'll back you whether you break the verbal agreement or not. It doesn't sound like they have any legal recourse, and it wouldn't make sense that one department of the same school would frown on others knowing about your arrangement. If I were you, I wouldn't worry about it, and I'd strategize to go where the richer opportunity could be." He then continues, "Regarding competence, I trust that you can handle yourself, but why don't you talk with some of the other departments and consider bringing some additional people into the initial meetings regarding this larger project?"

Ethical Issues to Be Considered

At first glance, this case may seem to be rather straightforward. Rita agreed at the beginning of the work to be quiet about her arrangement with Craig; therefore, she has a moral and ethical obligation to keep her word. As a result, failure to maintain confidentiality of her work, and even the nature of her work, with Craig can trigger a violation of ethical codes, including 4.01 Maintaining Confidentiality; 4.02 Discussing the Limits of Confidentiality; 4.04 Minimizing Intrusion on Privacy; and 4.06 Consultations (APA, 2010). However, three more pressing ethical issues appear to be salient in this case, including concerns regarding (3.08) Exploitative Relationships, (2.01) Boundaries of Competence, and (3.06) Conflict of Interest, as Rita would clearly benefit not only from discussing her relationship with Craig, but also from associating her program with Craig and his staff (even if she was not the one who first disclosed the relationship; APA, 2010).

Despite the fact that Rita certainly does not want to violate any ethical codes or lose the trust of the people with whom she has been working in Craig's department, she also wants to put some thought into how she responds to this new request. Clearly she should work to move forward with this opportunity, but she must first gain Craig's buyoff while also recruiting qualified colleagues to assist her efforts. This becomes a greater challenge to navigate because openly admitting that Rita actually worked with Craig will result in a violation of the ethical codes listed earlier. Additionally, she is concerned about how the president found out about her relationship with Craig, and what the perception will be amongst Craig and his colleagues if it leaks back that other departments on campus know about their relationship.

This is a potentially damaging scenario for four reasons: (1) Rita has yet to do anything wrong, but may have difficulty proving otherwise; (2) there is room for others to call Rita's professionalism and word into question; (3) Rita seems to lack the confidence and/or expertise to manage this new request adequately; and (4) Rita has an obligation to her company to pursue the best opportunity possible, especially when that opportunity does not breach any law or general business ethics.

Possible Solution

Once again, the best tool for avoiding more complex ethical dilemmas is communication. While Rita may be limited with what she can say, she can still take proactive measures to communicate her conscientious concerns. Her first step toward avoiding any ethical miscues might be to call Craig and say, "I just received a call from the president regarding our work. While I don't have many details to offer, I want to get your approval to continue the conversation as it seems that she is interested in contracting me in a capacity that extends beyond the athletic department." When making these types of calls, it's always a good idea to take notes and document that conversation. Second, it may then make sense for Rita to call the president back, and explain that she was engaged in a confidential arrangement with Craig and does not feel comfortable discussing details without Craig present. Additionally, she would be smart to invite a meeting to further discuss her work more generically and how it might benefit from this new direction. Rita should also assure the president that while some of the stated objectives of this new program may fall out of her line of competence, she will be assembling a small team to assist her with the project. Additionally, Rita should begin assembling her in-house team of experts who can assist her with this new program and specialize in moderating meetings, negotiations, etc. This approach is extremely proactive, but will likely preserve Rita's reputation as a fair and considerate businessperson who strives to stay ahead of challenges and potential issues.

While it is suggested that Rita assemble a team of trusted colleagues, this could present ethical concerns. It is certainly true that different education programs offer varying types of ethical training, but Rita would be making a mistake if she thought she had to partner with and/or consult colleagues who also had backgrounds in sport psychology. In fact, Hays (2006) advocated for developing and maintaining a "peer culture," or a professional network of like-minded people who could provide ethical guidance in the emerging field of performance psychology (and by no means did she limit this network to sport psychology professionals).

While it is true that the rigor professionals put into understanding ethics and their importance varies dramatically, this is true even within a specific discipline. Fortunately for Rita, ethics transcend work environment and business type. Although Rita may have received a response from her immediate supervisor that could raise some ethical concerns, she certainly has an opportunity to ask questions of other resources. Additionally, she always has her training to fall back on, and in special occasions can reconnect with trusted professors and colleagues from the graduate school. Although Rita may not have the benefit of calling up another consultant trained in sport psychology, she does have the benefit of hearing varying responses from consultants with different types of training. In fact, Rita's efforts to answer her questions may even provide more robust responses than if she limited her search to one discipline.

In considering Rita's dilemma, a key takeaway is that consultants and professional coaches benefit from strategizing and consulting before taking action. A consultant who simply tries to clear, protect, or promote her name may cause more harm than benefit in the long run. It's critical to be open, honest, tactful and considerate with clients. Business is built on relationships, and if one consistently strives to do good work and maintain honest and open relationships, she can trust that her fan base will drown out any negative feedback.

RELATIONSHIPS AND ETHICAL PITFALLS

The ability to develop and maintain a trusting partnership is generally considered a critical barometer for how successful a practitioner can be. In exploring how professional relationships can quickly become unintentionally convoluted, the following case study serves to identify how ethical dilemmas can arise through professional relationships that are not governed by strict and explicit boundaries. Ethical boundaries can be gray. At times, no clear line is crossed, and nothing extraordinarily "wrong" ever occurs. However, as explored, there is reason to continually be sensitive to professional interactions so that a practitioner can avoid ethical dilemmas while also maintaining strong and trusting relationships with key business contacts and clients.

CASE STUDY #2: TROUBLING RELATIONSHIPS

Background

The vice president of human resources (HR) at a global financial firm hires you to work with Susan, contracting you to consult her through a professional development plan and more individualized skills common to sport psychology (e.g., goal setting, team cohesion, etc.). Susan is a mid-level producer who has been identified as a key performer with potential to advance into a more senior leadership role, and an old friend of yours from a completely different level and department within the firm has confided in you that your work with Susan is intended to serve as a pilot for a more expansive commitment to identify and develop internal talent. Although unconfirmed by the VP of HR, your friend assures you that a job well done with Susan will likely lead to more work and a robust and continual contract for years to come.

You work with Susan for six months, meeting with her up to three hours a week via a combination of onsite meetings, emails and phone conversations. During this time, she makes substantial improvements, and the firm has acknowledged noticeable, measurable, and desirable advances. The VP of HR has met with you three times during your work with Susan, and in the last meeting suggested that the firm would like you to continue your efforts for six more months, after which they would like to review results and discuss a more extensive program for high performers. Your friend has also called you recently, kidding you to "not screw this up, as the word on the street is that you're a lock for an extensive contract that's being built into the budget for next year."

Word seems to be spreading fast regarding your efforts and Susan's development, but in an unexpected twist Susan is getting a reputation outside the firm as a top talent in her space. Recruiters begin calling, and Susan is offered a number of lucrative and attractive offers to leave her firm. Through your work with Susan, she has come to trust you as a confidant and advisor, and begins one of your sessions by asking, "Should I consider taking an offer to leave the firm? I have an opportunity to make more money at an executive level, and I'm seriously considering it. What do you think?"

Ethical Issues to Be Considered

First and foremost, the APA Ethics Code is explicit about avoiding the pitfalls of multiple relationships (APA, 2010; Standard 3.05), and you are juggling multiple relationships. While you may not have done anything wrong, the fact that you have a relationship triangle to manage (i.e., Susan, the VP of HR, and your friend) puts you in a difficult position. Who and what are you committed to: the VP, the firm, Susan, or the possibility of getting more work from this firm? In this scenario, the allure of more work is intoxicating as it might help stabilize or, better yet, grow your practice. However, further work will be unlikely if you consult top talent to leave the firm or merely have knowledge that top talent might leave. On the other hand, you have an ethical obligation to serve your client to the best of your ability, and Susan is looking to you for your best guidance and advice.

The crux of the matter is, who is your client—the firm, Susan or both? To avoid this relationship conundrum you must discuss expectations with the firm up front. In ethical terms, a third party has requested your service (APA, 2010; Standard 3.07). A third party, in this case the VP of HR, requested that you work with Susan. It is your obligation to talk with the VP of HR about the scope and limitations of your work, the confidential nature of the relationships you develop, and how you plan to conduct your dual relationship with the paying client (VP of HR/firm) and your consulting client (Susan). If you do not initiate this type of conversation at the onset, the multiple relationships you are developing can become more complex and this early error on your part can easily and quickly spiral into a muddy and confusing dynamic where your professional allegiances and obligations could be compromised.

During this initial conversation it is also recommended that you explicitly explore the parameters of what is confidential, what they expect you to report, what you are comfortable disclosing, how often, in what form and to whom (APA 2010; Standard 4.01 and 4.02). If the VP of HR wants to be informed of the content of your conversations with Susan, then it becomes your obligation to inform Susan from the onset about the nature of confidentiality for your sessions so that she knows what will stay between the two of you, and what others may find out. It may even be worthwhile to develop a form that explicitly outlines the limitations of confidentiality, so that your client is fully informed (APA, 2010; Standard 3.10).

Clearly, it would have been ideal if you had laid out this "what-if" scenario of Susan being recruited to other firms at the beginning of the relationship. However, even if you had put forth this exact account when you discussed the limits of what you can and cannot communicate at the beginning of the consultation, when it comes to something like talent retention, a firm is going to be much less interested in what was discussed six months ago in light of what is happening now. Keep in mind that firms spend a significant amount of money to attract and develop talent, and if you assume that you will be absolved from any responsibility by simply reminding the VP of HR that, six months ago, you forewarned them that this kind of situation could develop, you will be sadly disappointed. In fact, you may very well make the situation worse, sounding selfish and insensitive to their concerns. Their primary concern is that a competitor might now have the benefit of a valued employee in whom they invested a great deal of money, time and effort to develop. To make matters worse, the consultant they invested in, you, not only failed to convince her to stay, but also failed to immediately bring it to the attention of the VP of HR.

Let us assume that you are on top of your game and introduce your concerns about multiple relationships, allegiances, and confidentiality up front. Even with a surgically delivered effort, this particular case still offers some serious ethical roadblocks. The issue of Susan wanting to use you as a sounding board and coach about leaving the firm that hired you is still a sticky situation. If you do not honor your relationship with Susan by coaching her through this difficult decision, she might get offended, lose trust in you, and perhaps even end your work with her. Should this happen, the ramifications may extend beyond your work with her, as your six months of excellent results will be nullified if she is disinterested in openly endorsing your efforts. Conversely, if you coach Susan through the decision and she decides to leave, the firm may turn their back on you for future work, and may even terminate your existing contract the minute Susan announces her resignation; after all, no one likes having a Trojan horse inside their walls. The issue with this particular scenario could become incredibly serious if not dealt with carefully, as you want to avoid the ethical misstep of engaging in an exploitative relationship (APA, 2010; Standard 3.08) while also managing the very real ethical concern of balancing conflicts of interest (APA, 2010; Standard 3.06).

Regardless of the relationship you are working to preserve, you could be exploiting either party for future work, and that is certainly not how you want to gain clients. Every consultant wants to be talked about positively so that word-of-mouth marketing can lead to additional business because that is the single most powerful marketing tool you can employ. However, if you are making decisions about how you consult with future paydays in mind, your priorities may need some tweaking. Even if something as serious as engaging in an exploitative relationship is not at work, and you are not encouraging Susan to stay with the hopes of a more lucrative contract from the existing firm, you still have to deal with your clear conflict of interest. Your personal interests and benefits may interfere with your ability to be objective in this situation because the promise of more work with the firm could sway your approach with Susan. On the other hand, if you do help Susan, the firm will likely retain a different consultant in the future.

Finally, there is yet another layer to this ethical quagmire. What if you really think it might be useful for Susan to consider taking the other job with the competing firm? In addition, you know if she does go there that you have an automatic "in" with the new firm because she will be in a senior role. Once again, you are presented with a conflict of interest, but it is compounded by the fact that you also really believe it is best for the client. What do you do?

Possible Solution

The APA has dedicated a section of its ethics code to addressing the potential pitfalls of consulting within an "organization." Standard 3.11 recommends that a consultant outline the nature of services, who is/are the clients, the relationship the consultant will have with each person, the probable uses of the information obtained, who will have access to the information, and the limits of confidentiality (APA, 2010; Standard 3.11). Each of these is predicated on clear communication up front. As mentioned throughout, it is critical that you communicate with all relevant parties at the onset of a professional arrangement, and continue communicating throughout the contract. Talking with Susan, your contact at the company, and others with whom you develop relationships about your role, confidentiality, and concerns when they arise will not only put you in good standing as an ethical consultant or coach, but will likely strengthen the relationships you are working to develop. Additionally, it is imperative that at the beginning of the coaching relationship, you discuss with the firm how they expect you to deal with a "situation" should it come up. Potentially developing a form for all parties to sign that outlines confidentiality and the use of information may also be helpful. Furthermore, using a case study like this as an example may demonstrate that you are proactive, sincerely have the client's best interests in mind, and are dedicated to working with the client to overcome the complex issues that can arise during a consultation. While these initial conversations are unlikely to completely shield you from scrutiny if a situation does ensue, it is beneficial that you lay it out early so the firm never questions, "Why didn't you clarify your role in the beginning?"

Discussing with Susan that you believe it is in the best interest of the coaching relationship for you to avoid discussing her possible resignation and acceptance of another position because of its compromising nature is a good place to start. Explaining to her that you have a dual relationship and you do not want to jeopardize anyone's trust may put her at ease. Let her know that you are not going to say anything to anyone else at this point, and encourage her to seek out the counsel of a trusted mentor, her supervisor, or even HR. Additionally, assure her that you would be happy to strategize with her about speaking with her colleagues, as it may be an uncomfortable conversation. You can also offer to facilitate the dialogue if she thinks it would be of benefit. Finally, continue to check in with the VP of HR, and if there are ever questions about Susan moving on, suggest that you would not consult with Susan on such a move and it is best to talk with her directly. Should anyone ever confront you about not choosing a side, sharing information, or becoming more involved, you now have an opportunity to cite the APA Ethics Code while assuring that you are a professional bound to an ethical framework that simply prohibits such actions.

SUMMARY

As sport psychologist Kate Hays (2006) pointed out, "ethics can be described as a continuing process of attending to one's knowledge, beliefs, values, and practices" (p. 224). Accordingly, the purpose of this chapter is to encourage you to take stock of these factors and consider the nuances of the process of consulting in business and the types of challenges you might face. Whatever you take from this chapter, stay open to making new mistakes. It is not the mistake that results in ethical concerns, but often the manner in which a consultant deals with the mistake. Is it communicated well? Is it dealt with appropriately? Is it reported and discussed with qualified peers? These are the questions that often require the diligence and rigor needed to maintain an ethically sound practice and reputation. Additionally, ask questions and reach out to peers and mentors, as they can be invaluable to your practice and development. They can serve as essential resources with whom to consult when ethically challenging dilemmas are anticipated and encountered, which, you can be sure, they will.

REFERENCES

American Psychological Association. (2010). American Psychological Association ethical principles of psychologists and code of conduct: Including 2010 Amendments. Retrieved from http://www.apa.org/ethics/code/index.aspx

Brenkert, G. G. (2010). The limits and prospects of business ethics. *Business Ethics Quarterly, 20*(4), 703–709.

Hays, K. F. (2006). Being fit: The ethics of practice diversification in performance psychology. *Professional Psychology: Research & Practice, 37*(3), 223–232.

Jones, G. (2002). Performance excellence: A personal perspective on the link between sport and business. *Journal of Applied Sport Psychology, 14,* 268–281.

Lowenstein, R. (1996). *Buffet: The making of an American capitalist.* New York, NY: Random House.

Martens, R. (1987). Science, knowledge, and sport psychology. *The Sport Psychologist, I,* 29–55.

Meyers, A., Coleman, J., Whelan, J., & Mehlenbeck, R. (2001). Examining careers in sport psychology: Who is working and who is making money. *Professional Psychology: Research and Practice, 32*(1), 5–11.

Watson, J., & Etzel, E. (2000). Considering ethics: Using the Internet in sport psychology. *AAASP Newsletter 15,* 13–16.

WVU College of Physical Activity and Sport Sciences. (2011). Bachelor of science in sport and exercise psychology. Retrieved from http://cpass.wvu.edu/academic_programs/bachelors/sep/sep

CHAPTER 9

SPORTS MEDICINE: THE ETHICS OF WORKING AS PART OF A UNIVERSITY MEDICAL TEAM

James C. Moncier

INTRODUCTION

Katzenbach and Smith (1993) define a team as "a small number of people with complementary skills who are committed to a common purpose, performance goals, and approach for which they are mutually accountable" (p. 112). While this definition was originally used to describe a business team, it can easily describe other types of teams including athletic teams, teaching teams, and legal teams.

Another type of team that fits the above definition is a medical team. One such medical team includes a group of professionals working within a college athletic setting, also known as a university sports medicine team. In the author's experience of working as a sport psychologist and member of such a team for a number of years, the composition of a university sports medicine team can be both diverse and dynamic depending upon the circumstances. Members may include the athlete and, often, his or her parents, plus professionals such as primary care physicians (e.g., a family physician, internist, and/or pediatrician who has also completed training in sports medicine), athletic trainers, sport psychologists, dieticians, orthopedists and physical therapists (in cases of injury), coaches, administrators, and additional professionals as applicable (e.g., neurologists, neuropsychologists, radiologists, etc).

Working as part of a university sports medicine team can be very instructive and rewarding as it offers the members of the team a rare chance to observe, often directly, how their interventions link with interventions from other professionals. However, the work can also be challenging, as different professionals can have differing philosophies and ethical responsibilities related to issues such as when an athlete is ready to return to play, confidentiality, where and how treatment is provided, and who is the actual client. It is critical that the sport psychologist, as a member of a university sports medicine team, be alert and ready to respond to these potential conflicts.

THE CASE OF STACEY

The following case study will help illustrate a university sports medicine team in action. Stacey is a 19-year-old outfielder on her college softball team. She originally came to the attention of the team physician soon after returning for the fall semester of her sophomore year. She complained of significant back pain "all the time." Stacey stated that the back pain started at the end of the previous school year following a collision with a teammate during a game, approximately four months prior. She stated that the pain was interfering with her sleeping habits and noted that it regularly takes her about an hour to fall asleep once in bed. She related that on an average night she wakes up frequently due to pain, as much as every hour after initially falling asleep some nights.

Stacey also reported losing weight over the past 18 months—she dropped from 145 pounds to 120. She denied any eating issues such as binging, purging, using diuretics or laxatives, or starving herself. Instead, she attributed her weight loss to "not eating healthy." She reported that she had cut out all fat in her diet and mainly ate fruits and vegetables. She noted that she did eat lean meat occasionally, usually turkey or chicken. She said that since she had returned to school for the fall semester, several teammates and members of the training staff mentioned to her that she looked thin. She stated that she did not see herself as thin but acknowledged that the comments from others made her self-conscious. Stacey also reported that she had had only two menstrual periods during the past year, and therefore was prescribed birth control pills by her hometown physician to help regulate her cycle. She denied any other chronic health issues and any surgical history. Finally, Stacey reported that she was experiencing decreased energy, speed, strength, and "fight at the end of practice."

At the team physician's request, the athletic trainer set up referrals for Stacey for an X-ray of her back and for a consultation with a sports dietician. When Stacey returned the next week, the team physician told her that the X-ray had revealed a posterior rib fracture on her right side. Stacey noted that this made sense since she usually slept on her back. She also related that she had met with the local sports dietician, who had suggested a 2400 calorie diet that included more protein than she was currently ingesting. She reported being ambivalent about trying the diet mainly due to her concern that she would "end up getting fat." The team physician pointed out that the rib fracture should have healed within two months and that Stacey's decreased caloric intake was likely impeding the process. He also stated that until there was evidence that the rib was healing, she would be unable to practice or play with the softball team. Stacey acknowledged that she plays and feels better when she weighs around 140 pounds. She voiced her desire to become "a force" on the team again and reluctantly agreed to comply with the diet. The head coach was consulted and agreed with the plan. Within three weeks, Stacey had gained eight pounds, the pain in her back was lessening, and a subsequent X-ray confirmed that the rib was healing. The team physician released her to return to play and she earned a starting position. By the end of the fall season, she weighed 135 pounds and denied having any pain in her back. She also noted that sleep had improved considerably, as had her general energy and stamina levels. After completing the fall semester, Stacey returned home for Christmas break.

Upon her return from Christmas break, Stacey asked the head athletic trainer to help her work out several knots in her back. While doing this, the trainer noticed that Stacey had very poor musculature and appeared to have lost weight again. When asked about her diet, Stacey responded that she started to lose weight almost immediately after returning home. As a result, Stacey noted that both she and her parents concluded that the diet was not solving the problem. She then stopped complying with the prescribed diet and returned to her previous low fat/low calorie diet. A subsequent weight check indicated a drop from 135 pounds to 126. She again denied actively trying to lose weight and voiced her concern that she was heading back to the problems she faced in the fall. The athletic trainer, also concerned about the weight loss, suggested a meeting with the team physician. At this meeting, both Stacey and the trainer passed on the updated information. Stacey added that, for the first time, she had trouble following the off-season training plan. She said, "[I] just could not seem to hold myself to the training schedule coach gave us." Instead, she stated that she had spent much of her time at home "just sitting around the house." The team physician became concerned that Stacey's problems were beginning to look like they were influenced by emotional issues. He suggested that Stacey meet with the sport psychologist who consulted with the athletic department and explained that this person was a professional who specialized in helping athletes improve their sport performance using mental skills. She agreed to the referral.

Stacey met with the sport psychologist in an office within the athletic training room. They spent the beginning of the first session discussing confidentiality and its limits. As part of this discussion, the sport psychologist acknowledged that they were meeting in an office within a busy athletic training room. Others, including teammates, were likely to know with whom Stacey was meeting. However, the sport psychologist emphasized that, even though Stacey was referred by the team physician, Stacey was the client and had control over who knew what was discussed in these meetings. She was told that she even had control over whether the coach and/or the team physician knew the information. She voiced her understanding. Finally, they discussed how others may have a negative view of her simply because she was meeting with a sport psychologist. Stacey acknowledged that she was a bit nervous and was not certain what to expect.

Stacy stated that she was not "crazy." The sport psychologist emphasized that his role within the athletic department typically focused on helping athletes improve their performance using mental skills. This seemed to help her relax and she stated that she wanted to continue. She admitted that she was frustrated that she was unable to perform as well as before and would welcome any help in improving her softball performance. They spent the bulk of the initial session discussing the events that had led to the team physician recommending the referral to the sport psychologist. The sport psychologist concluded the session by reminding her that she had control over what others knew about what they discussed in session. She was asked to consider who, if anyone should also have the information and was given examples of possible recipients including the team physician, the team athletic trainer, her coach, and/or her parents. She agreed to consider this for the following session.

In the subsequent session, Stacey reported participating in softball for 11 years. She reported having difficulty developing friends from fifth until seventh grade following a family move. She reported that she felt drawn to sports (especially softball) as a way of coping with the resulting loneliness. She was asked how the transition from high school to college had gone and she responded that it had been "rough." She stated that her home town was about five hours away from the college. She was only able to visit home during holidays. Her freshman year was a bit overwhelming, but she had slowly adjusted. She rated her performance on the field as "good" and stated that she performed well enough to earn significant playing time. During her freshman year, she felt that she had related best with the juniors and seniors on the team and tended to socialize with them. Unfortunately, that meant that she had lost many of her friends to graduation now that she was a sophomore. She felt that she had really not "connected" with the newer members of the team. As a result, her support system at college was characterized as "poor."

Ironically, she noted that over the semester break, she felt lonely at home since she had grown apart from many of her friends from high school. She reported that while at home she was frequently not hungry, but she recognized that she needed to eat and would often eat "something" as opposed to the past when she would miss meals regularly. She admitted her doubts that she was even close to consuming the 2400 calories per day recommended by the dietician last semester and assumed this was the reason for her recent weight loss.

As part of the session, the sport psychologist evaluated Stacey for depressive symptoms. Stacey reported decreased energy and concentration since returning from the break. She also noted that she usually enjoyed exercising and working out, but felt a real lack of interest in either since the end of the last semester. Stacey denied any crying spells or feeling sad, but did acknowledge that she did not really seem to be enjoying anything. She also noted that she had been short tempered with teammates upon her return. She denied any thoughts of suicide. She was asked if she had any family history of depression and acknowledged that a paternal uncle had been treated in the past. Finally, Stacey noted that she was prone to being "brutally critical" of herself, especially when many responsibilities were going on at once, such as practices, games, and tests during the season. She noted that she even went so far as calling herself names, such as "stupid," after making mistakes.

The session ended with an agreement to meet the following week. She was given a copy of the Beck Depression Inventory (BDI-II; Beck, 1996) with instructions to complete it for next session. At the next appointment, the BDI-II was scored. Her resulting score of 26 placed her solidly in the moderately depressed range. Stacey seemed very surprised at this result and restated that she did not feel depressed. The symptoms of depression were discussed and she admitted that many of them fit, especially when the symptoms she mentioned during the last session were considered. The relationship between depression and performance was discussed, especially how decreased energy, appetite, and interest appeared to be impacting how she was performing during the fall season.

Finally, the sport psychologist stated that since it appeared depression was a major factor in Stacey's declining performance, and since depression was more formally a clinical issue, he suggested that two additional recommendations be considered. The first was that Stacey consider a referral to a mental health professional outside of the athletic department who had expertise in treating depression. The sport psychologist voiced his concern that, even though he was experienced in treating depression and is licensed as a psychologist, switching from a sport performance focus to a clinical focus might be a difficult change for Stacey to make. Stacey disagreed and stated that she felt comfortable working with the sport psychologist. She pointed out that, since her performance was being negatively impacted by depression, work to lessen the impact of depression would enhance her sport performance. She stated that she did not want to "have to tell my story to someone new." After fully discussing the pros and cons in detail, they agreed to continue to work together.

The second recommendation was that Stacey be referred for a medication evaluation. Since the team physician was trained in sports medicine and also had experience with prescribing anti-depressants, he was suggested as an appropriate referral source for this evaluation. Stacey agreed with this recommendation. Finally, they looked at options for communicating with the main members of the sports medicine team. In this case, team comprised the head coach, the team physician, and the head athletic trainer. Stacey suggested a group meeting and stated that she was comfortable discussing the plan to get her back to being a "force" on the team with the group as a whole. The two discussed what Stacey wanted addressed and a plan was made to focus on the need for the medication evaluation and treatment for depression. She signed releases of information to allow the sharing of information. Stacey also asked if the sport psychologist would explain to her parents what was happening. They agreed upon setting up a conference call to do so and Stacey also signed a release of information for her parents.

The meeting with the sports medicine team was held several days later. All team members were updated on her eating issues and how these appeared to be a side effect of the larger issue of depression. The head coach stated that Stacey was not the player she had been in the past. She noted that Stacey was especially not as aggressive at the plate. A strong recommendation was made for her to continue to consult with the dietician. Stacey agreed. The depressive symptoms were also discussed and the recommendation was made for the team physician to conduct a medication evaluation. He agreed and the evaluation was scheduled. Finally, the sport psychologist stated that he would continue to work with Stacey on performance issues, in addition to helping her manage her depressive symptoms.

Following the medical team meeting, Stacey and the sport psychologist had a conference call with Stacey's parents. Stacey's parents were updated on their daughter's condition and the medical team's recommendations. Both parents stated that they had suspected "something was going on." However, when they voiced their concern to Stacey, she regularly minimized how she was feeling (Stacey acknowledged this). They voiced relief that Stacey was getting help. Stacey met with the team physician and was started on a trial of anti-depressant medication to which she responded well. She also started a course of psychotherapy focused on relief from both her somatic and cognitive symptoms of depression along with social skills building and self-talk management. Her play on the field improved gradually during the spring and she earned a starting position in the outfield. The sports medicine team continued to stay in contact informally through occasional meetings or by phone as needed. This lasted through the summer semester. By the time the fall softball season of Stacey's junior year began, she had gained much of her weight back (139 pounds) and was reporting a significant decrease in both her negative self-talk and in most of the somatic symptoms of depression that she had previously experienced. The last BDI-II she took resulted in a score of 10 ("minimal depression"). She continued to take the anti-depressant and contact with the sport psychologist dropped to a maintenance level of approximately one meeting per month. She also joined several campus activity groups and reported enjoying meeting new people. Finally, her menstrual cycle was occurring regularly and she reported that the pain in her back was completely gone.

DISCUSSION

As the case study suggests, being a member of a university sports medicine team affords the sport psychologist the opportunity of working alongside a unique and frequently dynamic configuration of professionals with complementary skills who have the common goal of helping the athlete perform at his or her best. The case study presented describes one fairly common path (in the author's experience) by which an athlete is referred for sport psychology services within a college athletic department. The scenario also presents several ethical challenges that require some consideration before entering the sports medicine setting. These challenges fall under the following ethical standards from the American Psychological Association's (APA's) most recent ethical code (2002): (1) competence, (2) human relations, and (3) privacy and confidentiality.

Competence
Per APA (2002), "psychologists provide services . . . with populations and in areas only within the boundaries of their competence, based upon their education, training, supervised experience, consultation, study, or professional experience" (p. 1063). Previous authors have discussed the need for specialized education, training, and supervision in order to develop competence in sport psychology (American Psychological Association, n.d.; Brown & Cogan, 2006; Hays & Brown, 2004; Stapleton, Hankes, Hays, & Parham, 2010). Stapleton and colleagues (Stapleton et al., 2010) argue that an individual developing a specialty in sport psychology should include training in the fields of sport science and medicine, as well as in areas such as clinical or counseling psychology. In the scenario, competence in the diagnosis and treatment of depression was required for effective treatment. An additional, but no less important, level of competence is systemic in nature and includes developing an understanding of the context and culture in which a sports medicine team functions, a concept referred to as contextual intelligence (Brown, Gould, & Foster, 2005).

The purpose of licensure is to ensure that the licensee has obtained the minimum education and training expected of those in the field. According to Dr. Steve DeMers, Executive Officer of the Association of State and Provincial Psychology Boards, the boards of psychology in the United States and Canada only currently offer generic licenses to practice psychology (personal communication, September 7, 2010). No specialty licenses for psychologists are currently offered, including in sport psychology. Therefore, the burden of proof of competence in sport psychology ultimately rests with the clinician (Brown & Cogan, 2006) and can be accomplished through a variety of methods including formal study (e.g., coursework and/or continuing education workshops), informal study, consultation, and supervised experience.

Human Relations

Several subsections within the Human Relations standard of the APA Ethics Code (2002) have application within this scenario. These include avoiding harm (section 3.04), cooperation with other professionals (3.09), informed consent (3.10), and psychological services delivered to or through organizations (3.11).

Avoiding Harm/Cooperation With Other Professionals

Per the APA Ethics Code (2002), "psychologists take reasonable steps to avoid harming their clients/patients" (p. 1065) which, as noted by Whelan, Meyers, and Elkins (2002), is "the primary goal of the [ethics] code" (p. 508). In the case scenario, cooperating and collaborating with the other members of the sports medicine team is one of the more obvious ways that beneficence is demonstrated. APA (2002) states "when indicated and professionally appropriate, psychologists cooperate with other professionals in order to serve their clients/patients effectively and appropriately" (p. 1065). Using the definition of a team from Katzenbach and Smith (1993), in order to best serve Stacey, the sport psychologist must communicate with the other members of the university sports medicine team. In fact, in this case, if the team members do not communicate, there is a high probability that Stacey's problem will only be partially treated since each of the team members had important information that added to the larger clinical picture.

Informed Consent

Informed consent refers to the presentation of "all the information necessary for a client to make an educated, informed decision about the likely benefits and risks of the specific intervention to be used and the development of a professional working relationship with the therapist/consultant" (Moore, 2003, p. 603). The APA Ethics Code (2002) adds that informed consent includes information about third party involvement and the limits of confidentiality. Johnson (2004) notes that "it is an ethical obligation to provide all the pertinent facts to enable the athlete to make an informed decision" (p. 177). The use of informed consent is evidenced through discussions between Stacey and the sport psychologist regarding the limits of confidentiality, involving members of the university sports medicine team and Stacey's parents, and discussing both the pros and cons of adding treatment for depression as part of their treatment plan and, as per Linder and colleagues (e.g., Linder, Brewer, Van Raalte, & De Lange, 1991), the pros and cons of being an athlete and working with a sport psychologist.

Psychological Services Delivered to or Through Organizations

When a third party requests that services be provided, several issues become relevant when working as part of a university sports medicine team within an organization. Such issues often include managing confidentiality, determining for whom the sport psychologist works (i.e., who is the client), and avoiding conflicts of interest. These and other potential issues often can be prevented from becoming problems by clarifying the role of the sport psychologist and establishing policies for managing information obtained during the provision of sport psychology services with the organization before the consultation starts (Andersen, Van Raalte, Brewer, 2001; Aoyagi & Portenga, 2010; Gardner, 2001; Moore, 2003; Whelan, Meyer, & Elkins, 2002).

For instance, Brown and Cogan (2006) note that the "psychologist must clearly establish the boundaries of confidentiality with consideration for the athlete-client, the psychologist, and any referral source who may be a coach, parent, teammate, team physician, or athletic administrator" (p. 17).

Determining who pays for the sport psychologist's services often answers the question of who is the identified client but this is not an absolute. In fact, in the case scenario, the sport psychologist donates his time to the university. Regardless, clarifying this issue up front both with the organization and with the individuals involved can eliminate misunderstandings as the consultation begins (Aoyagi & Portenga, 2010; Gardner, 2001; Haberl & Peterson, 2006; Johnson, 2004; Stainback, Moncier, & Taylor, 2007). Additionally, reminding all parties on an ongoing basis about who maintains the rights to the information gathered will help keep the issue clear. While this is not a direct issue in the scenario, it is a safe assumption in this instance that Stacey is the client.

While not an issue in the scenario, an additional, and frequent, situation facing sport psychologists is that of a mandatory referral. An example can include an athlete who is having significant personal problems which impact his or her performance and for which he or she has been unwilling to seek professional help. In this situation, a coach may step in and make further participation with the team contingent upon the athlete's meeting with a psychologist. Haberl and Peterson (2006) suggest clarifying realistic expectations for each party involved at the beginning and throughout the relationship, in this case with both the coach and the athlete. Included in this ongoing discussion should be a regular clarification about what information from the meetings with the athlete will be shared and with whom. Finally, it is crucial for the sport psychologist to remember to share only information which is relevant to the referral and "only with persons clearly concerned with such matters" (APA, 2002, p. 1066).

Privacy and Confidentiality

Koocher and Keith-Spiegel (2008) define privacy as "the basic entitlement of people to decide how much of their property, thoughts, feelings, and personal data to share with others" (p. 193). They define the ethical principle of confidentiality as "an explicit contract or promise not to reveal anything about a client except under certain circumstances agreed to by both parties" (p. 194). Understandings of both are critical to providing health and psychological services and have their roots in the APA (2002) ethical principle of respect for people's rights and dignity. It is this ethical promise and protection of confidentiality (tempered by the knowledge of the limits as required by state and federal law, the respect for client privacy, and the answer to the question of to whom the professional answers) that allow clients to feel safe in disclosing information that frequently leads to an understanding of the presenting issue and keys to potential solutions. All parties involved need to know who gets access to the information and what the limits are ahead of time (Aoyagi & Portenga, 2010; Dunn, George, Churchill, & Spindler, 2007). Suggestions for managing confidentiality as a member of a university sports medicine team include reviewing confidentiality with the referral source at the time of the referral (Brown & Cogan, 2006) and regularly reminding the athlete about to whom you answer (Tucker, 2004). Additionally, Brown and Cogan (2006) recommend discussing the parameters and limits of the disclosure when an athlete signs a release of information. The APA Ethics Code (2002) states that "psychologists include in written and oral reports and consultations, only information germane to the purpose for which the communication is made" (p. 1066). This is clearly relevant to the case scenario as shown, given the many parties involved in the consultation and by releases being signed for all members of the sports medicine team and Stacey's parents. Additionally, the sport psychologist discussed with Stacey the extent of the information she wanted passed on to the rest of the sports medicine team.

Boundaries

Managing boundaries is another issue relevant when working as a member of a university sports medicine team. Brown and Cogan (2006) note that boundaries are sometimes less rigid and more difficult to maintain in sport psychology settings than in traditional psychology or counseling settings. They explain this as partially the result of sport psychologists frequently practicing in non-traditional settings. Haberl and Peterson (2006) more directly state that some sport psychologists take their practice to where the athletes are. Meetings with clients in a gym, on a golf course, on a tennis court, in a training room or in any number of additional sport-specific venues are relatively common. In sport psychology practice, strict adherence to traditional boundaries may not be in the best interest of the client and can result in ineffective service provision (Stapleton et al., 2010). Brown and Cogan (2006) argue that avoiding invitations to non-traditional situations, such as dinner meetings or team gatherings, may not be necessary but knowing how to handle them is critical. Of course, clarifying the expectations for each party involved at the beginning and throughout the relationship is important as noted above by Haberl and Peterson (2006).

The issues of boundaries are addressed in two ways in the case scenario. The first relates to where Stacey and the sport psychologist meet for their sessions—in an office within the training room. The second is the switch from a focus on mental skills development to a more clinical focus in which depression is added to the treatment agenda. Both are handled through discussion.

The issue of the location of treatment focuses on confidentiality and its limits. As Andersen, Van Raalte, and Brewer (2001) state, because of the location of service delivery, it often becomes obvious who is being served. However, as described in the case scenario, Stacey is assured that while others may know that she is seeing a sport psychologist, she has control over who knows what she discusses in the sessions. Andersen et al. (2001) also discuss how in the case of a change of service focus, a referral to another service provider may not work because the athlete may not have an interest in starting a new relationship with another service provider. In the above scenario, the boundary is maintained by an open discussion of the pros and cons of changing the focus of the work. Stacey, in this case, made the decision to continue working with the original provider through the process of informed consent. It should be noted that if the sport psychology consultant was not trained in the treatment of mental health issues, a referral to a mental health professional would have been made.

Multiple Relationships

While the case scenario does not feature multiple relationships as an issue, multiple-role relationship precursors are inherent in onsite applied work (Andersen, Van Raalte, & Brewer,

2001) and are often unavoidable (Moore, 2003). An example can be a situation in which a sport psychologist is hired by the head coach to provide services to a team and also works with individual athletes on the same team. If an individual athlete has a problem with the head coach, how might the sport psychologist help the athlete and remain objective?

It is important that the practitioner remember that multiple roles can increase the potential for conflicts of interest. A conflict of interest occurs when two (or more) roles interfere with each other and can reasonably be expected to (1) impair the psychologist's objectivity, competence, or effectiveness in performing his or her functions as a psychologist, or (2) "expose the person or organization with whom the professional relationship exists to harm or exploitation" (APA, 2002, p. 1065). However, Aoyagi and Portenga (2010) remind us that we do not work in a vacuum and that, while working within the culture can lead to multiple roles, instead of avoiding these, it is important to maintain appropriate boundaries. Managing multiple roles and boundaries can be aided through the use of supervision and consultation (Van Raalte & Andersen, 2002). Watson and Clement (2008) also suggest that practitioners avoid becoming involved in multiple roles unless the potential for harm to the client is minimized and they have taken all reasonable steps to avoid such problems. This is especially important as the consultant is responsible for personal oversight since he or she is likely to be the only person in the environment knowledgeable of his or her own professional roles, responsibilities, and ethics (Aoyagi & Portenga, 2010). Additionally, and as with the other issues discussed in this chapter, proactively managing the potential for problems can be helped by the sport psychologist clarifying his or her role, the expectations for managing information, and who is the client in each situation prior to the beginning of service provision with all those involved.

SUMMARY

In summary, being a part of a sports medicine team at a university offers the members an opportunity to work alongside a unique and often dynamic team of professionals with complementary skills that have the common goal of helping athletes perform at their best. The case scenario provides an example of a relatively traditional university sports medicine team in action and demonstrates some of the issues a sport psychologist is likely to have to manage as a member of the team. These issues frequently include being competent on several levels, maintaining confidentiality, assuring that the athletes with whom he or she works are able to exercise autonomy in their work together (by providing information regarding informed consent), and managing the multiple roles that are frequent within the athletic arena. Many ethical problems can be avoided by discussing them up front with those involved. Similarly, and as suggested by Stainback, Moncier, and Taylor (2007), by thinking about the ethical issues unique to sport psychology consultation within a sports medicine setting and the possible options for their successful resolution before being confronted with them, the sport psychologist will increase the likelihood of being an integral member of the university sports medicine team through effective and ethical practice.

REFERENCES

American Psychological Association. (2002). Ethical principles of psychologists and code of conduct. *American Psychologist, 57,* 1060–1611.

American Psychological Association (n.d.). *Public description of sport psychology.* Retrieved from http://www.apa.org/ed/graduate/specialize/sports.aspx

Andersen, M. B., Van Raalte, J. L., & Brewer, B. W. (2001). Sport psychology service delivery: Staying ethical while keeping loose. *Professional Psychology: Research and Practice, 32,* 12–18.

Aoyagi, M. W., & Portenga, S. T. (2010). The role of positive ethics and virtues in the context of sport and performance psychology service delivery. *Professional Psychology: Research and Practice, 41,* 253–259.

Beck, A. T., Steer, R. A., & Brown, G. K. (1996). *Manual for the Beck Depression Inventory-II.* San Antonio, TX: Psychological Corporation.

Brown, C. H., Gould, D., & Foster, S. (2005). A framework for developing contextual intelligence (CI). *The Sport Psychologist, 19,* 51–62.

Brown, J. L., & Cogan, K. D. (2006). Ethical clinical practice and sport psychology: When two worlds collide. *Ethics & Behavior, 16,* 15–23.

Dunn, W. R., George, M. S., Churchill, L., & Spindler, K. P. (2007). Ethics in sports medicine. *The American Journal of Sports Medicine, 35,* 840–844.

Gardner, F. L. (2001). Applied sport psychology in professional sports: The team psychologist. *Professional Psychology: Research and Practice, 32,* 34–39.

Hays, K. F., & Brown, C. H. (2004). *You're on! Consulting for peak performance.* Washington, DC: American Psychological Association.

Hays, K. F., McCann, S. M., Cogan, K. D., Peterson, K. M. (2009, September). Doing performance psychology: Working with athletes, performing artists, and business leaders. Lecture presented at the annual meeting of the Association for Applied Sport Psychology, Salt Lake City, UT.

Johnson, R. (2004). The unique ethics of sports medicine. *Clinics in Sports Medicine, 23,* 175–182.

Katzenbach, J. R., & Smith, D. K. (1993). The discipline of teams. *Harvard Business Review, 71*(2), 111–120.

Koocher, G. P., & Keith-Spiegel, P. (2008). *Ethics in psychology and the mental health professions: Standards and cases* (3rd ed.). New York, NY: Oxford University Press.

Linder, D. E., Brewer, B. W., Van Raalte, J. L., & De Lange, N. (1991). A negative halo for athletes who consult sport psychologists: Replication and extension. *Journal of Sport and Exercise Psychology, 13,* 133–148.

Moore, Z. E. (2003). Ethical dilemmas in sport psychology: Discussion and recommendations for practice. *Professional Psychology: Research and Practice, 34,* 601–610.

Stainback, R. D., Moncier, J. C., & Taylor, R. E. (2007). Sport psychology: A clinician's perspective. In G. Tenenbaum & R. C. Eklund (Eds.), *Handbook of sport psychology* (3rd ed., pp. 310–331). Hoboken, NJ: John Wiley & Sons, Inc.

Stapleton, A. B., Hankes, D. M., Hays, K. F., & Parham, W. D. (2010). Ethical dilemmas in sport psychology: A dialogue on the unique aspects impacting practice. *Professional Practice: Research and Practice, 41,* 143–152.

Tucker, A. M. (2004). Ethics and the professional team physician. *Clinics in Sports Medicine, 23,* 227–241.

Van Raalte, J. L., & Andersen, M. D. (2002). Referral process in sport psychology. In J. L. Van Raalte & B. W. Brewer (Eds.), *Exploring sport and exercise psychology* (2nd ed., pp. 325–337). Washington, DC: American Psychological Association.

Watson II, J. C., & Clement, D. (2008). Ethical and practical issues related to multiple role relationships in sport psychology. *Athletic Insight, 10*(4). Retrieved from http://www.athleticinsight.coom/Vol10Iss4/Multiple.htm.

Whelan, J. P., Meyers, A. W., & Elkins, T. D. (2002). Ethics in sport and exercise psychology. In J. L. Van Raalte & B. W. Brewer (Eds.), *Exploring sport and exercise psychology* (2nd ed., pp. 503–523). Washington, DC: American Psychological Association.

CHAPTER 10

ETHICAL CHALLENGES FOR MENTAL SKILLS TRAINERS WORKING WITH SOLDIERS IN THE UNITED STATES ARMY

Tiz A. Arnold, Marjourie B. Fusinetti, and Keith A. Wilson

INTRODUCTION

The United States Army strives to develop soldiers and leaders who are both physically and mentally tough, and has recently come to recognize the importance of deliberately training the force's mental toughness just as it trains their physical toughness. Consequently, the Army has begun to rely on mental training to supplement its well-known and rigorous physical, technical, and tactical training. While mental skills training has been conducted with cadets at the United States Military Academy since 1993, not until 2006 were sport psychology practitioners employed to provide mental skills training (e.g., building confidence, enhancing focus, using imagery, setting goals, managing energy and arousal, etc.) to soldiers Army-wide, with the ultimate goal of enhancing their performance in training exercises, on the battlefield, and on the home front. Civilian mental skills trainers (MSTs) are now stationed at Army posts across the United States, and the types of performances they target varies by their location and the populations with whom they work, potentially including marksmanship, the Army Physical Fitness Test, tactical maneuvers, field artillery operations, scout and sniper operations, healing and recovery, and learning and comprehension.

The program's MSTs come from a variety of backgrounds and have different educational experiences and credentials. All of the trainers are required to hold a masters or doctoral degree, an increasing number are Certified Consultants within the Association for Applied Sport Psychology (AASP), and some hold state licensure in their specific professional field, which allows them to legally perform counseling/psychology skills. However, none of the MSTs are permitted to conduct any clinical work as part of the Army's mental skills training program, and all share the common goal of helping soldiers and Army leaders perform at the highest level through education and application of concepts from the fields of sport and performance psychology. Trainers conduct this work in a number of formats and settings (e.g., formal classroom instruction, individual consultations, training during field exercises, and mobile training teams), and as with practitioner-client relationships in any setting, the potential exists for ethical dilemmas to occur.

The mental skills training program's headquarters has produced and occasionally revises the curriculum used by its trainers at their respective Army posts. However, the sites have some leeway to determine the best methods for implementing the program at their locations and for the specific populations with whom they work (e.g., tactical units, wounded soldiers, schoolhouses), and the sites may differ in the structure of their training. For example, some sites require all soldiers to initially participate in a formal group training (e.g., approximately 15-30 soldiers) in a classroom setting. This training is a 16-hour course, generally taught over two consecutive days, that introduces the mental skills and their applications for soldiers, with a primary focus on performance enhancement. During this interactive training, soldiers are educated about various concepts and theories from the field of sport and performance psychology, and are also given the opportunity to engage in hands-on practical exercises that facilitate their learning, acquisition, and application of the skills. Some sites also require MSTs to conduct the group training using a team-teaching style; one trainer teaches a lesson while the other observes the training, tracks the group dynamics, and is available to deal with any unusual circumstances that may arise (e.g., assist a soldier who arrives late, deal with a medical problem, escort a soldier out of the training). Only following the completion of this formal training are soldiers permitted to opt into working with an MST in a one-on-one format. Soldiers may seek to engage in mastery training to mentally prepare for a specific performance (e.g., a shooting competition, the Warrior Games, test-taking) or simply desire to master skills such as relaxation or increasing confidence.

The Army's MSTs are required to be current AASP members, and some belong to other organizations such as the American Psychological Association (APA) and the National Association of Social Workers (NASW). Each of these organizations provides guidance (AASP, n.d.; APA, 2010; NASW, 2008) to its members pertaining to what professional behaviors are and are not ethically appropriate, and all of them encourage their members to perform their duties in an ethical manner. Because all of the trainers belong to AASP and none of them, regardless of their education, experience, and credentials, engage in clinical work, the AASP ethics code (AASP, n.d.) is particularly relevant to the discussion of sport and performance psychology as it is practiced within the military environment. The AASP code is based on six general principles and contains 25 general ethical standards to guide practitioners' work. Those sections of the code that appear to have particular relevance to MSTs practicing in the Army today are: (1) competence, (2) roles and boundaries, (3) maintaining confidentiality, (4) exploitation and harassment, (5) multiple relationships, and (6) referral. This chapter will discuss these ethical issues and the measures the program has taken to minimize problems related to these issues, and will conclude with a case study.

ETHICAL ISSUES FACED BY MSTS IN A MILITARY SETTING

The military environment has characteristics, demands, and restrictions that make it a unique setting in which to operate as an MST. While sport and performance psychology practitioners in all environments face ethical dilemmas, the Army's MSTs encounter certain dilemmas regularly. The most prevalent ethical issues are addressed below.

Competence

AASP's Principle A (Competence) and General Ethical Standard 2 (Boundaries of Competence; AASP, n.d.) emphasize that all professionals must recognize their limitations and be cognizant of the areas that are within and outside of their areas of current expertise. For example, individuals with clinical backgrounds may be limited in terms of their knowledge of sport science, while those with a sport science background must know their limits when it comes to counseling and clinical work. In addition to simply being aware of their limitations, this standard mandates that professionals in the field only practice within their areas of competence. Consequently, the Army's MSTs, because of their diverse backgrounds, must practice within the limits of competence set forth by their education, training, supervision, and licensure. In addition to the guidance given to practitioners by the AASP ethical guidelines, the Army provides MSTs with additional clarity related to their roles and responsibilities.

The U.S. Army strictly regulates who may provide clinical services to its soldiers, as well as the protocols to which they must adhere when doing so. Specifically, civilians must receive clinical privileges from an Army installation's medical treatment facility. The Army's mental skills training program was established as an educational program and, therefore, neither the program nor its trainers are approved clinical providers. The professional role of its trainers, therefore, is defined to a great extent by what it *excludes:* diagnosing, or providing family, clinical, or other counseling services to soldiers. Regardless of a trainer's education, experience, and/or licensure, he or she is to operate only in an educational capacity, training soldiers and leaders to use mental skills for non-clinical, performance-related purposes. Despite this guidance for trainers, dilemmas can occur when clients seek to apply mental skills training to clinical issues (e.g., a soldier who wants to learn relaxation skills to help manage his panic attacks). Trainers are still able to work with these individuals. However, they are to teach mental skills only as they apply to non-clinical performances. Soldiers who want to make use of the skills related to their clinical issues are encouraged to discuss the mental skills they have learned with their clinical healthcare providers to determine whether they may be used to supplement a treatment plan already in place.

Enforcing the requirement that soldiers attend formal classroom training prior to working individually with an MST is one way the mental skills training program's sites attempt to prevent ethical dilemmas related to competence. At the outset of the formal training, the trainers introduce themselves and briefly highlight their education, personal performance endeavors, and experience working with athletes, soldiers, and other performers. What is notably missing during these introductions is any reference to functioning in a clinical capacity. Throughout the training, as soldiers learn about mental skills, they become aware of the role and capabilities of the trainers and, ideally, come to realize that the trainers are not working in clinical roles.

Finally, soldiers are not asked to identify or describe any physical or mental health issues they may experience. Soldiers generally leave the training with an understanding of which topics are appropriate to address with the MSTs in mastery work. As a result, the likelihood of a soldier discussing clinical issues or expecting that a trainer can help them with clinical issues in a one-on-one session is reduced.

MSTs are clearly limited by the AASP code of ethics (n.d.) to operate only in the areas in which they are competent, and even further by the U.S. Army to provide only educational services related to performance enhancement. As would be expected, trainers must also be competent in the mental skills they teach and coach soldiers to apply, and the mental skills training program has established several requirements to ensure that MSTs maintain a high level of competence. The program requires applicants to hold either a masters or doctoral degree in performance, sport, cognitive, social, or human factors psychology. Once hired, all MSTs who have not already done so are expected to complete the requirements necessary for AASP certification, and are provided with the necessary supervision opportunities by AASP-certified trainers within the program. This certification ensures that trainers have met certain academic and experiential standards in the field of sport and performance psychology. Additionally, shortly after gaining employment with the program, all trainers attend a two-week initial training course at the program's headquarters; this serves to introduce them to the program's curriculum, provide an introduction to the Army culture, and allow new trainers to practice presenting the material and receive feedback from the program's master trainer. Finally, MSTs are required to engage in professional development activities (e.g., reading textbooks and journal articles, observing field trainings) on a regular basis in order to continually expand and update their knowledge.

In addition to recognizing and adhering to their boundaries of competence, and in accordance with AASP's General Ethical Standard 2 (Boundaries of Competence; AASP, n.d.), MSTs must also understand the military environment, both in terms of its structure and culture. A trainer's level of understanding of the dynamics and customs of this setting can quickly cause him or her to either gain or lose credibility. Becoming familiar with the Army culture and the experiences of soldiers, and subsequently maintaining that familiarity, is an important component of working effectively with military personnel. MSTs are responsible for learning the rank structure and being able to call soldiers by the appropriate title, becoming accustomed to Army terminology and using it appropriately when teaching, providing military-specific examples of applying mental skills, adhering to the formalities and customs of the Army (e.g., standing when a general enters the room), following the rules specific to working with soldiers who are considered students (e.g., soldiers in Basic Combat Training or who are in training to learn a military "job") versus those who are not, and understanding what is expected of soldiers with different military occupations and leadership positions.

While some MSTs have past military experience, which is certainly beneficial in terms of understanding the military culture and environment, it is not a requirement. Similarly, although it is important for practitioners to have a basic understanding of the tasks soldiers perform (e.g., rappelling, firing a weapon, navigating an obstacle course, entering and clearing a room), it is not necessary to have engaged in these soldiering activities to effectively teach and coach soldiers to apply the principles of sport and performance psychology to these performances.

In fact, very few trainers have both military experience and training in the field of sport and performance psychology. As a result, it is essential that a novice MST quickly gain a thorough understanding of the military culture. This can be achieved by reading military books and training manuals, watching military movies, receiving mentoring from an experienced trainer, observing soldiers in training exercises, or simply asking soldiers about their experiences.

Military competence is also essential so that the MST can avoid offending military personnel. Soldiers engage in different *performances* than athletes, and there is much more at stake for soldiers as compared to athletes (i.e., soldiers' performances can have life or death consequences). While trainers do not need military experience to work with soldiers, those MSTs who lack military experience must realize that they may never fully grasp what it means to be a soldier, or the experience of dealing with the outcomes that often result from performing in the military.

Civilian MSTs must also understand that when soldiers perform their duties, it may necessitate killing another person, which could result in an ethical and/or moral dilemma for some trainers. Employment by the mental skills training program demands that trainers do outstanding work regardless of their personal views on this issue. Standard 24 of the AASP ethics code (Conflicts between Ethics and Organizational Demands; AASP, n.d.) encourages practitioners to "seek to resolve the conflict in a way that permits the fullest adherence to the Ethics Code." If practitioners cannot reconcile or put aside their own beliefs about this matter, this conflict has the potential to lessen their effectiveness when working with soldiers. This dilemma may also diminish a trainer's ability to build rapport with soldiers, especially if the trainer appears uncomfortable or judgmental should a soldier unexpectedly share a story related to his or her own experience of being in combat. Ultimately, if a trainer cannot find a way to resolve the conflict between his or her personal ethical beliefs and the work soldiers are called upon to do, the trainer may need to seek work outside of the military environment.

Roles and Boundaries

A major challenge faced by MSTs involves defining their role in working with soldiers. While the trainers are aware that they are functioning in an educational rather than clinical capacity, they must also clearly convey this to those with whom they work. In accordance with AASP Ethics Code Principle B (Integrity; AASP, n.d.), which encourages practitioners to "clarify for relevant parties the roles they are performing and the obligations they adopt," the mental skills training program and its trainers must ensure that their clients understand the trainers' areas of expertise and what topics are appropriate for discussion during mental skills training. As will be discussed in more depth later, one way this is accomplished is by requiring potential mastery clients to first attend a group training course. This simple precaution facilitates the maintenance of appropriate boundaries between the trainer and his or her client, and also assists the trainer in staying well within his or her professional lane.

Maintaining Privacy and Confidentiality

Confidentiality is an ethical concern for any practitioner, and it is a significant concern in the military environment. Through their work with soldiers, MSTs could potentially encounter classified information. Consequently, obtaining the necessary security clearance is a prerequisite for beginning to work in this environment. Because the Army values protecting certain information, it has developed protocols to ensure that the confidentiality of classified information is maintained, and every employee receives annual training in these procedures. AASP Ethics Code Standard 5(b) (Personal Problems and Conflicts; AASP, n.d.) also indicates that protecting "privileged information about clients or client organizations" is not just a safety or legal issue, but an ethical one as well. The restrictions put in place by the Army clarify what information is considered sensitive and indicate how to handle and label such information, resulting in very straightforward guidelines for maintaining the integrity of important information.

MSTs are also responsible for the protection of clients' personal information and information related to military operations. AASP Ethics Code Standard 18 (Maintaining Confidentiality; AASP, n.d.) indicates that members should "take reasonable precautions to respect the confidentiality rights of those with whom they work," as well as ensure that clients understand the limitations of confidentiality. One difference between the training conducted by the Army's MSTs and that of sport psychology consultants outside of the military is that the trainers cannot guarantee the confidentiality of information revealed in a group setting. Because the program is educational in nature as opposed to a form of group therapy, participants in group settings (e.g., a classroom setting, a field training targeted at improving basic rifle marksmanship performance) are not asked or encouraged to reveal any personal information or stories they consider too private, nor are they instructed to maintain the privacy of others in the group. However, a soldier has the right of confidentiality when he or she is working in a mastery setting (i.e., one-on-one) with an MST. The five exceptions to confidentiality occur when: (1) a soldier indicates that he or she intends to inflict self-harm or to harm others, (2) the trainer suspects child abuse or neglect, (3) the soldier's records are subpoenaed for a court case, (4) the participant is a minor and his or her parent(s) or legal guardian(s) request his or her records, or (5) if the participant lodges a complaint against the mental skills training program or one of its trainers that results in a review of the incident by a third party. In the first two cases, the MST would be required to report the information to the individual's chain of command; for the remaining situations, the MST would have no choice but to break confidentiality and provide the requested information to the party requesting the records.

MSTs take several deliberate precautions related to maintaining the confidentiality and privacy of the soldiers with whom they work. As proscribed by AASP Ethics Code Standard 17(a) (Informed Consent to Practice; AASP, n.d.), all soldiers who seek individual sessions with a trainer are required to sign a consent form during their initial session. This form explains what the soldier can expect from the mastery sessions, but also identifies the limitations of confidentiality mentioned above. Trainers also keep documentation or notes from mastery sessions in locked drawers and/or offices to reduce the risk of private information becoming public.

Exploitation and Harassment

According to the AASP Ethics Code Standard 4 (Exploitation and Harassment; AASP, n.d.), practitioners are directed not to exploit or otherwise take advantage of clients or anyone over whom they have authority. Many of the soldiers who are instructed by MSTs are relatively young (i.e., in their late teens and early twenties). Since these soldiers are still "learning the ropes" of the Army system and often feel overwhelmed and nervous about their new environment, they do not hesitate to consider MSTs as members of the official training cadre. With this cohort of young soldiers, in particular, any cadre member is seen as an authority figure; therefore, it is important that trainers not abuse that authority. Because new soldiers are accustomed to taking and following orders from cadre members without hesitation, MSTs find themselves in positions where they could easily take advantage of trainees. In order to protect this particularly vulnerable group, the Army requires all cadre members who work with soldiers in Basic Combat Training or who are in a schoolhouse environment, not just MSTs, to complete a training session prior to having contact with these soldiers. The Army's Support Cadre Training Course, which echoes the AASP guidance, familiarizes cadre members with the rules and regulations related to training and maintaining appropriate relationships with these young, often naive soldiers.

Multiple Relationships

Standard 9 of the AASP ethics code (Multiple Relationships; AASP, n.d.) indicates that engaging in nonprofessional relationships with clients can be detrimental to the client and/or the client-practitioner relationship. Consequently, professionals are not to socialize, engage in romantic relationships, or establish additional relationships, professional or otherwise, with individuals with whom they have worked. Many MSTs perform counseling or sport and performance consulting services, based on their training and/or licensure, outside of the military system. The AASP standards indicate that it would be unethical for MSTs to establish these kinds of professional relationships with soldiers with whom they work currently or have worked previously. In addition, MSTs are not permitted to solicit clients or offer their private services to soldiers, family members, or Army civilians, even those whom they have not trained; this restriction comes from the contracting companies that employ the MSTs.

MSTs may find themselves in a unique situation related to multiple relationships, specifically romantic relationships. First, because the group training is educational rather than clinical in nature, it is possible that an MST could develop a relationship with a soldier who has completed the mental skills training course and is not continuing a professional relationship with the trainer (i.e., the soldier does not pursue mastery) and, technically, not be in violation of the ethical guidelines. Certainly this kind of relationship is not encouraged by the program, but it could occur. Second, there is the potential for an MST to start a nonprofessional relationship with a soldier who has had no exposure to the mental skills training program, but who may at a later time. If this were to happen, the soldier should receive training from a different MST to prevent the occurrence of ethical dilemmas related to multiple relationships.

Practitioners are very clearly instructed not to engage in sexual relationships with current clients by Standard 9 of the AASP ethics code (Multiple Relationships; AASP, n.d.), Standard 10.05 of the APA ethical principles (APA, 2010), and Standard 1.09(a) of the NASW code of ethics (NASW, 2008). In addition, Standard 10.08 of the APA principles and Standard 1.09(c) of the NASW code both clearly state that practitioners are discouraged from engaging in sexual relationships even with previous clients. These standards also apply to the MSTs working in the military environment. In addition, one specific Army regulation (United States, 2010) indicates that it is not acceptable for a cadre member to become friends with, date, or engage in any relationship with a soldier other than what is required for his or her training. This regulation, in combination with the ethical guidelines described above, specifically directs MSTs to avoid forming multiple relationships with the soldiers with whom they work.

Referral

According to the AASP Ethics Code Standard 11 (Consultations and Referrals; AASP, n.d.), members should make referrals and "cooperate with other professionals in order to serve their patients or clients effectively and appropriately." MSTs are responsible for recognizing situations that are beyond the scope of their competence or job description and referring these soldiers to the appropriate resource. A growing number of soldiers who deployed to Iraq and Afghanistan have been diagnosed with post-traumatic stress disorder (PTSD), depression, and traumatic brain injury (Hoge, Auchterlonie, & Milliken, 2006), and the Army's mental skills training program has been tasked to focus much of its efforts on working with soldiers as they rehabilitate from both physical and mental injuries sustained in combat settings. As a result, MSTs will likely find themselves working with soldiers who have clinical issues even though the trainers are not permitted to provide clinical services. Often, these soldiers are already being treated by Army-approved practitioners. However, when this is not the case, MSTs may have to refer soldiers for clinical counseling. Some MSTs, based on their education, training, and prior experience, can easily recognize the indicators that a soldier requires a referral, and would be expected to do so appropriately. Many MSTs, on the other hand, lack the knowledge and experience to know when a client does or does not need to be referred. These trainers would be expected to consult with other MSTs when they suspect a referral might be necessary, and err on the side of caution if they believe, but are not certain, that a soldier needs immediate attention from another professional.

Within the structure provided by the Army, soldiers have a number of options for receiving clinical care, including seeing a counselor in Army Behavioral Health, using Military One Source (a free service provided to service members and their families to assist with a broad range of concerns) to gain access to a non-military provider in the local community, and talking to a chaplain. While there is no single correct process for referring a soldier, MSTs are responsible for maintaining an awareness of the referral options so that they are prepared to contact an approved Army practitioner directly, assist the soldier in contacting a practitioner, or offer to accompany the soldier to a clinical practitioner's office.

While all professionals in the fields of sport and performance psychology encounter ethical dilemmas, MSTs working with the military population face somewhat unique challenges as a result of the environment in which they operate. The following case study illustrates that several ethical dilemmas can arise when working with a single military client.

CASE STUDY: FACING ETHICAL ISSUES

The MST is a female with a doctorate in counseling psychology. During her graduate education, she focused on sport psychology and accrued the hours and supervision necessary to become an AASP-certified consultant. She is licensed to do clinical work in the state in which she also provides mental skills training services to soldiers on an Army post. During her post-doctoral internship, she gained experience doing assessments and making PTSD diagnoses. Prior to taking the position as an MST, she worked with veterans, focusing most of her time and effort on patients with PTSD at a Veterans Affairs hospital. In her current position, she works to improve soldier performance using sport psychology techniques. She continues to perform a limited amount of clinical work with non-military personnel outside of her official capacity working with the Army.

Presenting Information

After completing the two-day training, a soldier, who the trainer estimates to be in his early thirties, schedules a mastery session with the MST. The soldier states that he wants to work to overcome his fear of public speaking; ultimately, he would like to be more confident and composed when giving military briefings and when speaking at his church. The soldier responds well to the mental skills training provided in the initial mastery sessions. The trainer is impressed with the soldier's willingness to practice the skills and complete homework assignments between sessions, and notes that by the fourth session he is becoming noticeably more optimistic about his potential to successfully engage in public speaking.

In the fifth mastery session, however, the soldier's optimism has obviously faded. He mentions to the trainer that following his second deployment he was diagnosed with PTSD and experiences severe anxiety attacks. He explains his fear that he will have a flashback during a public speaking engagement, and that this is his real motive for seeking mastery. He is concerned that if he unexpectedly hears a loud noise while speaking, he will throw himself to the floor. He worries about the embarrassment and ridicule he will experience if this were to occur, and it is this fear that has made it nearly impossible for him to imagine speaking in public in the future. The soldier believes the relaxation skills that he was exposed to during the two-day training will help him avoid or deal with flashbacks and anxiety attacks. His medical provider within the Army Behavioral Health system has given him medication specifically to contain his anxiety, which he reports taking as prescribed, but the soldier indicates that the medication is not always effective.

Discussion of Ethical Considerations

Several potential ethical issues are evident in this case study. These include: (a) in what capacity, if any, the MST can continue to work with this soldier; (b) to what extent, if any, the trainer needs to communicate with the soldier's Behavioral Health counselor; and (c) how to protect the soldier's personal information. Each of these issues is discussed below.

The primary ethical concern for the MST relates to whether she can work with this soldier and, if so, in what capacity. As this soldier has been diagnosed with and is already receiving treatment for PTSD, he obviously does not require a referral. According to AASP Ethics Code Standard 2 (Boundaries of Competence; AASP, n.d.), this particular trainer has the education, experience, and licensure necessary to effectively and ethically work with this individual on those clinical issues; however, as one of the Army's MSTs, her job description restricts her from doing so. She may not work to treat any aspect of this soldier's PTSD, which means she cannot tailor the mental skills training she provides to the alleviation or reduction of flashbacks or anxiety related to PTSD. She can, however, continue to work with the soldier in a non-clinical capacity. In other words, she may teach him relaxation and other skills for the targeted perfor-mance of public speaking and related performance anxiety. The MST has the responsibility to make this distinction to the soldier and ensure he understands what is and is not appropriate to discuss if they decide to continue their mastery work together.

Because of her credentials (i.e., her psychology licensure in the state in which she works) and because she still conducts counseling to supplement her work with the military, the trainer may be tempted to offer her services to the soldier outside of the official Army environment. This would violate a number of codes of conduct. First and foremost, taking on or simply at-tempting to recruit a client from the Army environment for her personal gain is a conflict of interest as it would be defined by the contracting company for which she works. In addition, it also violates AASP Ethics Code Principle B (Integrity; AASP, n.d.), which states that "mem-bers are honest and fair . . . they clarify for relevant parties the roles they are performing and the obligations they adopt. They function appropriately in accordance with those roles and obligations."

Because the soldier has made it clear that his intent is to apply the mental skills in the hopes of managing his symptoms of PTSD, additional measures are necessary. The trainer should have a discussion with the soldier about establishing communication between herself and the soldier's Behavioral Health counselor. If the soldier agrees, he should be asked to com-plete a consent form that will allow the trainer to speak with his counselor and release infor-mation related to the skills she is teaching in the mastery sessions. Acting in accordance with AASP Ethics Code Standard 11 (Consultations and Referrals) and 18 (Maintaining Confidential-ity; AASP, n.d.), the trainer will not release information to the counselor without the soldier's consent, and will seek to avoid releasing more information to the counselor than is necessary. The MST should also encourage the soldier to share the mental skills he is learning with his counselor, giving him or her the opportunity to assess whether the skills may be beneficial for other purposes, including managing PTSD symptoms; the Behavioral Health counselor can decide if and how to build those skills into the soldier's treatment plan. If the trainer is able to take these steps (i.e., recognize her limited capacity to work with this soldier, ensure she and the soldier only target non-clinical performance, and coordinate with the clinical counselor), she will be well within the ethical standards that have been created to guide her work in the field of sport and performance psychology, especially within the military environment.

SUMMARY

Working with soldiers in a military environment has the potential to generate various ethical dilemmas for MSTs. While these challenges are not drastically different from those faced by sport and performance psychology practitioners in other settings, the characteristics of the military environment create a unique set of circumstances in which to function. The Army's MSTs have the responsibility of familiarizing themselves with the protocols specific to this en-vironment and gaining an appreciation for the kind of work soldiers do and the tasks in which they engage. In addition, it is important for trainers to understand the ethical dilemmas they may encounter and the guidelines that exist to influence their work. When MSTs anticipate ethical dilemmas and strive to prevent and respond to them appropriately, they can deliver both ethical and effective performance enhancement strategies to help soldiers save lives, prepare for missions, and manage the demands of the home front.

REFERENCES

Association for Applied Sport Psychology. (n.d.). *Ethics code: AASP ethical principles and standards.* Retrieved from http://appliedsportpsych.org/about/ethics/code

American Psychological Association. (2010). *American Psychological Association ethical principles of psychologists and code of conduct.* Retrieved from http://apa.org/ethics/code/index.aspx

American Society of Exercise Physiologists. (1997). Code of ethics. Retrieved from http://www.asep.org/organization/ethics

Hoge, C. W., Auchterlonie, J. L., & Milliken, C. S. (2006). Mental health problems, use of mental health services, and attrition from military service after returning from deployment to Iraq or Afghanistan. *Journal of the American Medical Association, 295,* 1023–1032.

National Association of Social Workers. (2008). Code of ethics of the National Association of Social Workers. Retrieved from http://www.naswdc.org/pubs/code/code.asp

United States. (2010). Army Command Policy: Army regulation 600-20, Washington, DC: Headquarters, Dept. of the Army.

CHAPTER 11

ETHICAL ISSUES IN CONSULTING WITH PERFORMING ARTISTS

Kate F. Hays

INTRODUCTION

As a practicing psychologist, Jan is known for her expertise in sport psychology. Jasper, a 25-year-old singer, contacts her after browsing her website. He would like assistance in figuring out the discrepancy between practice and performance. Jasper says that he sings well during practice and rehearsals but experiences tremendous performance anxiety, especially before auditions.

Jasper's initial description seems familiar to Jan from her work with athlete clients. Maybe, she thinks, it's time to expand her practice into "performance psychology." And besides, it's been kind of a slow year in terms of sport psychology clients and income.

A client such as Jasper may be the impetus for changing or expanding one's practice to include performing artists. Other practitioners may be more deliberate in their decision making. This chapter is designed to respond to questions such as: How is performing arts consultation similar to or different from sport psychology practice? From counseling or clinical psychology? What should one know about this particular area of performance? What ethical obligations and issues apply in performing arts consultation?

As Jan responds to these questions, what factors might determine her conclusions? The initial contact and service request? Might it be a differential fee that she has specified for performance consultation in contrast to therapy? How was she trained, and with what range of skills and competencies? Would it make a difference if her primary training in psychological skills methods for athletes was through a department of kinesiology rather than clinical or counseling psychology?

The definitive answers to these questions are not yet carved in stone—but then, ethics is an always evolving and reflective process. Attending to some of the most salient issues can help us practice in responsible ways to assist our clients and allow us to understand diversification in a constructive and ethical manner. As Haberl and Peterson point out in relation to sport psychology practice, "the lack of structure should be a cue for ethical practitioners to tread carefully, seek consultation regularly, and strive to keep the interests of their athlete or coach clients in the foreground at all times" (2006, p. 39).

Before addressing the ethics of practice directly, it is useful first to define performing arts consultation. What is performance psychology for performing artists, described here interchangeably as "performing arts psychology" and "consulting with performing artists?" Who can practice it? What kind of training is needed in order to perform it?

PERFORMANCE PSYCHOLOGY AND PERFORMING ARTS CONSULTATION

In a somewhat tautological (or facetious) definition, performance psychology can be considered the psychology of performance, that is, what people do when they are *doing,* i.e., behaving purposely. It is not just any kind of performance, however. Performance psychology typically refers to the striving for *excellent* performance within a field where excellence counts. Regardless of field, performers "must meet certain performance standards: They are judged as to proficiency or excellence, there are consequences to poor performance, [and] good coping skills are intrinsic to excellent performance" (Hays & Brown, 2004, p. 19). This type of performance also has a temporal dimension: The performer's particular talents and skills must be delivered at a specific point in time (Brown, 2001). Competence at a particular activity while in the presence of others is often a central defining feature, especially in the performing arts (Emmons & Thomas, 1998). One can also consider performance to be a combination of the development and execution of knowledge, skills, and abilities in a given performance domain (Aoyagi & Portenga, 2010).

These definitions apply to at least four general areas or domains of performance: (1) sports, (2) performing arts, (3) business, and (4) high-risk professions (e.g., public safety, emergency room physicians, surgeons; Hays, 2009). The task of the performance consultant is to assist in the development of more effective performance within the particular domain (Kampa & White, 2002).

Performing arts psychology draws its knowledge base, energy, and legitimacy from four, somewhat distinct traditions: (1) sport psychology, (2) psychotherapy, (3) performing arts medicine, and (4) consultation. Sport psychology, with its long history of research and practice regarding the mental skills associated with excellent athletic performance, is a field rich in relevant information concerning performance issues, albeit relatively unknown within the field of psychology (Hays, 2006). Psychotherapy brings to the mix various bases of knowledge. Among its many contributions, most relevant to performance psychology, are: practical, short-term, and positive applications, such as CBT, solution-focused therapy, and positive psychology; the value of accurate assessment to relevant practice; and the finely-tuned awareness of human interaction (De Shazer, 1985; Meyers, Whelan, & Murphy, 1995; Murphy, 1995; Seligman & Csikszentmihalyi, 2000). Although performing artists experience some medical issues similar to those among athletes, a number of differences have also been noted (Hamilton, 1997; Mainwaring, Krasnow, & Kerr, 2001; Sataloff, Brandfonbrener, & Lederman, 2010). Consultation and executive coaching derive from a mix of family systems theory, mental health consultation, organizational development, and life coaching (Dean, 2001; Jones, 2002; Kampa-Kokesch & Kilburg, 2001; Newman, Robinson-Kurpius, & Fuqua, 2002; Wynne, McDaniel, & Weber, 1986).

Comparable to applied sport psychologists, performance psychologists practice in a number of different settings. Among the most common are: counseling in university counseling centers, teaching classes or workshops or providing assistance such as in a professional school or performing arts department, offering consultation in one's private practice office, or going on the road, whether literally or figuratively (electronically). As with applied sport psychology, services potentially offered may include educational workshops, assessment, clinical treatment, and individual and systems consultation.

When conducting (generic) performance consulting, some psychologists, conscious of the potential for stigma especially amongst athletes or business executives, deliberately choose to refer to themselves as coaches or consultants. The issue may be less fraught with performing artists: "psychologist" is a much less stigmatized label—in fact it may well add cachet (Hays, 2002). Aside from label, what is one actually doing? Is one a consultant, a coach, or a therapist? For any individual practitioner, the answer involves a mix of skill, focus, definition, legal regulation, clientele or setting, and common usage, as well as advertising and marketing. Coaching or consultation has been differentiated from psychotherapy by: a limited time frame, a goal or outcome focus, less interpersonal intimacy, a decreased focus on relational dynamics, and—at least in theory—work with clients who have less diagnosable psychopathology than those seeking psychotherapy (Aoyagi & Portenga, 2010; Harris, 2002; Younggren & Gottlieb, 2004).

ETHICAL PRACTICE IN CONSULTING WITH PERFORMING ARTISTS

"Ethics is defined as the rules or standards governing the conduct of members of a profession" (Committee on Professional Practice and Standards, 2003, p. 595). Although ethical codes are both prescriptive and proscriptive (principle ethics), ethics more broadly refers to both practice and process. Positive ethics and virtue ethics emphasize proactive rather than reactive thoughts and behavior on the part of the practitioner (Aoyagi & Portenga, 2010). Ethics can be described as a continuing process of attending to one's knowledge, beliefs, values, and practices, "a process through which we awaken, enhance, inform, expand, and improve our ability to respond effectively to those who come to us for help" (Pope & Vasquez, 1998, p. xiii).

Whether preparing for a practice in performing arts psychology or maintaining such a practice, the ethical practitioner needs to attend to the interwoven issues of training, competence, and ethics. These concerns include: preparation for practice, competence, interpersonal and relational issues of practice, and those connected to the ways in which performance psychologists present themselves to the public. Various emerging ethical factors also bear reflection.

PREPARATION FOR PRACTICE

Jan is aware of her background, training, and skills regarding both psychotherapy and mental skills training with athletes. She also is an avocational singer, and this experience seems relevant to her. It may enhance rapid rapport development as well as increased credibility as she works with Jasper. Jan understands first-hand about the audition process; she recognizes shifts in attention when on stage; she can appreciate the tension and tempo of a dress rehearsal.

But change the scenario a bit and then what? What if Jasper were a drummer in an R&B band instead of a classically trained singer? What if, instead of being a musician, the performing artist were an actor? Supposing that Jan's performance background is in modern dance?

In a field as loosely organized, minimally defined, and emergent as performing arts psychology, what defines adequate professional preparation? Much of the preparation for a performing arts consultant will involve extrapolation from areas of expertise other than performing arts psychology per se (Hamilton, 1997; Hays, 2000, 2002; Hays & Brown, 2004). Performance consulting preparation generally involves a combination of both formal and informal knowledge and skill. Formal elements include those derived from one's academic degree preparation and subsequent structured training. Informal preparation may include performance experience, informal training opportunities, and pertinent formative life experiences (Hays & Brown, 2004).

Within an emergent area of practice in particular, informal preparation may be especially salient (Belar et al., 2001; Brown, Gould, & Foster, 2005; Glueckauf, 2003). Effective learning can occur through a mixture of relevant reading, observation, and/or direct experience in the domain. Other elements of informal training may involve being coached, mentored, or supervised. A vital aspect of competent consultation includes the development of a network of colleagues who can serve as a sounding board, resource, or means of "peer review" when the consultant encounters challenging situations. The expansion, breadth, and depth of informal training gives the practitioner the opportunity to understand commonalities across domains and gain specific knowledge within particular domains.

COMPETENCE

Competent practice involves three levels of knowledge and skill—foundational skills, domain-specific knowledge, and contextual intelligence (Brown, Gould, & Foster, 2005; Hays & Brown, 2004; Sternberg, 1985). The five essential skills for performance psychology, typically learned during graduate training, include: (1) relationship or clinical/counseling skills, (2) change skills, (3) knowledge of performance excellence, (4) knowledge of the physiological aspects of performance, and (5) knowledge of systems and systems consultation (Hays & Brown, 2004). In addition to these foundational skills, a performance consultant needs to understand the specific domain within which the performer conducts him or herself—in this case, the performing arts (Hays, 2000, 2002; Jones, 2002; Martin & Cutler, 2002; Poczwardowski & Conroy, 2002; Weinberg & McDermott, 2002). At the most specific level of knowledge, in regard to a particular consultation situation, the practitioner needs to have "contextual intelligence," "knowing the culture and context of the specific setting in which the individual operates" (Brown, Gould, & Foster, 2005, p. 54).

Whether or not one is engaging in a new area, "practicing psychologists must continually deal with the ethical and professional issues involved in expanding and updating their services" (Belar et al., 2001, p. 136). Most relevant to this issue is APA's Standard 2.01, relating to the Boundaries of Competence. This standard lists a number of methods that may be important to the development of competence. Similarly, the AASP Ethics Code (Standard 2) emphasizes the importance of maintaining awareness and competence in regard to relevant scientific and professional information and relevant skills.

Although formal graduate or post-degree training is readily available in sport psychology and organizational psychology, performing arts consultation is typically dependent on extrapolated learning and adaptation. The onus rests on the practitioner to develop and maintain the relevant competence. Regular self-assessment is thus critical in determining the particular practitioner's formal and informal knowledge and skills, as well as goals and plans for further development (Hays & Brown, 2004).

Jan can rely to some degree on her knowledge of mental skills techniques and her own experience in the music world to adapt her work to assist Jasper. She may still need to learn about such aspects as the physiology of music production, the systems and culture of conservatory programs, or the rampant use of Beta blockers amongst musicians (Isaacs, 2006). As a performing arts consultant, Jan will find that the more that her client's experience differs from her own, the more she will need to supplement knowledge based solely on her personal experience. On the other hand, the more similar her client's experience is to her own, the more she will need to assess the degree to which she is only extrapolating from her own experience, over-identifying with her client, or subjecting herself to boundary slippage.

INTERACTIONAL OR RELATIONAL ISSUES IN CONSULTING WITH PERFORMING ARTISTS

The practitioner's knowledge and skills—competence—is vitally important. At the same time, consultation is an interactional process. It is "the cornerstone ingredient for any successful outcome" (Parham, 2010, p. 151). In order to reflect that interactional context, this section clusters a number of aspects of ethical practice that are inherently relational: informed consent, confidentiality, boundaries, the often triadic nature of consultation, multiple role relationships, and fees. Although in actual practice these issues are often intertwined, for clarity of discourse they are discussed separately.

Informed Consent
In any type of professional interpersonal situation, whether counseling or consultation, clients are entitled to understand the anticipated benefits, risks, and expectations of service. Consultants working with performing artists need to have a clear understanding of the ways in which informed consent for consultation is both similar to and different from that for psychotherapy. The complexity of the organizational context often complicates informed consent (Newman

et al., 2002). In consultative situations, the degree to which consent is truly voluntary may be altered by subtle systemic pressure (Koocher, 2004). To the extent that the client can accurately understand and choose to engage with the consultant, the client's self-determination is increased and some of the inherent systemic power imbalance may be rectified (Newman et al., 2002).

Confidentiality

"Except for the ultimate precept—above all, do no harm—there is probably no ethical value in psychology that is more inculcated than confidentiality" (Bersoff, 1999, p. 149). Yet confidentiality in consultation is more complicated than the mere question of whether one is or is not working with an individual (Koocher, 2004). Particularly in situations where the consultant works with a group of performers, confidentiality becomes more multifaceted (Haberl & Peterson, 2006; Hamilton, 1997; Parham, 2010).

Confidentiality in performance consulting may revolve more around *what* is being shared than *that* it is being shared (Andersen, Van Raalte, & Brewer, 2001; Hamilton, 1997; Van Raalte, 1998). As McCann noted in relation to sport psychology, "Practitioners learn to perfect the ski-lift consult, the bus-ride consult, the 10-minute breakfast table team-building session, the confidential session in . . . hotel lobbies, parking lots, and trainers' tables" (2000, p. 211). Different norms of time and space may need to be developed and discussed (Andersen et al., 2001; Moore, 2003).

The confidentiality needs of stars or celebrities, whether athletes or performing artists, must be handled with particular awareness and tact (Gould & Damarjian, 1998; Hamilton, 1997). AASP's Standard 5.b. speaks to the "extreme visibility and notoriety of some clients and organizations" in sport. Similarly, the performing arts consultant needs to maintain sensitivity and vigilance regarding the privacy and confidentiality of well-known performing artists.

Boundaries

Professional boundaries "derive from the rules of the professional relationship that distinguish it from business or social relationships" (Knapp & Slattery, 2004, p. 553). Traditional training as a psychotherapist and the APA Code reflect boundary regulation appropriate to the therapy office. With nontraditional settings or services, boundaries are more complex and boundary issues potentially can be more of a concern (Knapp & Slattery, 2004; Koocher, 2004).

A useful distinction has been made between boundary crossings and boundary violations (Guthiel & Gabbard, 1993). Although a boundary crossing occurs when a professional deviates from the absolute professional role, the crossing in itself may be helpful, neutral, or harmful. "Boundary crossings can become boundary violations when they place clients at risk for harm" (Knapp & Slattery, 2004, p. 554).

"Natural environments" such as the playing field or stage, the locale for some aspects of performance consultation, may increase the potential for loosened boundaries. "This does not mean that the rules are different, but that the structure, expectations, and outcomes may be, thus leading to different guidelines governing the choice of interventions" (Knapp & Slattery, 2004, p. 554).

Triadic or Systems/Organizational Context

Who is consenting to the service and who is the service for? Psychotherapy (at least in theory) is dyadic, involving the therapist and client. In contrast, "a distinguishing feature of consulting relationships is their triadic nature" (Newman et al., 2002, p. 733).

Within the APA Ethics Code, Standard 3.11(a) speaks directly to systemic and organizational issues. Issues of confidentiality, power, financial remuneration, or impact and effectiveness are all made more complex by context (Brown, Gould, & Foster, 2005). A systemic issue may be as (seemingly) simple as the influence of a pushy stage mother who is paying for performance consultation for her stage-frightened daughter (Hamilton, 1997). It may be as multi-layered and financially fraught as being hired by a professional arts school to teach mental skills classes, consult with administration, interact with other faculty (e.g., teachers, arts coaches, physical therapists), and conduct one-on-one sessions with students. The more embedded the consultant is within a performance system, the more ambiguous the consultant's role and relationships may be (Haberl & Peterson, 2006). The performing arts consultant can draw on systems theory and practice (Education and Training Committee, Division 13, 2000). The experience of sport psychologists who have learned to work with managers, staff, team members, and individual players is also informative (Haberl & Peterson, 2006; McCann, 2005; Moore, 2003).

Multiple Role Relationships

Jan is a member of an auditioned chorus that holds social activities as well as rehearsals and performances. At the first rehearsal of autumn, Jasper (already her client) is introduced to the chorus as the new bass section lead. Should Jan resign from the chorus?

Alternatively: Jan first met Jasper in the chorus. Knowing her expertise, he requests performing arts consulting. Is it appropriate for Jan to take him on as a client?

One can envision many other complex scenarios, whether involving only the hypothetical Jan and Jasper or their friends, partners, choral personnel, or singing coaches. "Psychologists who are in professional roles or relationships with clients, supervisees, or students may intentionally, unintentionally, or unforeseeably find themselves in a second role or relationship with that same individual" (Lamb, Catanzaro, & Moorman, 2004, p. 248). Although one might attempt (or be tempted) to avoid *any* such additional role or relationship, rigid maintenance of a singular role or relationship potentially can become unhelpful, harmful, or destructive (Younggren & Gottlieb, 2004). In fact, the APA code recognizes that practitioners can be nuanced in their response: "Multiple relationships that would not reasonably be expected to cause impairment or risk exploitation or harm are not unethical" (APA, 2010, p. 6). Similarly, Standard 9 of the AASP Ethical Code notes the need for sensitivity and awareness of multiple role relationships, including the potential for altering the consultant's objectivity, or for exploitation or harm. Whether a particular relationship or action is or might be exploitative or harmful "remains ambiguous" (Lamb et al., 2004, p. 253). Certain multiple relationships, particularly in consultative situations, may be unavoidable, normative, obligatory, or beneficial (Andersen et al., 2001; Haberl & Peterson, 2006; Koocher, 2004; Lamb et al., 2004; Stapleton, Hays, Hankes, & Parham, 2010; Younggren & Gottlieb, 2004).

Sexual relationships are specifically eschewed in both codes, but nonsexual multiple role relationships are potentially normative in settings such as small, isolated, rural, or closed communities (Andersen et al., 2001; Aoyagi & Portenga, 2010; Campbell & Gordon, 2003; Lamb et al., 2004). As with athletics, many performance settings and circumstances take on qualities of being isolated and self-contained (Hamilton, 1997; Hays, 2002; Moore, 2003; Van Raalte, 1998). Using a military analogy as an example, the dance community often views non-dancers as "civilians" (Hays, 2002). The more closed or insular a system is, the more likely it is that contractual consultative relationships will develop out of a prior relationship with some member of that system. In fact, multiple role relationships may be "more the norm than the exception" in some settings (Newman et al., 2002, p. 740).

Fee Setting and Barter

Fees for consultation vary widely, depending in part on the performance domain, the size and type of project, the presenting issues, and the credentialing and experience of the consultant. As with athletes, issues of diagnosis and third party billing may be relevant (Brown & Cogan, 2006).

In working with performing artists, it is important to be aware that, for a variety of cultural reasons, the vast majority of performing artists are systematically underpaid for their services (Sidimus, 1998). Unless they are high-ranking within their profession, engaged in high-visibility popular culture, or insulated to some degree through union membership, performing artists may be more likely than other types of performers to have limited funds for services. Because of these potential financial limitations, the consultant working with performing artists will need to be particularly mindful of both the APA Code (6.04) and AASP Code (Standard 15) with regard to fees and financial arrangements.

In contrast to psychotherapy clients but similarly to athletes, performing artists may be used to operating within a "barter" culture, in which goods or services might become the means of "payment" for services. It may be tempting to contemplate free tickets or entrée to the upper echelons of culture. The APA Code (6.05) notes that such barter is acceptable only if not clinically contraindicated nor exploitative. The AASP Code (Standard 10) more explicitly considers such barter to be inherently problematic and counsels against such arrangement.

THE CONSULTANT'S PRESENTATION OF SELF TO THE PUBLIC

Consultants working with performing artists need to address various aspects of their manifested professional self. Four ethical concerns of particular relevance include issues of: (1) advertising, (2) marketing, (3) title, and (4) applicability.

Advertising, Marketing, and Title

APA Standard 5 addresses the issue of advertising in relation to avoiding false or deceptive statements (as does AASP Standard 16), as well as media statements, testimonials, and solicitation of business. Specific state or provincial laws regarding title or scope of practice may further regulate the ways in which psychologists are legally bound in describing themselves to the public.

Performing arts consultants might hope that, in contrast to clinical practice, and as consultants rather than clinicians, they could be given leeway in regard to advertising and marketing their practice. Licensed psychologists in particular may feel frustrated by the strictures that limit their self-promotion; non-licensed practitioners at times make misleading claims and do not have to meet the same exacting standards and limitations. These constraints, while challenging, are nonetheless ethically binding.

Applicability

If a psychologist is functioning in a role as a consultant or coach, does the Ethics Code even pertain? The Ethics Code is explicit in acknowledging that its scope applies to psychologists only in relation to their professional roles. Those roles, however, are not limited to the times when psychologists call themselves psychologists. Applicability is not merely a matter of how one labels oneself in a particular professional circumstance: The Code applies to psychologists' behavior in all of their professional roles (Hays & Brown, 2004; Koocher, 2004; Levant, 2005).

EMERGING ISSUES IN PERFORMING ARTS CONSULTATION

Not surprisingly in an emergent field, some practitioner issues are just now being articulated, developed, and acknowledged. Particularly salient are those regarding multicultural competence, technology, and risk management.

Multicultural Competence

The 21st century is seeing the rapid development of awareness of culture and cultural context. Multicultural competence is increasingly recognized as a critically important component of psychotherapy training and practice, whether in regard to the student, client, or therapist (Kaslow & Kelly, 2010; Schwartz, Domenech Rodriguez, Satiago-Rivera, Arredondo, & Field, 2010).

Similarly, sport and performance consultants need to be able to understand and work with various cultures, including those that may or may not have sensitivity to diversity (Education and Training Committee, Division 13, 2000; Etzel et al., 2004; Kraus et al., 2004; Pope & Vasquez, 2005; Sachs, 1993). AASP's Principle D and APA's Ethical Principle E both speak directly to awareness and respect for cultural, individual, and role differences.

In addition to the intersectionality of the individual and specific system, consultants need to recognize that various performance domains contain within them different cultures and perspectives with regard to diverse social, environmental, and political contexts (Parham, 2010). Adding to the complexity, boundary crossings are culturally consistent in some performance domains (Gottlieb & Younggren, 2009).

Technology

Jan and Jasper may also differ along the "digital divide." How should Jan respond if Jasper wishes to "friend" her on Facebook? If he travels for an audition, should they schedule a VoIP session?

Technology, and especially rapidly changing technology, has an impact on consultation in a variety of ways. Increasingly, performance consultants provide some or all of their services via telephone or Internet. Methods of social networking proliferate, adding both options and dilemmas. "We have this wonderful new technology . . . [but] the ethical, legal and regulatory infrastructure to support the technology is not yet in place" commented Stephen Behnke, the director of APA's Ethics Office (Martin, 2010, p. 32).

These services and their potential and limits add another layer of complexity to those described in earlier sections of this chapter. Among the most challenging are issues of technical competence; confidentiality, security, and privacy; and record keeping (Etzel, Watson, & Zizzi, 2004; Hamilton, 1997; Kraus, Zack, & Stricker, 2004; Taylor, McMinn, Bufford, & Chang, 2010; Zur, Williams, Lehavot, & Knapp, 2009). "It is essential that psychologists develop a clear understanding of the ethical, technological, and regulatory issues associated with new practice methods and, in the case of telehealth, the advantages and limitations of specific delivery systems" (Glueckauf, 2003, p. 159).

Risk Management

In an increasingly litigious society, for one's own sanity as well as the welfare of one's clients, the ethical consultant needs to act "to anticipate reasonably foreseeable risks and make every effort to avoid, minimize, and manage them" (Younggren & Gottlieb, 2004, p. 256). Imagining the worst possible scenario and making decisions that take that into account, although sobering, can allow for decision-making that recognizes the best interests of all the players—including the consultant (Campbell & Gordon, 2003).

IMPLICATIONS AND RECOMMENDATIONS FOR PERFORMING ARTS CONSULTANTS

Practicing in new or nontraditional ways holds considerable excitement and promise. It has been suggested here that it is possible to develop and maintain a practice in performing arts consulting in a competent and ethical manner. The increasing number of presentations, publications, conversations, and websites would suggest that this is a growing field.

Ethical practitioners who diversify their practice to address the needs of performing artists will give careful attention to a number of elements, including appropriate preparation and supports, the various interactional issues that are especially relevant to consultation or coaching, and their public presentation of self and persona. The following suggestions are designed to underscore the pivotal elements for developing and maintaining such a practice:

1. *Regularly conduct a "fearless inventory" of one's knowledge and skills.* It is important to build on what one knows and to broaden and deepen what is yet to be learned. The many paths to effective performance consultation suggest that graduate education alone will rarely suffice (Belar et al., 2001; Glueckauf et al., 2003).

2. *Obtain additional training, knowledge, and skills.* Some of this may be formal and some, informal. Practitioners should systematically close the gap between what they already know and what they need to learn.

3. *Document additional training.* Careful compilation of accumulated learning provides recognition of one's competence and serves as a useful risk management procedure.

4. *Recognize that performing artists may have financial constraints.* Practitioners should be aware of funding options for performing artists, including organizational contracting for services, or union or insurance benefits that may be accessed by performing artists.

5. *Develop and maintain a peer culture.* Like-minded practitioners involved in similar work can provide support, supervision, peer consultation, and referral opportunities. Organizational involvement at local, national, and international levels can be a rich source for the development of these connections (Hays & Brown, 2004; Koocher, 2004). In regard to performing arts consulting, both APA's Division 47 and AASP—via journal titles and contents, relevant presentations, sub-groups and interpersonal connections—offer a variety of methods for the enhancement of peer culture.

6. *Create a network of referral resources.* Informal networks are an important element of a successful practice for a number of reasons. Network members might include clinicians; if the client needs psychotherapy during the consultative relationship, the practitioner can choose to refer for that task (Aoyagi & Portenga, 2010; Van Raalte, 2010). It is also useful to develop a network of practitioners in adjunctive professions, such as physical therapists, massage therapists, Pilates or yoga instructors, voice coaches, nutritionists, or accountants. These professionals are capable of performing many of the functions that the performing arts client may need. Collaboration with adjunctive professionals can increase the practitioner's knowledge and understanding. Further, these colleagues may provide such practice-related benefits as new client referrals.

7. *Maintain an active means of learning, questioning, and reviewing.* In order to maintain competence, performance consultants have a responsibility to remain current regarding research and practice in their consulting domains (Winum, 2003). This may occur through conferences, courses, or workshops, via colleagues, or through self-directed reading and training. Some of the literature will even provide practitioners with checklists or questions that can be used to help shape accurate self-reflection (e.g., Belar et al., 2001; Brown, 2001; Glueckauf et al., 2003; Moore, 2003; Pope & Vasquez, 1998, 2005; Younggren & Gottlieb, 2004).

SUMMARY

The ethical issues in performing arts consulting bear considerable similarity to those encountered by sport psychologists. These include concerns related to appropriate preparation, recognizable competence, the relational elements of practice, and the consultant's presentation of self in relation to advertising, marketing, and title. At the same time, performing arts consulting involves a different domain of performers. They may have different expectations and needs. Further, since performing arts psychology is an emerging field, appropriate training to work with performing artists may rely more on informal learning methods than does sport psychology. Without set guidelines and standards, the ethical practitioner will enter this new and exciting field with due care for continual learning and collegial support.

REFERENCES

APA. (2010). Ethical principles of psychologists and code of conduct. Retrieved from www.apa.org/ethics/code/principles.pdf

Andersen, M. B., Van Raalte, J. L., & Brewer, B. W. (2001). Sport psychology service delivery: Staying ethical while keeping loose. *Professional Psychology: Research and Practice, 32,* 12–18.

Aoyagi, M. W., & Portenga, S. T. (2010). The role of positive ethics and virtues in the context of sport and performance psychology service delivery. *Professional Psychology: Research and Practice, 40,* 253–259.

Association for the Advancement of Applied Sport Psychology. (n.d.). Ethics code. Retrieved from http://www.aaasponline.org/governance/committees/ethics/standards.php

Belar, C. D., Brown, R. A., Hersch, L. E., Hornyak, L. M., Rozensky, R. H., Sheridan, E. P., . . . Reed, G. W. (2001). Self-assessment in clinical health psychology: A model for ethical expansion of practice. *Professional Psychology: Research and Practice, 32,* 135–141.

Bersoff, D. N. (1999). Confidentiality, privilege, and privacy. In D. N. Bersoff (Ed.), *Ethical conflicts in psychology* (2nd ed.), pp. 149–150. Washington, DC: American Psychological Association.

Brown, C. H. (2001). Clinical cross-training: Compatibility of sport and family systems psychology. *Professional Psychology: Research and Practice, 32,* 19–26.

Brown, C. H., Gould, D., & Foster, S. (2005). A framework for developing contextual intelligence (CI). *The Sport Psychologist, 19,* 51–62.

Brown, J. L., & Cogan, K. D. (2006). Ethical clinical practice and sport psychology: When two worlds collide. *Ethics & Behavior, 16,* 15–23.

Campbell, C. D., & Gordon, M. C. (2003). Acknowledging the inevitable: Understanding multiple relationships in rural practice. *Professional Psychology: Research and Practice, 34,* 430–434.

Committee on Professional Practice and Standards (2003). Legal issues in the professional practice of psychology. *Professional Psychology: Research and Practice, 34,* 595–600.

Dean, B. (2001, January/February). The sky's the limit. *Family Therapy Networker,* 36–44.

De Shazer, S. (1985). *Keys to solution in brief therapy.* New York, NY: Norton.

Education and Training Committee, Division 13 (2000). Principles for education and training at the doctoral and post-doctoral level in consulting psychology/organizational. In R. L. Lowman (Ed.), *Handbook of organizational consulting psychology* (pp. 773–785). San Francisco, CA: Jossey-Bass.

Emmons, S., & Thomas, A. (1998). *Power performance for singers: transcending the barriers.* New York, NY: Oxford.

Etzel, E. F., Watson, J. C., & Zizzi, S. (2004). A Web-based survey of AAASP members' ethical beliefs and behaviors in the new millennium. *Journal of Applied Sport Psychology, 16,* 236–250.

Glueckauf, R. L., Pickett, T. C., Ketterson, T. U., Loomis, J. S., & Rozensky, R. H. (2003). Preparation for the delivery of telehealth services: A self-study framework for expansion of practice. *Professional Psychology: Research & Practice, 34,* 159–163.

Gottlieb, M. C., & Younggren, J. N. (2009). Is there a slippery slope? Considerations regarding multiple relationships and risk management. *Professional Psychology: Research and Practice, 40,* 564–571.

Gould, D., & Damarjian, N. (1998). Insights into effective sport psychology consulting. In K. F. Hays (Ed.), *Integrating exercise, sports, movement, and mind: Therapeutic unity* (pp. 111–130). Binghamton, NY: Haworth.

Guthiel, T., & Gabbard, G. (1993). The concept of boundaries in clinical practice: Theoretical and risk management dimensions. *American Journal of Psychiatry, 150,* 188–196.

Haber, S., Rodino, E., & Lipner, I. (2001). *Saying good-bye to managed care: Building your independent psychotherapy practice.* New York, NY: Springer.

Haberl, P., & Peterson, K. (2006). Olympic-size ethical dilemmas: Issues and challenges for sport psychology consultants on the road and at the Olympic Games. *Ethics & Behavior, 16,* 25–40.

Hamilton, L. H. (1997). *The person behind the mask: A guide to performing arts psychology.* Greenwich, CT: Ablex.

Harris, E. (2002). *Risk management for therapists who coach.* (Recording available via telephone). Retrieved from MentorCoach.com

Hays, K. F. (2000). Breaking out: Doing sport psychology with performing artists. In M. B. Andersen (Ed.), *Doing sport psychology: Process and practice* (pp. 261–274). Champaign, IL: Human Kinetics.

Hays, K. F. (2002). The enhancement of performance excellence among performing artists. *Journal of Applied Sport Psychology, 14,* 299–312.

Hays, K. F. (2006). Being fit: The ethics of practice diversification in performance psychology. *Professional Psychology: Research and Practice, 37,* 223–232.

Hays, K. F. (Ed.). (2009). *Performance psychology in action.* Washington, DC: American Psychological Association.

Hays, K. F., & Brown, C. H. (2004). *You're on! Consulting for peak performance.* Washington, DC: American Psychological Association.

Isaacs, D. (2006, July 21). Where even pros pay to play. *Chicago Reader: The Business.* Retrieved from http://www.chicagoreader.com/features/stories/thebusiness/060721/

Jones, G. (2002). Performance excellence: A personal perspective on the link between sport and business. *Journal of Applied Sport Psychology, 14,* 268–281.

Kampa, S., & White, R. P. (2002). The effectiveness of executive coaching: What we know and what we still need to know. In R. L. Lowman (Ed.), *Handbook of organizational consulting psychology* (pp. 139–158). San Francisco, CA: Jossey-Bass.

Kampa-Kokesch, S., & Kilburg, R. R. (2001). Executive coaching: A comprehensive review of the literature. *Consulting Psychology Journal: Practice and Research, 53,* 139–153.

Kaslow, N. J., & Kelly, J. F. (Eds.). (2010). Special section: The diversity status of the psychotherapist. *Psychotherapy: Theory, Research, Practice, Training, 47,* 143–197.

Knapp, S., & Slattery, J. M. (2004). Professional boundaries in nontraditional settings. *Professional Psychology: Research and Practice, 35,* 553–558.

Koocher, G. P. (2004, September). *Staying inside the safety zone: Ethical dilemmas in sport psychology.* Keynote presentation at the annual conference of the Association for the Advancement of Applied Sport Psychology, Minneapolis, MN.

Kraus, R., Zack, J., & Stricker, G. (Eds.). (2004). *Online counseling: A handbook for mental health professionals.* London, UK: Elsevier.

Lamb, D. H., Catanzaro, S. J., & Moorman, A. S. (2004). A preliminary look at how psychologists identify, evaluate, and proceed when faced with possible multiple relationship dilemmas. *Professional Psychology: Research and Practice, 35,* 248–254.

Lesyk, J. J. (1998). *Developing sport psychology within your clinical practice: A practical guide for mental health professionals.* San Francisco, CA: Jossey-Bass.

Levant, R. F. (2005, July 7). Letters: Codes of ethics and detentions. *New York Times,* p. A22.

Lowman, R. L. (Ed.). (1998). *The ethical practice of psychology in organizations.* Washington, DC: American Psychological Association.

Mainwaring, L. M., Krasnow, D., & Kerr, G. (2001). And the dance goes on: Psychological impact of injury. *Journal of Dance Medicine & Science, 5,* 105–115.

Martin, J. J., & Cutler, K. (2002). An exploratory study of flow and motivation in theater actors. *Journal of Applied Sport Psychology, 14,* 344–352.

Martin, S. (2010, July/August). Questionnaire: The Internet's ethical challenges. *Monitor on Psychology,* 32–35.

McCann, S. (2005). Roles: The sport psychologist. In S. M. Murphy (Ed.), *The sport psych handbook* (pp. 279–291). Champaign, IL: Human Kinetics.

Meyers, A. W., Whelan, J. P., & Murphy, S. (1995). Cognitive behavioral strategies in athletic performance enhancement. In M. Hersen, R. M. Eisler, & P. M. Miller (Eds.), *Progress in behavior modification* (pp.137–164). Pacific Grove, CA: Brooks/Cole.

Moore, Z. E. (2003). Ethical dilemmas in sport psychology: Discussion and recommendations for practice. *Professional Psychology: Research & Practice, 34,* 601–610.

Murphy, S. M. (Ed.). (1995). *Sport psychology interventions.* Champaign, IL: Human Kinetics.

Newman, J. L., Robinson-Kurpius, S. E., & Fuqua, D. R. (2002). Issues in the ethical practice of consulting psychology. In R. L. Lowman (Ed.), *Handbook of organizational consulting psychology* (pp. 733–758). San Francisco, CA: Jossey-Bass.

Parham, W. D. (2010). Ethical considerations in applied sport psychology: Culture, communications, and going the extra mile. *Professional Psychology: Research and Practice, 41,* 151–152.

Poczwardowsi, A., & Conroy, D. E. (2002). Coping responses to failure and success among elite athletes and performing artists. *Journal of Applied Sport Psychology, 14,* 313–329.

Pope, K. S., & Vasquez, M. J. T. (1998). *Ethics in psychotherapy and counseling: A practical guide* (2nd ed.). San Francisco, CA: Jossey-Bass.

Pope, K. S., & Vasquez, M. J. T. (2005). *How to survive and thrive as a therapist.* Washington, DC: APA.

Sachs, M. L. (1993). Professional ethics in sport psychology. In R. N. Singer, M. Murphey, & L. K. Tennant (Eds.), *Handbook of research on sport psychology* (pp. 921-932). New York: MacMillan.

Sataloff, R. T., Brandfonbrener, A. G., & Lederman, R. J. (Eds.). (2010). *Performing arts medicine* (3rd ed.). San Diego, CA: Singular.

Schwartz, A., Domenesch Rodriguez, M. M., Santiago-Rivera, A. L., Arredondo, P., & Field, L. D. (2010). Cultural and linguistic competence: Welcome challenges from successful diversification. *Professional Psychology: Research and Practice, 41,* 210–220.

Seligman, M., & Csikszentmihalyi, M. (2000). Positive psychology. *American Psychologist, 55,* 5–14.

Sidimus, J. (1998, April). The artist in society: Prejudices, myths and misconceptions. Paper presented at *The Dance Goes On...* The Conference, Toronto.

Stapleton, A. B. (2010). Ethical considerations in applied sport psychology. *Professional Psychology: Research and Practice, 41,* 143–149.

Stapleton, A. B., Hays, K. F., Hankes, D. M., & Parham, W. D. (2010). Ethical dilemmas in sport psychology: A dialogue on the unique aspects impacting practice. *Professional Psychology: Research and Practice, 41,* 143–152.

Sternberg, R. J. (1985). *Beyond IQ: A triarchic theory of human intelligence.* New York, NY: Cambridge University Press.

Taylor, L., McMinn, M. R., Bufford, R. K., & Chang, K. B. T. (2010). Psychologists' attitudes and ethical concerns regarding the use of social networking web sites. *Professional Psychology: Research and Practice, 41,* 153–159.

Terenzini, P. T. (1993). On the nature of institutional research and the knowledge and skills it requires. *Research in Higher Education, 34,* 1–10.

Van Raalte, J. L. (1998). Working in competitive sport: What coaches and athletes want psychologists to know. In K. F. Hays (Ed.), *Integrating exercise, sports, movement, and mind* (pp. 101–110). Binghamton, NY: Haworth.

Van Raalte, J. L., (2010). Referring clients to other professionals. In S. J. Hanrahan & M.B. Andersen (Eds.), *Routledge handbook of applied sport psychology* (pp. 205–213). New York, NY: Routledge.

Weinberg, R., & McDermott, M. (2002). A comparative analysis of sport and business organizations: Factors perceived critical for organizational success. *Journal of Applied Sport Psychology, 14,* 282–298.

Winum, P. C. (2003). Developing leadership: What is distinctive about what psychologists can offer? *Consulting Psychology Journal: Practice and Research, 55,* 41–46.

Wynne, L. C., McDaniel, S. H., & Weber, T. T. (1986). *Systems consultation: A new perspective for family therapy.* New York, NY: Guildford Press.

Younggren, J. N., & Gottlieb, M. C. (2004). Managing risk when contemplating multiple relationships. *Professional Psychology: Research and Practice, 35,* 255–260.

Zur, O., Williams, M. H., Lehavot, K., & Knapp, S. (2009). Psychotherapist self-disclosure and transparency in the Internet age. *Professional Psychology: Research and Practice, 40,* 22–30.

ACADEMIC ISSUES

ETHICAL ISSUES AFFECTING THE USE OF TELETHERAPY IN SPORT AND EXERCISE PSYCHOLOGY

Jack C. Watson II, Robert J. Schinke, and James P. Sampson, Jr.

INTRODUCTION

Professionals in sport and exercise psychology (SEP) are being presented with new opportunities based upon the constant improvements in technology. As we progress deeper into the 21st century, technology changes and adapts almost daily, and many of these new and developing technologies (e.g., Skype, smart phone applications, texting) are available to the average working professional. SEP practitioners are forced to decide if and how to use this new technology. While it may seem a logical next step to make the most of these advancements, practitioners are faced with questions about the ethical use of these new technologies, as ethical standards governing the practice of psychology and sport psychology have not for the most part provided clear standards or guidelines to address these advancements (Mallen, Vogel, & Rochlen, 2005). Instead of directly addressing the use of these new and emerging technologies for fear that new technologies would develop so quickly that the codes would become outdated, the American Psychological Association (APA) ethics code revision in 2002 added a section stating that "This Ethics Code applies to these activities across a variety of contexts, such as in person, postal, telephone, Internet, and other electronic transmissions" (p. 2). This addition was intended to alert practitioners that the use of the Internet and other electronic technologies, if used for professional purposes, does involve their professional life and is therefore required to meet the standards put forth within the ethical code of conduct for psychologists. No such updates or clarification statements regarding the use of technology have been created by the Association for Applied Sport Psychology (AASP) or other international sport psychology organizations, with the exception of a position stand related to the use of technology by the International Society of Sport Psychology (Watson, Tenenbaum, Lidor, & Alfermann, 2001).

The initial development of the Internet in the 1970s and its evolution into a global interconnection of computer networks used for quick and reliable information was a major technological advancement that continues to significantly affect the practice of SEP, directly and indirectly. Advancements in technology occur so quickly that it is commonly stated that computer technology is out of date within months of purchase. "As is true within other professions, sport and exercise psychology (SEP) professionals are finding the Internet to be a powerful and cost-effective tool that has the potential to help promote and develop the field as well as change the way SEP professionals conduct research, teach, and provide services" (Watson, Lubker, Zakrajsek, & Quartiroli, in press). While we do not know a great deal about the use of the Internet and other technologies in SEP, professions such as counseling and psychology have used it as a resource for over 30 years (Maxmen, 1978, as cited in Fisher & Fried, 2003). Further, the incidence of online counseling and therapy is predicted to increase in the future (Norcross, Hedges, & Prochaska, 2002), and technological developments will have a strong impact upon the future practice and training of psychology (DeLeon, Crimmins, & Wolfe, 2003).

Based upon the projected impact of new technology in the field of SEP, the current chapter outlines many of the ethical issues facing SEP professionals as they make decisions about if and how to use this advancing technology in their work. In this chapter, the term "teletherapy" refers to Internet and non-Internet related technology used to facilitate therapy with clients from a distance. Many other terms such as telehealth, e-therapy, and online counseling have also been used throughout the literature to discuss this concept.

While service delivery issues in SEP will be the primary focus of this chapter, the authors would be negligent if we did not mention the many other ways that technology can be beneficial to SEP professionals. Such uses include the marketing and dissemination of information about one's practice via websites and other electronic and social media. Technology can also be used to help professionals remain competent by providing opportunities for distance learning, online continuing education, consultation and collaboration with other professionals, as well as supervision. Additionally, practitioners are using electronic media to locate appropriate referrals for clients living, working and training in other regions of the country and across the world.

BENEFITS AND CONCERNS RELATED TO USING TECHNOLOGY IN SEP

It is clear that technology presents SEP practitioners with many new and positive options when it comes to deciding how to work best with clients. However, when considering the possibility of using the Internet and other related technologies within one's professional practice, it is important that the *benefits* and *concerns* of such decisions be considered.

Benefits
SEP practitioners are currently using technology to improve the efficiency, scope, and quality of services they provide to athletes and other clients. Among the many possible benefits to using technology in one's practice include: (1) improved service availability for clients who live

in remote locations, have disabilities, or are dealing with issues that are out of the ordinary, (2) cost-effectiveness of services, (3) ease of assessment, (4) more access to self-help resources, (5) access to culturally knowledgeable consultants, (6) clients' willingness to disclose, (7) more opportunities for supervision, (8) client anonymity, (9) decreased response time, and (10) collaboration (Mallen et al., 2005; Naglieri et al., 2004; Osborn, Dikel, & Sampson, 2011; Shaw & Shaw, 2006).

Concerns

While the use of this technology comes with obvious benefits to the practitioner and client, it is not without its concerns. The primary concerns involve ethical issues and questions about the quality of services (Bloom & Sampson, 1998). The primary ethical concerns include: (1) confidentiality, (2) relationship development, (3) computer mediated communication competency, (4) limited accessibility, (5) data transmission and storage issues, (6) credentialing across state and provincial lines, (7) quality and quantity of information provided to clients, (8) lack of local knowledge, (9) validation of resources and techniques, and (10) managing the ever-changing technology (Mallen et al., 2005; Shaw & Shaw, 2006; Watson, Tenenbaum, Lidor, & Alfermann, 2001). Concerns about service quality and effectiveness typically involve questions about the efficacy of online or technology-driven interventions. In many cases, older treatment interventions are being used with new modes of service provision with the assumption of efficacy, but little data supports this assumption.

DESCRIPTION OF THE CLIENT

While any person competing in a sport, seeking to perform a skill at a high level, or trying to change health and/or exercise behaviors is a good candidate for SEP services, it is probably a fair statement to say that the majority of SEP clients are younger individuals between the ages of 12 and 35 who compete in higher-level sports or other physical activities. In addition, adults are spending more and more time each year online, with adults spending an average of 13 hours a week online in 2009 (Harris Interactive, 2009). From this same survey, we also know that approximately 184 million adults were online in 2009, with over 100 million people using the Internet to look for health-related information in 2002 (Harris Interactive, 2002).

Major issues affecting practitioners' decisions about using new technology include the needs and perspectives of their clients. Given the advancements in technology since the mid-1990s, younger generations have embraced these advancements to a greater degree than older individuals. In fact, in 2009 it was estimated that 93% of youths aged 12-17 years used the Internet (Pew Internet & American Life Project, n.d.). Those currently in middle school, high school, college, and those in their twenties have grown up with technological options that have given them increased access to information (e.g., Internet), increased demands on their attention (e.g., cell phones, email, texting, instant messaging, social networking), and a cost-effective, almost immediate connection to those around them (e.g., cell phones, video conferencing). Because of their early and frequent connection to these technologies, many of these younger individuals have grown accustomed to and possibly dependent upon the availability of technology.

Beyond their strong connection with new and evolving technology, the athletes of today often have extreme demands upon their time (Pinkney & Tebbe, 2009). Especially within elite sport populations, athletes travel a great deal to compete in their sports. When they are not traveling, many also attend classes, do homework, practice their sports, seek employment, and have other time demands. Therefore, given their travel schedules and time demands, as well as their common use of digital media technology, many athletes may see technology as a viable means of receiving the services that they desire.

NEW TECHNOLOGY

As previously noted, new technology is developing at a staggering pace. Much of this technology can be used by SEP practitioners for distance consultations (e.g., email, cell phones/texting, video conferencing, social networking websites, Internet/chat rooms, listservs, instant messaging, blogging, webinars). Because of the long list of these types of technology, the pace at which each changes, and space requirements, full descriptions of each technology resource will not be included in this chapter. However, some of the more common forms of technology used for teletherapy within SEP will be briefly described below.

Email. Email communication is a technology that allows for text-based asynchronous chatting between individuals over the Internet. Email communication has many positive qualities for SEP consulting, such as allowing clients to take their time to write messages and send these messages at any time. Since these messages are asynchronous, the consultant can read the message at another time and respond effectively, perhaps upon reflecting. Email is a common form of communication, but it is not considered to be a secure form of communication without the use of encryption.

Cell phones/texting. Cell phones allow for synchronous text and verbal communication, as well as asynchronous text-based communication. While the text-based communication is often limited by the number of characters and the speed/ease of typing, the verbal communication allows for immediate synchronous communication, both lacking in visual feedback.

Websites. Internet websites provide a wide array of information in text and video format that can be used as learning resources to support SEP interventions. For example, viewing videos depicting various performance strategies can be used as a homework assignment between sessions with a SEP practitioner.

Video conferencing. While video conferencing technology has existed for years, it has been limited by cost and availability until recently. With the advent of new technology such as Skype, individuals can communicate in a synchronous verbal manner with visual feedback from a distance. Video conferencing requires a relatively inexpensive camera and microphone, and the security of such technology is often questioned.

Social networking. Social networking technologies allow individuals to connect electronically using synchronous and asynchronous text and pictorial information (e.g., Facebook, LinkedIn, Twitter). These networking opportunities encompass meeting people, exchanging ideas, and making and maintaining personal and professional contacts. These innovations are popular, as up to 35% of adults have an online profile (Lenhart, 2009). Further research with psychology doctoral students and psychologists has indicated that as many as 77% maintain a profile on a social networking site, with this percentage being much higher amongst younger participants (Taylor, McMinn, Bufford, & Chang, 2010). This data leads the authors to believe that the issue of social networking and the accidental and unintentional self-disclosures that result from involvement with technology will likely arise in the future.

LEGAL, ETHICAL AND PRACTICAL ISSUES

To date, the ethics codes created by the American Psychological Association (APA, 2002) and the Association for Applied Sport Psychology (AASP, 1996) have offered little guidance specifically directed at the work of SEP consultants regarding the use of the Internet and other forms of distance technology. Therefore, SEP practitioners have lacked clear guidelines and standards to help direct their practices in non face-to-face settings, and "as a result, psychologists and their clients are at a substantial risk of potential harm" (Ohio Psychological Association, 2010, p. 1). To help alleviate these concerns, guidelines need to be developed regarding how new technology can and should be applied (Maheu et al., 2005). The authors will provide a summary of the commonly identified legal and ethical issues that have emerged about teletherapy and identify the guidelines that practitioners should consult before providing teletherapy consultations.

Legal Issues
It is important for practitioners who are interested in providing psychological or psychoeducational services to be aware of the potential legal issues that they may face when providing these services. Knowledge of these issues will help practitioners develop strategies that allow them to avoid legal problems associated with their work.

Insurance. Practitioners would be wise to discuss, with their liability insurance providers, their stance related to services provided in non-traditional settings using the Internet and other technologies (Mallen et al., 2005; Ohio Psychological Association, 2010). If a malpractice case were to develop during teletherapy, practitioners should ensure that they are covered. As a common rule of thumb, malpractice insurance companies only cover their clients for services provided within the scope of their licenses. Therefore, if practitioners are practicing in an area outside of the scope of their license or competency, they may not be covered by their insurance company.

Cross boundary certification/licensure. If licensed, practitioners should also check state laws related to practicing in a state other than where they are licensed (Barnett, 2005). Practicing across state, provincial, or international boundaries raises legal concerns (APA Ethics Code 1.02). While practitioners have the ability to use technology to connect with clients around the world, they should realize that their license typically covers practice within one state, providence or country and may not be valid where a distant client is located. If providing teletherapy services to a client who is physically located in another jurisdiction, there is a possibility that insurance companies would not be responsible for covering any damages or legal expenses if sued.

Ethical Issues

Beyond the brief and non-descript 1997 APA Ethics Committee statement on using electronic services, guidelines for psychologists providing services via teletherapy did not exist until very recently (Ohio Psychological Association, 2010). Guidelines had been established for other closely aligned mental health professions (see section on Teletherapy Guidelines below). The remainder of this section will provide a brief overview of the common ethical issues raised in the discussion of teletherapy with regard to psychology and SEP. It is important to note that practitioners who provide teletherapy services need to take appropriate actions to remain in compliance with appropriate codes of ethics.

Marketing. Practitioners who market teletherapy services likely do so using the Internet. When marketing teletherapy services, practitioners should consider the APA Ethics Code 5.01-5.06. According to Shaw and Shaw (2006), information that practitioners should consider posting on their webpages includes:

- full name,
- state of operation,
- degrees earned,
- area of study and institution,
- address and phone number,
- a statement that clients must be over 18 or have consent from legal guardian,
- a statement that teletherapy is not the same as face-to-face counseling,
- a statement that not all problems are appropriate for teletherapy,
- referral options,
- a statement about inability to ensure confidentiality in teletherapy,
- a statement about use of encryption software,
- a statement about conditions for breaching confidentiality, and
- a waiver for teletherapy.

Other items of importance to consider having on one's webpage include a personal picture, a description of the scope of one's practice and competencies, and a description of possible technical difficulties that may occur with this technology (Mallen et al., 2005).

Intake information. The initial interview "intake" process for teletherapy clients should be different from the processes used with traditional consulting. The first step in this process should be gathering basic contact information that may include name, address, telephone number, physician, and emergency contacts (Mallen et al., 2005). Additionally, the practitioner should identify contact information for local emergency services, a local backup practitioner and/or hotline numbers, and ways to stay up-to-date on local events (Watson et al., 2001). Practitioners should also attempt to verify this information, as distance technology makes it possible for clients to misrepresent themselves. Having such information on file allows practitioners to have a means of contacting their clients or important others in case of emergency or technology breakdown.

Informed consent and disclosure. While the informed consent process for teletherapy should be similar to that of a traditional face-to-face consultation, some differences exist. In addition to the normal informed consent process, there is other information that practitioners should provide to their clients about themselves. First in this process is to ensure that informed consent is being provided by an appropriate person (i.e., the client is over 18, or a legal guardian is providing consent). Similar to traditional informed consent, practitioners should discuss the limits to confidentiality (e.g., supervision), but also how they would handle situations where the client presented a risk to him/herself or others (Mallen et al., 2005). However, the consultants would also need to provide information about how they use electronic communication, and their background and training with this technology.

Practitioners should also provide, as part of the informed consent process, information similar to what was suggested for use in electronic marketing. Such information may include risks to confidentiality, limitations associated with teletherapy, the possibility for misunderstandings due to a lack of visual cues, how often one will check for messages, how fast a response to expect, and the circumstances for use of alternative communication avenues should the technology malfunction (Ohio Psychological Association, 2010; Watson et al., 2001).

Confidentiality. Maintaining confidentiality appears to be the most commonly cited concern with teletherapy. Confidentiality is a basic tenant of psychology practice (APA Ethics Code 4.01). Practitioners need to take reasonable steps to maintain the confidentiality of information about their clients, including firewall protections for stored data and the use of encryption software. As per recommendations from section 4.02 of the APA Ethics Code, it is also important for practitioners to discuss the limits of confidentiality with their clients. In the case of teletherapy, these limits should involve issues beyond those discussed in a normal face-to-face setting and include hackers obtaining one's email, chat, or file storage information.

Appropriate use of services. Services provided via teletherapy should be engaged in on a case-by-case basis given that the appropriateness of such services varies based upon presenting concerns, time, setting, and circumstances (Ohio Psychological Association, 2010). Practitioners must judge the appropriateness of services based upon the concerns presented and the client's ability to communicate effectively with different technology. For example, clients with Axis II disorders or who may have suicidal/homicidal ideations may not be suitable for teletherapy given the likelihood of success or the dangers they present to themselves or others. Clients with limited technology backgrounds or motor problems also may not be good candidates for text-based consultations.

Competency. Consultants should be concerned with two areas of competency when providing teletherapy services (Mallen et al., 2005). The first area relates to the practitioners' ability to understand and effectively use the technology with which they intend to work. The second area is related to their ability to communicate effectively when using this technology.

Practitioners interested in teletherapy should make sure that they have the proper current training or support to use the technology effectively. They need to develop and maintain a level of competence with its use. It is a good idea to hire a technology expert to maintain any technology that is used in their practice. SEP practitioners are traditionally trained to work with clients in face-to-face settings. These skills do not necessarily transfer over to teletherapy consultations. Consultants should learn how to communicate effectively using text-based asynchronous and synchronous chat because some technology will not allow consultants to observe the non-verbal behaviors of the client, and some may not allow consultants to verbalize empathy the same way they would face-to-face. While many of the skills learned in school may transfer over to teletherapy, others will not. Thus, it is important for consultants to learn how to effectively work with clients from a distance.

Demonstrating and determining competence with regard to teletherapy is more difficult than it is with other specialties (Mallen et al., 2005). Training programs to help consultants develop these new skills exist primarily online. Those interested can do a Web search for such programs and may identify programs such as OnlineCounsellors and the Online Therapy Institute. In fact, the Florida Certification Board (n.d.) allows practitioners to obtain a Certified E-Therapist designation for providing direct care to individuals using distance technology.

Record keeping. The use of technology in one's SEP practice presents many ethical issues with regard to record keeping. Text-based and video sessions can be saved in their entirety by either party, which allows the practitioner to retain a detailed account of his sessions (APA Ethics Code 6.01). However, the electronic storage of such information leaves open the possibility that a stranger may access it. Therefore, before records are stored electronically, clients should be made aware of this and told how long such records will be kept, who has access to the information, and what steps will be taken to keep this information confidential (Watson et al., 2001).

Another potential risk to electronic communication is that clients also have the ability to save these sessions. Such information could be used against the consultant in a legal proceeding or could be accessed by another individual. Consultants should provide clients with a list of the risks associated with saving this information (Mallen et al., 2005).

Personal presence on the Internet. SEP practitioners often use self-disclosure only when appropriate for the consultation process. However, the Internet makes it difficult for SEP practitioners to control what clients may know about them. While personal webpages and other sources of information may be available on the Internet, one of the easiest ways for clients to find information is through social networking sites. Social networking sites offer benefits, but practitioners need to be cautious of how these sites are used in their practices and what information is available to clients. Professionals should remember that information that used to be considered private is now public when found on the Internet, and can be used by others to form an opinion about them (Behnke, 2008). Such technology can be used to help market and advertise for a practice, but if clients have access to this information, practitioners should certainly limit the amount and type of information to which clients have access (Plugging In to Social Networks, 2009; Taylor, McMinn, Bufford, & Chang, 2010).

Issues to consider when using social networking include boundaries, privacy and confidentiality, informed consent, marketing, and advertising. If using social networking personally and professionally, there can be a blurring of these lines. SEP consultants need to consider what information they will make available, and who they will allow to see their profiles. If using this communication medium with clients, one must make sure that clients are aware of the potential confidentiality risks. Practitioners must realize that information posted on social networking sites can be accessible to clients, even if they are not "friended" and privacy settings are high (Martin, 2010). These resources, if used for professional purposes, do fall under the auspices of the APA Ethics Code, so practitioners should be mindful of how they use these resources and the information posted on them.

Selection of websites as learning resources. Practitioners have an ethical obligation to recommend appropriate websites to their clients and to provide a useful level of support relevant to their clients' needs. Some websites present information that is inaccurate, out of date, and biased (Osborn, Dikel, & Sampson, 2011). Recommending a website as part of a between-sessions homework assignment represents an endorsement from the practitioner that the information on the website is accurate and appropriate. Clients also vary in their readiness for learning. Some clients have substantial anxiety about their physical performance that can translate into anxiety about learning. Such clients will need more support to make effective use of web-based information. One client may only need a recommendation for a relevant website, while another client may need specific recommendations regarding what portions of a website to use in what order, as well as some modeling in its use. These clients may also need more follow-up to ensure that their learning goals have been met (Osborn, Dikel, & Sampson, 2011).

TELETHERAPY GUIDELINES

Several organizations have developed teletherapy guidelines to provide proactive guidance for practitioners interested in providing such services, ethically. The Ohio Psychological Association's Communications and Technology Committee developed a set of "Telepsychology Guidelines," approved in 2010, to help guide the related behaviors of psychologists. While these guidelines were intended for those practicing in Ohio, they tie together well with the APA Ethics Code (2002). Other guidelines that should be considered include those written by the American Counseling Association (2005), the International Society for Mental Health Online (2000), and the National Board for Certified Counselors (2006).

CASE EXAMPLE

Dr. John, a licensed psychologist trained in a traditional counseling psychology program, has a private practice in New York City. In college, Dr. John was the captain of his tennis team and a nationally ranked competitor. Since completing his graduate training, Dr. John has worked with a few collegiate tennis players to help with their performance. On his practice website, Dr. John promotes himself as an internationally acclaimed psychologist and sport psychologist. One day, he is approached via email by the mother of a high-level high school tennis player in North Carolina and asked if he would work with her son to help improve his performance as he moves into his senior year and is looking for tennis scholarships. She portrayed her son as a good tennis player who does not always take good nutritional care of himself and sometimes struggles with performance anxiety. Given that Dr. John has worked with athletes in the past, and has at times consulted with athletes via the phone, he decides to work with this athlete and use a variety of technological advancements to do so effectively (e.g., phone, email, websites). What are the pertinent issues to consider in this case?

While there are many pertinent issues to consider, some of these issues will be outlined below:

- Is Dr. John appropriately trained and competent to provide services in sport psychology and use distance technology?
- As a licensed psychologist, can John provide services to a person who lives in a state other than the one in which Dr. John is licensed?
- Does Dr. John know the true identity of the client? How will he find this out?
- Has Dr. John's marketing overstepped ethical bounds with his claims?
- Does Dr. John provide enough appropriate information to the potential client about himself?
- How does Dr. John deal with the issues of confidentiality that may be associated with some of the forms of technology he is considering using?
- How, if at all, will the billing be changed as a result of this form of consultation?
- Is this client an appropriate choice for teletherapy?

The questions raised by this case are imperative for practitioners to consider if they are faced with the opportunity to consult with clients from a distance using technology. While these issues and questions do not always have clear answers, they are important issues to consider. The remainder of this chapter will be geared toward providing information to educate practitioners about the benefits and concerns of teletherapy, and will help to inform the reader about these important issues and possible resolutions.

CONCLUSION

The history of distance therapy originated with Freud's work conducted with "Little Hans" by way of letters sent to his father (Skinner & Zack, 2004). Current technologies used to provide services at a distance are much more advanced. SEP practitioners who use these technologies must take steps to ensure that they are providing the best quality services while remaining ethical in this new age of practice. Given that ethical guidelines directed at the provision of teletherapy services for SEP practitioners do not exist, this chapter is an attempt at identifying ethical issues that may be important to such practices. It is expected that the current state of technology will continue to change, promoting further need for such guidelines. Concurrently, there is also a need for practitioners to research the efficacy of different forms of teletherapy, and for graduate programs to offer coursework in teletherapy (Mallen et al., 2005; Taylor et al., 2010) to encourage practitioner competence for this emerging form of practice.

REFERENCES

American Counseling Association. (2005). ACA Code of Ethics. Retrieved from http://www.counseling.org/Resources/CodeOfEthics/TP/Home/CT2.aspx

American Psychology Association. (1997). APA statement on services by telephone, teleconferencing, and Internet. Retrieved from http://www.apa.org/ethics/education/telephone-statement.aspx

American Psychological Association. (2002). Ethical principles of psychologists and code of conduct. Washington, DC: Author.

Association for Applied Sport Psychology. (1996). Ethical principles and standards. Retrieved from http://appliedsportpsych.org/about/ethics

Barnett, J. (2005). Online counseling: New entity, new challenges. *The Counseling Psychologist, 33,* 872–880.

Behnke, S. (2007, July/August). Ethics and the Internet: Requesting clinical consultations over listservs. *APA Monitor on Psychology,* 62–63.

Behnke, S. (2008, July/August). Ethics in the age of the Internet. Retrieved from http://www.apa.org/monitor/2008/07-08/ethics.html

DeLeon, P., Crimmins, D., & Wolfe, A. (2003). Afterword—the 21st century has arrived. *Psychotherapy: Theory, Research, Practice, Training, 40*(1–2), 164–169.

The Florida Certification Board. (n.d.). *Certification operations: E-therapy.* Retrieved from http://flcertificationboard.org/Certifications_E-Therapy.cfm

Harris Interactive. (2002). Cyberchondriacs continue to grow in America. *Health Care News, 2,* 1–2.

Harris Interactive. (2009). Internet users now spending an average of 13 hours a week online. Retreived from http://www.harrisinteractive.com/vault/HI-Harris-Poll-Time-Spent-Online-2009-12-23.pdf

International Society for Mental Health Online. (2000). Suggested principles for the online provision of mental health services. Retrieved from https://www.ismho.org/suggestions.asp

Lenhart, A. (2009, January 14). Adults and social network websites. Retrieved from http://pewinternet.org/Reports/2009/Adults-and-Social-Network-Websites.aspx

Lenhart, A., Hitlin, P., & Madden, M. (2005, July 27). Teens and technology. Retrieved from http://www.pewinternet.org/Reports/2005/Teens-and-Technology/01-Summary-of-Findings/Summary-of-Findings.aspx

Maheu, M., Pulier, M., Wilhelm, F., McMenamin, J., & Brown-Connolly, N. (2005). *The mental health professional and the new technologies.* Mahwah, NJ: Lawrence Erlbaum Associates.

Mallen, M. J., Vogel, D. L., & Rochlen, A. B. (2005). The practical aspects of online counseling: Ethics, training, technology, and competency. *The Counseling Psychologist, 33,* 776–818.

Martin, S. (2010, July). The Internet's ethical challenges. *Monitor on Psychology, 41*(7), 32.

National Board for Certified Counselors and the Center for Credentialing and Education. (2006). *The practice of Internet counseling.* Retrieved from http://www.nbcc.org/Assets/Ethics/internetCounseling.pdf

Norcross, J. C., Hedges, M., & Prochaska, J. O. (2002). The face of 2010: A Delphi poll on the future of psychotherapy. *Professional Psychology: Research and Practice, 3,* 316–322.

Osborn, D. S., Dikel, M. R., Sampson, J. P. (2011). The Internet: A tool for career planning (3rd ed.). Broken Arrow, OK: National Career Development Association.

PEW Internet & American Life Project. (n.d.). Trend data for teens. Retrieved from http://pewinternet.org/Static-Pages/Trend-Data-for-Teens/Usage-Over-Time.aspx

Pinkney, J. W., & Tebbe, C. (2009). The college student-athlete experience and academics. In E. F. Etzel (Ed.), *Counseling and psychological services for college student-athletes* (pp. 257–282). Morgantown, WV: Fitness Information Technology.

Plugging In to Social Networks (2009, Spring/Summer). *GOOD PRACTICE,* 8–12.

Shaw, H. E., & Shaw, S. F. (2006). Critical ethical issues in online counseling: Assessing current practices with an ethical intent checklist. *Journal of Counseling & Development, 84,* 41–53.

Skinner, A., & Zack, J. S. (2004). Counseling and the Internet. *The American Behavioral Scientist, 48,* 434–446.

Taylor, L., McMinn, M. R., Bufford, R. K., & Chang, K. B. T. (2010). Psychologists' attitudes and ethical concerns regarding the use of social networking web sites. *Professional Psychology: Research and Practice, 41,* 153–159.

Watson II, J. C., Lubker, J. R., Zakrajsek, R. A., & Quartiroli, A. (in press). Internet usage patterns and ethical concerns in sport and exercise psychology. *Athletic Insight.*

Watson II, J. C., Tenenbaum, G., Lidor, R., & Alfermann, D. (2001). Ethical uses of the Internet in sport psychology: A position stand. *International Journal of Sport Psychology, 32,* 207–222.

CHAPTER 13

ETHICAL ISSUES IN SUPERVISION: CLIENT WELFARE, PRACTITIONER DEVELOPMENT, AND PROFESSIONAL GATEKEEPING

John R. Lubker and Mark B. Andersen

INTRODUCTION

Supervision of graduate students' and applied sport, exercise, and performance psychologists' (SEPP) work with athletes, exercisers, and performers is often a relatively long-term, intimate professional relationship that carries with it many of the joys, frustrations, desires, and hopes that can also be found in other relationships in our lives. In therapeutic relationships, one hopes that the therapist is a model of an ethical, rational, caring, genuine, empathic, and loving human being. One also hopes that the client, in some ways, will internalize the therapist as a model and incorporate some aspects of the practitioner as part of the change process. Similar experiences and expectations are also beneficial within a supervision relationship. Supervisors may become internalized by supervisees, and modeling supervisors is probably one of the central means by which students and practitioners develop. Supervisees may learn a great deal from studying ethical principles and codes of conduct (e.g., American Psychological Association, 2010; Association for Applied Sport Psychology, n.d.), but, arguably, they may learn even more from the model the supervisor represents in terms of ethics-in-practice. Just as supervisors can be models for ethical best practice, they can also be models of loose ethics, which can be passed down to their supervisees. Supervision is a central area of study in counseling and clinical psychology, but in applied sport, exercise, and performance psychology the topic of supervision has not been focused upon as much as it should be. Why supervision did not emerge in sport and exercise psychology as an area of research (e.g., Andersen, Van Raalte, & Brewer, 1994) or a topic of discussion (e.g., Andersen & Williams-Rice, 1996) until the mid 1990s may have been due, in part, to the field's origins in physical education and exercise science rather than in psychology and counseling. To examine supervision in SEPP, let's begin with some background.

SUPERVISION IN APPLIED SPORT, EXERCISE, AND PERFORMANCE PSYCHOLOGY

Investigation and discussion of supervision for trainees and practitioners engaged in applied sport psychology work appeared relatively late in the history of the field. We mention only *sport psychology* here because supervision in exercise and performance psychology does not appear, to date, to have been addressed in the literature in any consistent or substantive way. The first appearance of supervision in applied sport psychology literature was an abstract for a workshop at a sport psychology conference (i.e., Carr, Murphy, & McCann, 1992). Given that the field of sport psychology has roots in academic departments of the 1960s and 1970s, which often trained physical education (PE) teachers, it seems unusual that the supervision of PE educators (student-teacher supervision) did not translate into the then psycho-educational practice of sport psychology service delivery.

In the clinical and counseling psychology literature, the topic of supervision goes back, at least, to Sigmund Freud (1909/1977). Today, there are scores of books, numerous journals, and thousands of book chapters and journal articles on supervision in mainstream psychology. Over two decades ago, Robiner and Schofield (1990) published a reference bibliography for supervision that contained over 700 entries. The number of professional journal articles on supervision in sport psychology, however, remains quite small (e.g., Watson, Lubker, & Zakra-jsek, 2007; Watson, Zizzi, Etzel, & Lubker, 2004), especially in the area of ethics in practice and training (see Andersen, 1994; Andersen, Van Raalte, & Brewer, 2000; Petitpas, Brewer, Rivera, & Van Raalte, 1994).

DEFINING SUPERVISION

Many definitions of supervision exist. Bernard and Goodyear (1998) defined supervision as

> an intervention provided by a senior member of a profession provided to a junior member, or members of that same profession. This relationship is evaluative, ex-tends over time, and has the simultaneous purpose of enhancing the professional functioning of the junior member(s), monitoring the quality of professional services offered to those clients she, he, or they see(s) and acting as the gatekeeper for those who are to enter that particular profession. (p. 6)

What is curiously missing from the above definition is that one of the main goals of super-vision is to ensure the health and welfare of the supervisee's clients. Van Raalte and Andersen (2000) described supervision as a long-term interpersonal relationship designed to foster the growth and development of a trainee's skills as a helping professional, but with the "primary purpose . . . to ensure the care of the athlete-client" (p. 153). The common thread tying these descriptions together is that supervision is important in the field of sport, exercise, and performance psychology (SEPP) because it is a means for protecting clients and for training and integrating practitioners into the profession. Within the context of this relationship, it is the supervisor's responsibility to provide a supervisee with both support and training in the interventions that will be used with their clients (Blocher, 1983; Kurpius & Morran, 1988; Milne & James, 2000).

HEALTH, WELFARE, AND SAFETY OF CLIENTS

The primary ethical consideration in supervision is the health, welfare, and protection of the clients under the supervisee's care. The professional and ethical growth and development of new practitioners is also a central outcome of the supervisory relationship. Through the supervision process, supervisees can achieve a greater sense of self-knowledge, a clearer understanding of the therapeutic process through close contact with the supervisor, and training in proper legal and ethical professional behavior (Andersen, 1994; Van Raalte & Andersen, 2000). These outcomes and processes directly influence service delivery and should play key roles in the training of new practitioners in SEPP (Andersen et al., 1994). A secondary function of the supervisor is to serve as a gatekeeper in charge of service provision quality control with respect to new practitioners (Feasey, 2002). Through the progressive development of supervisees' skills, this responsibility helps ensure the health, welfare, and safety of clients from providers who are insufficiently skilled to deliver services in a competent manner. Ideally, supervisors would be well trained in dealing with incompetent or even dangerous supervisees, but we know that many supervisors have no formal training in supervision (see Andersen et al., 1994; Watson et al., 2004)

COMMON MODELS OF SUPERVISION

Models of supervision vary greatly and are discussed in depth in other texts for the interested reader (e.g., Bernard & Goodyear, 1998; Falender & Shafranske, 2004; Stoltenberg, McNeill, & Delworth, 1998). In SEPP, most practitioners providing supervision appear to use derivations of cognitive-behavioral therapy (CBT) supervision. Although this seems to be the most commonly used model in our field, there have been some discussions and case studies using psychodynamic approaches (e.g., Andersen, 2005). Both models provide a solid framework for engaging in ethical supervision practices. We briefly outline the CBT (e.g., Kurpius & Morran, 1988) and psychodynamic models below.

Cognitive-Behavioral Supervision
The CBT model of practice has had a long-standing history in the field of sport psychology (Van Raalte & Andersen, 2000). It should come as no surprise that many practitioners employ this model when they provide supervision to students and fellow practitioners. Proponents of the CBT model of supervision maintain that supervisors need to be expert practitioners who

are responsible for the skills supervisees acquire and the mastery with which they practice from this theoretical perspective (Bernard & Goodyear, 1998).

Just as in the practice of CBT, the supervision process places a premium on the supervisor's ability to assist the supervisee by identifying adaptive and maladaptive behaviors and cognitions in practice, teaching/reinforcing those that should continue, and extinguishing those that are counterproductive (Rosenbaum & Rosen, 1998)

Psychodynamic Model of Supervision

Many counseling and clinical psychologists conduct supervision using a psychodynamic model, but only a small number of sport psychology supervisors employ this approach with their supervisees and students (Andersen & Williams-Rice, 1996). Psychodynamic models of supervision stem from Freudian (Freud, 1909/1977), Neo-Freudian, and object-relations theories. Although there is a focus on teaching and learning skills and competencies (as in CBT supervision) in this approach, there is a stronger emphasis on closely examining the relationships of the supervisee (e.g., supervisee and client, supervisee and supervisor, supervisee and family of origin; Andersen, Van Raalte, & Harris, 2000). The function of psychodynamic supervision is to increase supervisee awareness and insight into their relationship patterns through exploration of their interpersonal histories. This exploration centers on how the positive and negative patterns of behavior that have developed from their experiences may affect their current and future interactions with clients (Campbell, 2000).

The awareness and understanding of transference and countertransference are central factors in the supervisory relationship. Transference refers to the redirection (and projection) of the supervisee's feelings, behaviors, reactions, and thoughts about a historically significant other (e.g., mother), or fantasized other (e.g., the "good mom" one wishes one had), onto the supervisor. Similar (and parallel) processes occur between the practitioner and the client. Countertransference mirrors transference, but stems from the supervisor's history and projections onto the supervisee. This process can parallel the transference and countertransference phenomena in the supervisee-client relationship, which is also deeply examined in this type of supervision. For example, a client who was neglected by her father may respond to a psychologist as a "good father" figure whom she wished she had. In supervision, the same psychologist may respond with similar parental transference needs to the supervisor.

Psychodynamic supervision often focuses on resistance to self-understanding and, under the guidance of the supervisor, the removal of blind spots that result from unconscious factors. Once unconscious processes are identified, they are put into perspective to help the supervisee become more effective. Although there are many similarities, it is important to distinguish between psychodynamic supervision and therapy (Zaslavsky, Nunes, & Eizirik, 2005). Supervision may be therapeutic, but it is not therapy. In supervision, one may focus on the supervisee's unconscious motivations, transferences, and processes in terms of how they affect service delivery and the supervisee-client relationship, but exploring the roots of such processes lies in the realm of psychotherapy. It is a question of focus. Supervisees' strengths and weaknesses are examined in supervision to help supervisees use their strengths effectively with clients, and to recognize their weaknesses or neuroses and not let them interfere with or sabotage their working relationships with clients. In therapy, a person's weaknesses and strengths are examined in depth with the goal of changing maladaptive patterns. In supervision, those maladaptive patterns are recognized, but the job is to "walk around" them, or compensate, so they do not get in the way of practice.

ETHICAL ISSUES IN SUPERVISOR-SUPERVISEE RELATIONSHIPS

The supervisor-supervisee relationship can be like a fast-moving car. On a straight and narrow path, everything is humming along. However, add in a couple of sharp curves and some oil slicks, and the car is soon in danger of sliding out of control. The supervision relationship can make all the difference between doing productive, ethical work with clients and causing harm. This section will highlight the many common ethical issues that can arise in the supervisor-supervisee relationship and what can be done to stay on the ethical straight and narrow. Every successful journey begins with good directions, and the supervision relationship is no different. Understanding duties and establishing expectations is a best-practice starting point.

Duties and Expectations of Supervisors

The initial expectation of any supervisor is to have some training in supervision. Although neither the American Psychological Association (APA) or the American Association for Applied Sport Psychology (AASP) currently require supervisors to have a certain level of professional training in this area (AASP is poised to require some training in the near future), ethically a practitioner should be well-versed (coursework, continuing professional development) in the art and practice of supervision before engaging in it. The supervisor can then use this foundational training to establish, collaboratively with the supervisee, clear and coherent guidelines and expectations for the relationship in the initial meeting between the two. The guidelines and expectations will differ depending on the model employed. For example, in CBT supervision the supervisor might explain how there will be educational (e.g., teaching CBT skills and interventions) and self-reflective components (e.g., examining the supervisee's own maladaptive cognitions and behaviors when working with clients). Other duties include maintaining confidentiality for the supervisor-supervisee relationship, providing a warm but professional atmosphere that is free of threat, keeping written records of sessions, setting and evaluating the progress of the supervision goals, and modeling ethical behaviors. A supervisor is ultimately (and typically legally) responsible for the client's welfare, and that duty also extends to the supervisee's welfare. Supervisors are expected to seek out consultation relative to their supervision with trainees (meta-supervision) when difficulties in their relationships arise (see AASP Ethics Code, Principle C).

DUTIES AND EXPECTATIONS OF SUPERVISEES

No matter where along the continuum of learning supervisees are in the supervisory process, their primary responsibility is the welfare of the client. Therefore, the supervisee must be honest and open in supervision sessions when processing previous consultations, working on current therapeutic techniques, and formulating future interactions and interventions with clients.

Being honest and open in supervision and reporting successes, mistakes, frustrations, and confusion are types of self-reflection where supervisees can take an introspective approach to assess their own needs, motivation, and expectations. Another expectation of supervisees is to have an understanding of ethics and ethical behavior as well as acting in ways that reflect this understanding. It is also expected that supervisees maintain secure, comprehensive notes to assist in accounting for what occurs in consultations (see AASP General Ethical Standards, No. 14; APA Ethical Principles of Psychologists and Code of Conduct, Standard No. 6.01, 6.02).

Confidentiality

Confidentiality in supervision resembles the ethical agreement of confidentiality in general SEPP practice (e.g., confidentiality holds except for special cases such as harm to self or others, evidence of child abuse), but there are some differences. For example, if a coach-client of a SEPP practitioner (who is a licensed psychologist) revealed that he was having a romantic relationship with one of his adult athletes, the psychologist would be bound by confidentiality and would not be able to report him to a national or state governing body without breaching an ethical code. If, however, a supervisee (practitioner or student) reported that he was sleeping with one of his clients (or if information came to the supervisor that confirmed the liaison), then, in the role of gatekeeper, the supervisor would be ethically (and in some jurisdictions, legally) bound to report the misconduct to the appropriate body (e.g., state licensing board, educational institution). Confidentiality holds for most of supervision, but not when client health and safety are in jeopardy (see AASP General Ethical Standards, No.18; APA Standard No. 4).

Multiple Relationships

Supervisors in SEPP often find themselves in many roles, and multiple relationships are difficult to avoid given the structure of higher education. Supervisors are often professors who are advising/chairing theses and dissertations, teaching courses, supervising practica and internships, and consulting with athletes and teams. Quite often, supervisees will be graduate students in their supervisors' programs. For example, a supervisor may be the supervisee's classroom teacher and also the student's thesis advisor. The APA defines a multiple relationship as occurring

> when a psychologist is in a professional role with a person and (1) at the same time is in another role with the same person, (2) at the same time is in a relationship with a person closely associated with or related to the person with whom the psychologist has the professional relationship, or (3) promises to enter into another relationship in the future with the person or a person closely associated with or related to the person. A psychologist refrains from entering into a multiple relationship if the multiple relationship could reasonably be expected to impair the psychologist's objectivity, competence, or effectiveness in performing his or her functions as a psychologist, or otherwise risks exploitation or harm to the person with whom the professional relationship exists. Multiple relationships that would not reasonably be expected to cause impairment or risk exploitation or harm are not unethical. (APA, 3.05, 2010).

Multiple relationships are almost unavoidable in the university setting. This situation, however, does not mean that their existence should be treated lightly. Because of the complexity of some multiple relationships, both supervisors and supervisees need to recognize the potential for harm and adhere to the codes of ethics provided to members of professional organizations. For example, the AASP Ethics Code states:

(a) AASP members must always be sensitive to the potential harmful if unintended effects of social or other nonprofessional contacts on their work and on those persons with whom they deal. Such multiple relationships might impair the AASP member's objectivity or might harm or exploit the other party

(b) An AASP member refrains from taking on professional or scientific obligations when preexisting relationships would create a risk of such harm.

(c) If an AASP member finds that, due to unforeseen factors, a potentially harmful multiple relationship has arisen, the AASP member attempts to resolve it with due regard for the best interests of the affected person and maximal compliance with the Ethics Code. (AASP, 9, n.d.)

Sexual/Romantic Liaisons

A sexual/romantic multiple relationship is one that is undoubtedly unethical and should be avoided in both the supervisor-supervisee and supervisee-client relationships. Both APA and AASP explicitly state that sexual relationships have no place in the supervision process.

Psychologists do not engage in sexual relationships with students or supervisees who are in their department, agency, or training center or over whom psychologists have or are likely to have evaluative authority (APA, 7.07, 2010).

AASP members do not engage in sexual relationships with students, supervisees, and clients over whom the AASP member has evaluative, direct, or indirect authority, because such relationships are so likely to impair judgment or be exploitative (AASP, 9c, n.d.).

A supervisor or a counselor in a relationship with a supervisee or client has a substantial unequal power differential. Acting on one's romantic feelings and breaking professional boundaries is essentially abusing the power differential in the professional relationship to one's advantage. If feelings do begin to develop toward a supervisee or client, supervision needs to be sought (and possibly the relationship needs to be terminated) in order not to blur professional and ethical boundaries.

The topic of erotic attraction in clinical and counseling psychology has received extensive attention in the research and practice literature (e.g., Pope, Sonne, & Holroyd, 1993). Outside the work of Andersen and Stevens (e.g., Andersen, 2005; Stevens & Andersen, 2007a, 2007b) and Little and Harwood (2010), the erotic in SEPP has not been examined in depth. In SEPP, the issues of romance and the erotic have usually been handled with "Thou shalt not." Although this prohibition is proper, it is not instructive or helpful when romantic or sexual feelings occur. Ideally, supervisors should be equipped to help a supervisee when the erotic appears in service, but it is unclear how many supervisors in SEPP have the training necessary to navigate these issues effectively. Consult Andersen (2005) for a case study of how a supervisor helped a supervisee whose client was attracted to him.

Student Disclosure of Personal Information

In supervision, supervisees may explore their own histories, neuroses, and patterns of interpersonal behavior. Understandably, there has to be a good deal of personal information disclosed in supervision. This information, however, is to be carefully used only to determine how one's experiences affect interactions with clients. Such information is not used as it would be in personal therapy. Although revealing personal issues is appropriate in supervision, exploring the roots of those issues should, for the most part, be reserved for therapy. It becomes a question of multiple roles again in that a supervisor cannot be both supervisor and therapist for a student/supervisee.

> Psychologists do not require students or supervisees to disclose personal information in course- or program-related activities, either orally or in writing, regarding sexual history, history of abuse and neglect, psychological treatment, and relationships with parents, peers, and spouses or significant others except if (1) the program or training facility has clearly identified this requirement in its admissions and program materials or (2) the information is necessary to evaluate or obtain assistance for students whose personal problems could reasonably be judged to be preventing them from performing their training- or professionally-related activities in a competent manner or posing a threat to the students or others (APA, 7.04, 2010).

Supervisee Therapy

Sport psychology practitioners receive professional training and education in a variety of different disciplines. We do not know of any exercise science-based sport psychology programs that have a requirement that students enter into their own psychotherapy. In contrast, some counseling and clinical psychology programs do include such requirements. If therapy is required or strongly encouraged, this practice needs, at least, to be stated up front in the description of the program. If such programmatic requirements exist, then safeguards also need to be in place. For example:

> (a) When individual or group therapy is a program or course requirement, psychologists responsible for that program allow students in undergraduate and graduate programs the option of selecting such therapy from practitioners unaffiliated with the program.
> (b) Faculty who are or are likely to be responsible for evaluating students' academic performance do not themselves provide that therapy. (APA, 7.05, 2010)

As stated above, any supervisor or instructor in a graduate program in sport psychology who has had or will have responsibilities for evaluating a student cannot also provide therapy to that student because of the issues of power differentials and dual roles.

Assessing Supervisees

The assessment of supervisee performance, and the subsequent feedback, is an essential element of the gatekeeping function of the supervision process. If the expectation of supervision is to foster the growth and development of a trainee's skills as a helping professional (Van Raalte & Andersen, 2000), providing consistent, competent, and specific feedback is essential. The type and time of assessment, as well as the timeliness of the feedback, need to be established at the beginning of the supervisory relationship.

(a) In academic and supervisory relationships, psychologists establish a timely and specific process for providing feedback to students and supervisees. Information regarding the process is provided to the student at the beginning of supervision.
(b) Psychologists evaluate students and supervisees on the basis of their actual performance on relevant and established program requirements. (APA, 7.06, 2010)

A commonly used assessment includes the employment of pre/post self-rating of performance (by supervisee) and ratings of supervisee performance by the supervisor. During the supervision process, the ratings are completed and then discussed. This feedback may then, in turn, be used as a basis for future benchmarking and goal setting for skill and interpersonal development.

Impairment

Supervisors and supervisees can become impaired for a variety of reasons. When a sport psychologist's personal difficulties are having a negative influence on service delivery or a supervisor's problems are influencing supervisory sessions in ways that are counterproductive, then impairment has entered the therapeutic space. If practitioners are treating problems that are outside their areas of expertise, or supervisors are supervising cases with little knowledge of the presenting problems, then they would also be impaired by way of not being competent (see Andersen et al., 2000).

(a) Psychologists refrain from initiating an activity when they know or should know that there is a substantial likelihood that their personal problems will prevent them from performing their work-related activities in a competent manner.
(b) When psychologists become aware of personal problems that may interfere with their performing work-related duties adequately, they take appropriate measures, such as obtaining professional consultation or assistance, and determine whether they should limit, suspend, or terminate their work-related duties. (APA, 2.06, 2010)

CASE EXAMPLE

A male SEPP doctoral student has been working with a female field hockey team. His clients are the athletes. He chats often with the same-age new coach (female), but she is not really his client in any way. Over time, he and the coach find themselves attracted to each other; they have already been to dinner together alone, and it was not a "working dinner" about the team. He reveals to his supervisor that he thinks he will have to terminate his relationships with the athletes because he and the coach would like to start a romantic relationship. He wants to do the ethical thing, but may not have considered the potential harm to the clients, his reputation in the local sport world, and his damage to the reputation of the field as a whole. Below we present a brief fantasy dialogue between this doctoral student and his supervisor.

Doctoral student (DS): I didn't plan on this happening, but I think I am in love. She and I click in so many ways, but I want to do the right thing. I don't see how I can ethically continue working with the team. It would also be way too awkward.

Supervisor (S): So what would it be like leaving the team?

DS: It would be a bummer. I really like the group as a whole. They're a great bunch of gals, and I have worked closely with several members of the team one-on-one and have become very close to some of them. As you know, I have worked with some of them on some really intimate and painful stuff. I'll be sad to let go of them.

S: I would imagine so, but I think I worded my question poorly. I was thinking more about your clients than you. Maybe I should have said, "What will it be like for the team if you leave?"

DS: Oh, I guess several of the team would also be sad to see me go.

S: And?

DS: And what?

S: OK. And what do you know about what happens when a therapist initiates a sudden termination of treatment?

DS: (pause) You mean like feelings of abandonment, and resentment, and anger?

S: And regression, and acting out, and depression. Do you think there is a possibility of any of these reactions happening?

DS: Maybe there would be some minor sense of abandonment for some team members.

S: I think I am going to have to disagree with you on this one. Working as a team psychologist kind of diffuses one's view. Let's take another example. Say you have been working closely with a violin player for a year. There's lots of positive transference and countertransference going on. The therapeutic alliance is a strong one. Over the course of the year you have met with her violin instructor several times for conversations about how you both can help the artist. You and the instructor become attracted to each other, and then you cut off treatment and pursue a romantic relationship with the violin teacher. What happens to your client then?

DS: OK, OK, I think I see what you mean. She would probably feel really abandoned and even betrayed.

S: And what might your abandonment do to the relationship between the instructor and your now former client?

DS: There could be a big rupture in their relationship.

S: I think we need to entertain the possibility that your actions could harm the team as a whole, and some members may be seriously affected. I think we also need to recognize that your actions, and the coach's, could negatively affect the coach's relationship with the team.

DS: (long pause) It's getting messy, isn't it?

S: Yup, and it gets messier because team members talk; coaches talk.

DS: What do you mean?

S: There are few well-kept secrets in sport. Your story will come out and people will talk about the sport psychologist who had the hots for the coach. I don't think it will do your reputation, at least in field hockey, any good, and it could damage the coach's reputation too. You don't have to answer this next question, but how much risk are you willing to take for love? Risks for the team? Risks for you? Risks for the coach? Even risks for the field's reputation? Maybe take a few days to ponder, reflect, and "feel" about all the potential consequences.

DS: This is giving me a headache.

S: Or maybe a heartache. Love is a beautiful and terrible thing. Lord knows we all need more love and happiness in our lives. It is sometimes a question of costs and benefits or a question of joys and sorrows for us and for those in our care. I suggest you don't make any final decisions right now, but let's keep talking over the next week. OK?

DS: (long sigh) OK . . . yeah . . . let's do that.

CONCLUSION

The process of supervision and the quality of the relationships between the supervisors and supervisees are central to ensuring positive professional development, client welfare, and general ethical practice in the field of sport, exercise, and performance psychology. These relationships serve as the ethical foundations for future professional conduct. Competent supervisors use theory to guide their supervision practices and are aware of the expectations that come with this professional role. Supervisees also need to understand their roles and responsibilities when engaging in the supervision process. When ethical issues or concerns arise, it is important to use the professional codes and standards as guides to assist in the resolution of such occurrences. This practice can assist both supervisors and supervisees in navigating the sometimes ethically turbulent waters of working with athletes, exercisers, and clients in performing professions.

REFERENCES

American Psychological Association. (2010). *Ethical principles of psychologists and code of conduct: 2010 amendments.* Available from http://www.apa.org/ethics/code/index.aspx

Andersen, M. B. (1994). Ethical considerations in the supervision of applied sport psychology graduate students. *Journal of Applied Sport Psychology, 6,* 152–167.

Andersen, M. B. (2005). Touching taboos: Sex and the sport psychologist. In M. B. Andersen (Ed.), *Sport psychology in practice* (pp. 171–191). Champaign, IL: Human Kinetics.

Andersen, M. B., Van Raalte, J. L., & Brewer, B. W. (1994). Assessing the skills of sport psychology supervisors. *The Sport Psychologist, 8,* 238–247.

Andersen, M. B., Van Raalte, J. L., & Brewer, B. W. (2000). When sport psychology consultants and graduate students are impaired: Ethical and legal issues in graduate training and supervision. *Journal of Applied Sport Psychology, 12,* 134–150.

Andersen, M. B., Van Raalte, J. L., & Harris, G. (2000). Supervision II: A case study. In M. B. Andersen (Ed.), *Doing sport psychology* (pp. 167-179). Champaign, IL: Human Kinetics.

Andersen, M. B., & Williams-Rice, B. T. (1996). Supervision in the education and training of sport psychology service providers. *The Sport Psychologist, 10,* 278–290.

Association for Applied Sport Psychology. (n.d.). *Ethics code: AASP ethical principles and standards.* Available from http://appliedsportpsych.org/about/ethics/code

Bernard, J. M., & Goodyear, R. K. (1998). *Fundamentals of clinical supervision.* Boston, MA: Allyn & Bacon.

Blocher, D. H. (1983). Toward a cognitive developmental approach to counseling supervision. *The Counseling Psychologist, 11,* 27–34.

Campbell, J. M. (2000). *Becoming an effective supervisor: A workbook for counselors and psychotherapists.* Philadelphia, PA: Accelerated Development.

Carr, C. M., Murphy, S. M., & McCann, S. (1992, October). *Supervision issues in clinical sport psychology.* Workshop presented at the annual conference of the Association for the Advancement of Applied Sport Psychology, Colorado Springs, CO.

Falender, C. A., & Shafranske, E. P. (2004). *Clinical supervision: A competency-based approach.* Washington, DC: American Psychological Association.

Feasey, D. (2002). *Good practices in supervision with psychotherapists and counselors.* London, England: Whirr.

Freud, S. (1977). Analysis of a phobia of a five year old boy. In A. Richards (Ed.) & J. Stachey (Trans.), *The Pelican Freud library, Vol. 8, Case histories 1* (pp. 169–306). Toronto, ON, Canada: Penguin Books. (Original work published 1909).

Kurpius, D. J., & Morran, D. K. (1988). Cognitive-behavioral techniques and interventions for application in counselor supervision. *Counselor Education and Supervision, 27,* 368–376.

Little, G., & Harwood, C. (2010). Enhancing our understanding of the potential violation of sexual boundaries in sport psychology consultancy. *Journal of Clinical Sport Psychology, 4,* 302–311.

Milne, D., & James, I. (2000). A systematic review of effective cognitive-behavioural supervision. *British Journal of Clinical Psychology, 39,* 111–127.

Petitpas, A., Brewer, B. W., Rivera, P., & Van Raalte, J. L. (1994). Ethical beliefs and behaviors in applied sport psychology: The AAASP Ethics Survey. *Journal of Applied Sport Psychology, 6,* 135–151.

Pope, K. S., Sonne, J. L., & Holroyd, J. (1993). *Sexual feelings in psychotherapy: Explorations for therapists and therapists-in-training.* Washington, DC: American Psychological Association.

Robiner, W. N., & Schofield, W. (1990). References on research in clinical and counseling psychology. *Professional Psychology: Research and Practice, 21,* 297–312.

Rosenbaum, M., & Rosen, T. (1998). Clinical supervision from the standpoint of cognitive-behavior therapy. *Psychotherapy: Theory, Research, Practice, Training, 35,* 220–230.

Stevens, L., & Andersen, M. B. (2007a). Transference and countertransference in sport psychology service delivery: Part I. A review of erotic attraction. *Journal of Applied Sport Psychology, 19,* 253–269.

Stevens, L., & Andersen, M. B. (2007b). Transference and countertransference in sport psychology service delivery: Part II. Two case studies on the erotic. *Journal of Applied Sport Psychology, 19,* 270–287.

Stoltenberg, C. D., McNeill, B., & Delworth, U. (1998). *IDM supervision: An integrated developmental model for supervising counselors and therapists.* San Francisco, CA: Jossey-Bass.

Van Raalte, J. L., & Andersen, M. B. (2000). Supervision I: From models to doing. In M. B. Andersen (Ed.), *Doing sport psychology* (pp. 153–165). Champaign, IL: Human Kinetics.

Watson J. C., II, Lubker, J., & Zakrajsek, R. (2007, October). Supervision issues in applied sport psychology: An international survey. Paper presented at the annual conference of the Association for Applied Sport Psychology, Louisville, KY.

Watson, J. C., II, Zizzi, S. J., Etzel, E. F., & Lubker, J. R. (2004). Applied sport psychology supervision: A survey of students and professionals. *The Sport Psychologist, 18,* 415–429.

Zaslavsky, J., Nunes, M. L. T., & Eizirik, C. L. (2005). Approaching countertransference in psychoanalytic supervision: A qualitative investigation. *International Journal of Psychoanalysis, 86,* 1099–1131.

CHAPTER 14

ETHICS AND TEACHING IN SPORT AND EXERCISE PSYCHOLOGY

Michael L. Sachs

INTRODUCTION

Discussion about ethics in sport, exercise, and performance psychology typically centers on applied issues. Ethical issues arise in our relationships with our clients. These issues are often challenging, given the non-traditional consulting settings in which many of us practice. However, especially for those of us in academia, but also for those in private practice who teach courses occasionally, the ethics of teaching is a critical area that is often ignored.

Unfortunately, the American Psychological Association's (APA) Ethics Guidelines (2002) and the Association for Applied Sport Psychology's (AASP) Ethics Guidelines (2010) include relatively little that is directly related to teaching. Fortunately, there is an extensive body of work that does address ethical issues in teaching from which we can draw for this chapter. One can start with the premise that all of us wish to be ethical in our teaching in sport and exercise psychology, but we often do not get much instruction/mentorship in these ethical issues while in graduate school, just as we sometimes get very little instruction in how to be a "good" teacher in the first place (an ethical issue in itself!). The assumption seems to be that if we are good researchers (and practitioners), we will somehow be able to be good and ethical teachers when we have our doctoral degree and go out into the world of academia. Alas, this does not take place by osmosis, so some instruction in this area is warranted.

Keith-Spiegel, Whitley, Balogh, Perkins, and Wittig (2002) provide an excellent casebook on the ethics of teaching, and cover 22 areas of interest. These are listed here because, as you will see here and in other references listed below, there are numerous books on this topic and one needs to select just a few areas of particular/primary interest within sport and exercise psychology. The other areas may be of interest to you as well, and you are encouraged to explore Keith-Spiegel et al. (2002) and the other references for more information:

1) Instructors' Classroom Policies
2) Student Deportment in the Classroom
3) Instructors' Presentation Style and Content
4) Required In-Class Learning Activities
5) Testing and Other Academic Evaluations
6) Grading Methods
7) Feedback to Students
8) Writing Reference Letters for Students
9) Biased Treatment of Students
10) Academic Dishonesty
11) Availability to Students
12) Student-Faculty Interactions
13) Multiple Role Relations and Conflicts of Interest
14) Interprofessional Relations
15) Exploitation of Students
16) Discrimination
17) Manipulative Students and Instructors
18) Supervising, Advising, and Collaboration With Students
19) Instructor Competency
20) Confidentiality Issues
21) Political and Public Statements
22) Responsibilities to the Institution (pp. v–x)

As noted, there are numerous books that address ethics in teaching (Infantino & Wilke, 2009; Johns, McGrath, & Mathur, 2008; Macfarlane, 2004; Mackenzie & Mackenzie, 2010; Mahoney, 2008; Strike & Soltis, 2004). Many of these books contain engaging case studies, some of which can be easily transferred to sport and exercise examples. Drawing upon Keith-Spiegel et al. (2002) and these other texts, I have identified six topics to focus upon in this chapter:

1) Multiple Role relationships
2) Confidentiality
3) Competence
4) Biased treatment of students
5) Dealing with helicopter parents
6) Social networking

Other topics, such as academic dishonesty/plagiarism, testing/grading, dealing with manipulative students, etc., are certainly important areas within teaching, but are not necessarily especially connected to sport and exercise psychology, and so the reader is referred to the excellent resources listed above for more information on these more general topics.

MULTIPLE ROLE RELATIONSHIPS

Watson and Schinke (2010; see also Watson, Clement, Harris, Leffingwell, & Hurst, 2006) recently addressed the issue of multiple role relationships in academic settings. The APA Ethical Principles (2002) address the issue of multiple relationships directly:

> A multiple relationship occurs when a psychologist is in a professional role with a person and (1) at the same time is in another role with the same person, (2) at the same time is in a relationship with a person closely associated with or related to the person with whom the psychologist has the professional relationship, or (3) promises to enter into another relationship in the future with the person or a person closely associated with or related to the person. (p. 6)

Overall, this is probably the area that has the most potential impact on our work as teachers. One should note, however, that "multiple relationships that would not reasonably be expected to cause impairment or risk exploitation or harm are not unethical" (APA, 2002). So multiple role relationships in and of themselves are not unethical, but if not handled appropriately, they can easily wind up being unethical in our work in sport and exercise psychology.

These multiple-role relationships arise clearly in two realms within teaching: (1) the faculty member is the instructor in a class, or multiple classes; and (2) the student is (a) a student-athlete with whom the teacher is consulting individually or as part of a team, (b) potentially a participant in a research study the faculty member is conducting/involved in, (c) an advisee of the faculty member—generally a graduate student but could be an undergraduate as well, or (d) a fellow exerciser/sport participant of the faculty member (takes the same aerobics class, exercises at the same time in the fitness center, plays on the same intramural basketball team, competes for the same local field hockey club, runs in the same local road races, etc.).

Ideally, one avoids these situations as best one can by not having students with whom one is consulting in one's class(es), not including students one is teaching in one's research studies, etc. Alas, this is rarely feasible, given required classes students must take, faculty who are the only ones teaching certain classes, research studies drawing from particular pools of participants, etc. Therefore, one is sometimes forced to address these multiple role relationships up front as they arise. It should be further noted that in smaller communities it is not unusual to cross paths with one's students in local settings such as restaurants, malls, and movie theaters. These encounters are unavoidable and, as with individuals with whom you are consulting, one should simply be friendly/polite as the occasion warrants—clearly this is not the setting to discuss classroom issues (or continue talking about a consulting issue raised at the last session).

How should the ethical professional handle these dilemmas? The first step is for the faculty member to "understand and acknowledge the possibility of multiple-role relationships occurring within our professional lives" (Watson & Schinke, 2010, p. 6). Understanding that these relationships may/will arise and having a preemptive plan of action for dealing with them is key.

The second step, as Watson and Schinke note, is that "multiple-role relationships should be managed proactively" whenever possible (p. 6). This means discussing the multiple role relationship with the student-athlete with whom one is consulting and making clear that you will do your best to make sure there will be no connection between the consulting sessions and the classroom settings. As will be discussed later in the section on confidentiality, the faculty member must indicate clearly that she/he won't bring up the student-athlete's performance issues in class (as in an example of issues in arousal control, where one might be tempted to say "I have a perfect example right here. Jane is working with me on just such an issue..."). And consulting sessions are not the place to discuss academic questions about class material (save those for office hours/other appointments that address academic concerns specifically). But what if that athlete says she/he is feeling overly stressed and the main reason is all the work required in YOUR class? In this case, this issue should be discussed in the consulting sessions, but the academic side of things could perhaps be more directly addressed in an academic meeting. The sensitive and aware faculty member/consultant will handle these situations as ethically as possible, with the best interests of the student in mind.

In research situations, some universities already frown on doing research with one's classes, as the power differential is inherent in these settings and it is problematic to address these power differential issues effectively. Occasionally, an instructor can convince one's Institutional Review Board (IRB) that she/he will have others come into class and solicit research participants, as well as make participation anonymous (e.g., remove oneself from data collection), etc. These issues should be addressed up front with one's classes, and the use of others to solicit/collect data as well as anonymity should be embraced as effective strategies for dealing with these issues. Instructors should also check with their IRB to ascertain how "strict" they are on these issues.

Situations in which one is teaching students who are one's advisees are generally not seen as particularly problematic, but a normal state of affairs in academia. One should, however, be aware of, and take steps to deal with as necessary, issues that may arise in either setting that might influence one's advising and/or one's grading. This could encompass one's advisee not following through on recommendations for revising a research plan, or the student not doing well in class (seemingly uninterested and/or taking a good grade for granted without having to work hard because she/he is your "star" advisee). These types of situations can prove uncomfortable and, as noted, should be addressed in an ethical and professional manner.

Finally, there may be situations in which your exercise/sport participation brings you into direct (a teammate) or indirect (fellow exerciser in the gym or participant in a road race) contact with a student. These are best handled, as noted earlier, by simply being friendly/polite as the occasion warrants. This is not the setting to discuss classroom issues or continue talking about a consulting issue raised at the last session. One should be careful, especially with teammates, that these exercise/sport issues don't carry over to the classroom in terms of grading or in confidentiality issues ("John and I play on an intramural basketball team and he lost the game for us the other night by getting nervous at the end of the game and missing two free throws which would have won the game for us").

These types of multiple-role issues will arise during one's academic career. The ethical academician will be sensitive/aware of these multiple-role possibilities. She/he will need to take proactive steps to address these issues as they arise—discussing these issues with the student is called for, but taking care to avoid these situations in the first place, if possible, is advised.

CONFIDENTIALITY

Confidentiality is an ethical standard that is covered extensively in both the APA (2002) and AASP guidelines (2010). Within the context of teaching, we are concerned with sharing information in the classroom about individuals/teams with which we have had contact in applied settings and/or research. We strive to highlight our lectures with wonderful real-world examples, from applied settings and/or research, to bring home points "perfectly." However, if we do not have permission to share this information and the team is identifiable, then we are breaching confidentiality and providing private information that the individuals/teams may not wish to be shared with the rest of the world.

We may think that sharing this information is innocuous and will result in no harm to the individuals/teams, and this may often be the case. However, we have no way of knowing this for sure, and the "law" of unintended consequences dictates that even such well-meaning sharing of information may have negative consequences. You may think that mentioning that "Amy [a field hockey player who happens to be a student in your class] and I discussed her issues with arousal control during games in our consulting session the other day. . . ." is perfectly fine, not remembering/realizing that Amy hadn't shared this with her teammates/coaches and this information was definitely NOT for public consumption.

There are abundant examples in the published literature (e.g., newspapers, magazines, books, research articles, web sites, movies, YouTube clips) that we can use to make our points in the classroom. You may also get permission from someone in your research/with whom you've worked in an applied setting to use an example in your classroom if you feel the example is that critical—but remember the power differential issue raised earlier and the potential hesitancy of that person to say "no" to your request. You might be tempted to use old examples of athletes from years ago, perhaps changing the athlete's gender and other identifying information, but this still has the potential to be a breach of confidentiality. Ideally, avoid this path and use publicly available sources for those perfect examples to include in the classroom.

COMPETENCE

Some individuals like to think they are competent in whatever they do, but this isn't the case (as in "We can't all be perfect"). Competence herein focuses upon how current one is in one's area of expertise—sport and exercise psychology. Most of us keep up with the latest theories and research in our field. This is especially true in our specific areas of expertise, but applies as well to the field in general.

Both the APA and AASP codes of ethics comment upon issues of competence. The APA states in section 2.01 that "(a) Psychologists provide services, teach, and conduct research with populations and in areas only within the boundaries of their competence, based on their education, training, supervised experience, consultation, study, or professional experience" (2002, p. 5). AASP's (2010) Principle A under General Principles addresses competence:

AASP members maintain the highest standards of competence in their work. They recognize the boundaries of their professional competencies and the limitations of their expertise. They maintain knowledge related to the services they render, and they recognize the need for ongoing education. AASP members make appropriate use of scientific, professional, technical, and administrative resources. They provide only those services and use only those techniques for which they are qualified by education, training, or experience. AASP members are cognizant of the fact that the competencies required in serving, teaching, and/or studying groups of people vary with the distinctive characteristics of those groups. In those areas in which recognized professional standards do not yet exist, AASP members exercise careful judgment and take appropriate precautions to protect the welfare of those with whom they work.

This standard of being up to date is the essence of competence in knowing one's subject matter. Keeping on top of current advances in pedagogy is critical as well—do you use Power-Point as appropriate, Blackboard (or some related system), the latest YouTube clips, classroom clickers, and other related technologies? Information sharing can be enhanced by using the latest technological advances that will facilitate communicating this information to your technologically savvy students. This does not mean you need to be using your iPad with one hand, your iPhone with the other, while listening to your iPod, but it does mean appropriately using technology that enhances your ability to teach effectively.

Maintaining competence on the technology side means keeping an eye out for advances that your university's technology center notes (and has workshops to help with), as well as noting occasional developments cited in your local newspaper, on the Internet, in magazines such as *Wired,* and so on. Asking your students about recent developments can sometimes bring enlightening ideas. Of course, if you tend toward the "geekish" side of the technology continuum you will be doing this anyway. If you do not tend toward that end, just ask those on your faculty who do, to let you in on the latest and greatest to help you communicate and teach more effectively and competently.

Maintaining competence in the knowledge base encompasses reading the literature (perhaps serving on an editorial board or two or as an occasional guest reviewer), as well as the latest books and textbooks (serving as a reviewer is helpful). Maintaining competence may also involve attending conferences, participating in continuing education workshops and webinars, maintaining networks with other researchers (especially in your area of expertise), and keeping up with the latest developments on listservs such as SPORTPSY and other Internet venues.

Competence in teaching extends beyond technology and content knowledge, to our teaching skills. Consider having a colleague or staff member/faculty member from your university's teaching center observe you teaching a class or two and provide feedback. Attend the center's seminars and review materials they make available on up-to-date teaching practices. Keeping up on this information will help make us more effective in the classroom and, therefore, more competent in communicating the knowledge within sport and exercise psychology that we wish to share with our students.

BIASED TREATMENT OF STUDENTS

An area of particular concern in academia is the possibility of playing favorites. While faculty will usually be vociferous in indicating they are objective in class and do not play favorites (in classroom settings and/or grading), we all have a "natural tendency" to like some students more, for a variety of reasons that may relate to exercise/sport, gender, ethnicity, religion, etc. Most of us probably do an excellent job of fighting this tendency, but it bears noting.

The first step, as with most of these ethical challenges, is understanding and acknowledging this as a potential issue. Accept that the student in the first row of your class, a basketball star at your university, is someone you admire (perhaps even envy), but you are going to be objective in treating her/him the same as all the other students in your class. The fact that your tennis doubles partner is now a student in your graduate sport psychology class must have no effect on how you treat her/him in class or grade her/his papers.

The second step, similar to earlier points, is to address these issues with the student as necessary. In the case of one's doubles partner, one should be up front about the issues and clarify that you intend to treat her/him fairly and equitably in class and in your grading. One may also emphasize the fact that the low grade on a recent paper has nothing to do with the fact that she/he has been playing poorly lately in tournaments. This type of situation can be problematic (one could suggest not playing with one's students on teams or in tournaments as the best way to deal with these potential issues) and must be addressed as needed.

If you find yourself struggling with these issues for whatever reason, having a supervisor/ mentor to discuss this with is extremely helpful (having such a person in any case is advisable)—we all need mentoring as we progress through our careers. On occasion one can have another individual grade papers (for example, one might have a relative in class—spouse, child, etc.— and this would certainly be necessary) or evaluate work done in class. Another suggestion would be to blind papers before grading to help make the process more objective.

DEALING WITH HELICOPTER PARENTS

Helicopter parents hover around their children, refusing to let them venture out into the world without close parental supervision. Helicopter parents have become the bane of our existence in recent years, not nearly as badly as when they appear in youth sport, but still annoying/ troubling. Such parents have been known to sit in on freshman orientation, and even attend classes with their children. Some universities have had to have separate orientations, one for new students and one for parents, at which they provide the parents with some information, thank them for their support, and send them on their way so the students can have the place to themselves.

Helicopter parents may feel that, because they are paying the bills (in many cases), they are entitled to keep close tabs on their children and be informed of anything and everything whenever they want such information. Confidentiality (as noted earlier) is the key ethical standard applicable here. Fortunately, you have a short acronym that will save you—FERPA, which stands for Family Educational Rights and Privacy Act (2011). You can check at your institution for the specifics of how to apply FERPA, but the bottom line is you can simply tell parents that you appreciate their call but that federal law in the form of FERPA prohibits your sharing any information about the student's educational records with them (assuming the student is 18 years of age or older—most are). You can recommend they talk with their child to get whatever information they need. This has the added advantage of facilitating communication between parent and child.

I have had parents accompany their children to interviews for our graduate program, in some cases sitting in on our informational session as the student explores our program and others. I find this perfectly fine, as I want to be sure the students and parents are comfortable with where the students might be spending a few years of their lives, especially if the parents may be paying for some or all of the students' education. Fortunately, I have never had a parent call me asking for information after the student has enrolled.

Helicopter parents are related to snowplow parents, who plow right into situations in which they do not belong. This, again, is usually found in youth sport situations, but hopefully you won't get any in your office or on the telephone. Parents these days can and do stay connected, via phone calls, emails, texts, and tweets, in ways unimaginable a decade or two ago. But, if handled correctly, this shouldn't affect you or your role as a teacher.

SOCIAL NETWORKING

Social networking sites are becoming ubiquitous in our society, with many of us having Facebook pages (as well as other social networks, but we will focus on Facebook here). Some universities have specific policies concerning using social networking sites to communicate with one's students, but most do not. So, do you "friend" your colleagues, graduate students, undergraduate students, etc.? Some faculty take special care to separate their private and professional lives so that this is not an issue—they do not friend colleagues or students. They may take the position that they are not here to be your friend, but to be friendly and professional while maintaining the role of professor and keeping the friendship circles separate.

But for many of us, our colleagues and students are our friends, and so we may be tempted to embrace them as friends on Facebook. Friending colleagues seems reasonable for those comfortable with this arrangement. The question of students is more problematic, given the inherent power differential that exists. This power differential may also exist with colleagues— if you are a senior colleague, a junior, pre-tenured colleague may feel uncomfortable saying no to a friend request because you still hold their future in your hands with your future tenure vote.

In the end, this may come down to personal preference/comfort level, and may differ by undergraduate/graduate level. If you are the "friendly" type who has lots of Facebook friends, then friending all your graduate students seems reasonable (but do not friend some and not others, as this raises favoritism issues). Some of the graduate students may decide they do not want to friend you back, which is perfectly fine (and you must take care not to be offended). This does not mean they do not like you, but simply want to keep their personal and professional lives separate.

One could suggest that having graduate students as friends can help keep one up to date on how they are doing and what's happening in their lives (some may not feel comfortable sharing things with you that they are fine with broadcasting to the world on Facebook—go figure!). This can also be a means to assess how they are presenting themselves to the world. Some students are very comfortable presenting their pictures of the wild parties they had on vacation, with many pictures of alcoholic beverages being consumed, wild outfits, etc. Alas, prospective employers have been known to check Facebook about applicants, and that front picture of the student with a big glass of beer in her/his hands doesn't make a great first impression. This can be a good occasion for quality mentoring, done tactfully, of your graduate students, as well as impression management. Additionally, Facebook has enhanced their privacy settings (and continues to do so), so students can block "outsiders" (the public in general or specific groups or individuals) from seeing any piece of content, such as pictures, if they wish to do so.

It should be noted that some students may still see these boundaries of friendship and advising/mentoring as being more solid than you do. Friending your graduate students is something to carefully consider, and also to potentially discuss with each of them to be sure they are comfortable with the arrangement and note that you will not be offended at all if they do not wish to do so.

The issue of friending undergraduate students strikes me as more problematic. A 50-year-old faculty member friending a 19-year-old student may raise a bit of a concern, but can be tempered by certain factors. The easiest way to address this issue/concern is not to friend undergraduate students. However, at some universities perhaps the culture is to friend all your students. In other cases one could be flexible—for example, one could decide not to friend undergraduate students, but with two exceptions: one has formed a connection with them for whatever variety of reasons (mutual interest in running, for example) and they have recently graduated, or the students are still in school but will not be taking any more classes with you. This may seem like the old "situational ethics" approach, and should be carefully considered. One has to explore what one feels comfortable with that still meets ethical principles (and any University guidelines) and hold to these principles. Other options could be explored—one might consider using a more professional networking site such as LinkedIn.

SUMMARY

There are numerous ethical issues that may confront the teacher of sport and exercise psychology. Six of them have been discussed here, but there are certainly many others listed that concern teaching in general, and which some of you may find relevant in your teaching experience. Keeping multiple role relationships to a minimum (eliminating them altogether if possible), maintaining confidentiality, staying competent in your field, avoiding biased treatment of your students, dealing effectively with helicopter parents, and using social networking judiciously will go a long way toward ensuring your success and respect as an ethical teacher of sport and exercise psychology.

REFERENCES

American Psychological Association. (2002). *Ethical principles of psychologists and code of conduct.* Retrieved from http://www.apa.org/ethics/code2002.html#3_09

Association for Applied Sport Psychology. (2010). *AASP code of ethical principles and standards.* Retrieved from http://www.appliedsportpsych.org/about/ethics

Family Educational Rights and Privacy Act. (2011). Retrieved from http://www2.ed.gov/policy/gen/guid/fpco/ferpa/index.html

Infantino, R., & Wilke, R. (2009). *Tough choices for teachers: Ethical challenges in today's schools and classrooms.* Lanham, MD: Rowman & Littlefield Education.

Johns, B. H., McGrath, M. Z., & Mathur, S. R. (2008). *Ethical dilemmas in education: Standing up for honesty and integrity.* Lanham, MD: Rowman & Littlefield Education.

Keith-Spiegel, P., Whitley, Jr., B. E., Balogh, D. W., Perkins, D. V., & Wittig, A. F. (2002). *The ethics of teaching* (2nd ed.). Mahwah, NJ: Lawrence Erlbaum Associates, Publishers.

Macfarlane, B. (2004). *Teaching with integrity: The ethics of higher education practice.* London, UK: Routledge Falmer.

Mackenzie, S. V., & Mackenzie, G. C. (2010). *Now what? Confronting and resolving ethical questions.* Thousand Oaks, CA: Corwin/A Sage Company.

Mahoney, D. (2008). *Ethics in the classroom: Bridging the gap between theory and practice.* Lanham, MD: Rowman & Littlefield Education.

Strike, K., & Soltis, J. F. (2004). *The ethics of teaching.* New York, NY: Teachers College Press.

Watson, II, J. C., Clement, D., Harris, B., Leffingwell, T. R., & Hurst, J. (2006). Teacher-practitioner multiple role issues in sport psychology. *Ethics and Behavior, 16,* 41–60.

Watson, II, J. C., & Schinke, R. (2010). Ethics in teaching: Multiple role relationships in academic settings from a faculty perspective. *AASP Newsletter,* 6–7.

CHAPTER 15

ETHICAL CONSIDERATIONS IN
SPORT AND EXERCISE PSYCHOLOGY RESEARCH

Gershon Tenenbaum, Selen Razon, and Lael Gershgoren

INTRODUCTION

When planning and conducting responsible research, it is of the utmost importance that re-searchers understand research ethics and the ethical dilemmas commonly associated with research. To protect humans, animals, and researchers engaging in research, several initiatives have been aimed at outlining the ethical considerations needed to guide experimentation. The Belmont Report (1979) in the United States, the Nuremberg Code (1949), and the Helsinki Declaration (1974) have been considered the gold standards in terms of ethical guidelines for conducting planned research. To this extent, these guidelines have formed the ethical corner-stones for many organizations that employ researchers in the biomedical and behavioral-social domains. Although the formation of an acceptable code of ethics is acknowledged, it is clear that a universality of ethics is likely impossible (Jago & Bailey, 2001; Pojman, 1995). For ex-ample, research in the sport and exercise domain seeks to explore the underlying mechanisms of people's behaviors when engaged in tasks, which entail physical, mental, and/or emotional effort. Consequently, research in this area requires domain-specific ethical guidelines to safe-guard the emotional, mental, and physical safety of its participants.

To introduce a more comprehensive conceptualization of ethical considerations in the sport and exercise domain, we break down the scientific issues associated with research in sport and exercise psychology (e.g., sampling, data, instrumentation, interventions, and publi-cation), and then present the ethical codes required for protecting the emotional, mental, and physical safety of the participants within the entire research process. To address the unique-ness of the sport and exercise domain as one which entails a unique set of ethics, we elaborate on the ethical codes associated with different experimental conditions and environments, research methods, and the ethical codes associated with stages of experimentation.

RESEARCH METHODS AND RELATED ETHICAL ISSUES

Research is the act of applying methods of inquiry aimed at testing hypotheses, or the act of exploration and describing the phenomena we observe. Research is often *complex* because there are unlimited questions to be answered and many methods, which vary in nature and essence, that can be used to provide answers. Research is *multi-dimensional* because it consists of many facets and concepts, and it is *relative* because questions, methods, and answers of the present day change completely in the future. However, the "investigation of what we know that we do not know" entails ethical consideration. There are, according to our conceptualization, two research paradigms; one is *impressionistic/descriptive/qualitative,* while the other is *quantitative.* The former is explorative and usually does not require prior assumptions about the world, while the second is inductive and consists of deterministic rules the researchers must follow if they wish recognition. Figure 15.1 presents the two research paradigms and attempts to associate the ethical issues that may be encountered while practicing them.

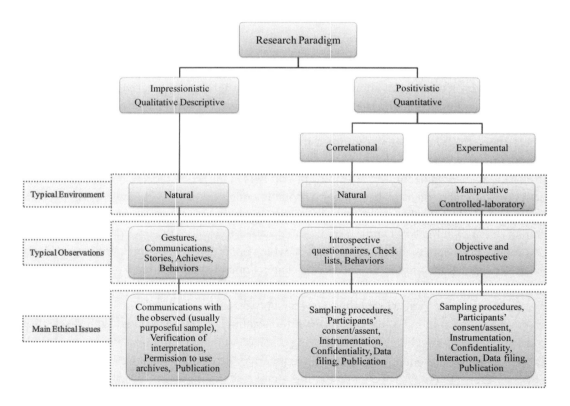

Figure 15.1. Research Paradigms and Associated Ethical Issues

The qualitative methods for research and exploration are performed in natural environments, and the researcher uses techniques, such as non-obtrusive observation, complete participation (action methodologies), interviews, archives, stories, and published materials to generate the "know-how" about the people or phenomenon he/she seeks to understand. Thus, the main ethical concerns in implementing methods classified in this paradigm relate to permission to conduct the study, use of authentic materials and observations, verification of interpretation with the observed, and permission for publication. The main ethical concerns are related to the safety and integrity of the individuals in the studied cultural setting.

THE CULTURAL TURN

A recent research trend in psychology and sport and exercise psychology is termed the *cultural turn* (see Ryba, Schinke, & Tenenbaum, 2010). It consists of critical inquiry and an expanded range of methodologies, such as ethnography, narrative inquiry, and biography. Accordingly, a special focus on ethics in these emerging methodologies was offered by Fisher and Anders (2010). They claim that

> the navigation of research positions in cultural studies—which are political and moral—are qualitatively different from ethics as an area of study in disciplines like psychology, philosophy, political theory, and sport psychology. Whereas ethics may *precede* an analysis of power and discourse in the above-mentioned disciplines, in cultural studies, power and discourse are always already situated culturally, historically, and politically. . . . Ethics is situated as well." (p.102)

Those who practice cultural turn methodologies in the sport psychology domain challenge the AASP set of ethical principles for being ambiguous and unclear. For example, Fisher and Anders (2010) raised concerns over several ethical issues, such as which knowledge is needed to acquire *competence* (1st AASP principal). What does appropriate use of scientific knowledge mean? Related to integrity (2nd AASP principal), what do terms such as *honest, fair, excessively emotionally involved,* and *objective* mean? They reject the universal acceptance of what these terms mean, and challenge researchers to find better operational definitions for them. Ethics is inherent in the cultural study and is part of the discursive meanings of lived experiences; thus, the role of discourse is essential and must be acknowledged. As a consequence, Fisher and Anders (2010) present four commitments inherent in cultural studies: (1) commitment to the generative meanings of violence and suffering among targeted groups and individuals; (2) commitment to working in the particular; (3) commitment to the intersectionality of identity; and (4) commitment to arduous, graceful, and sanctioned representations in theoretical and empirical work (Anders & Diem, 2008).

QUANTITATIVE RESEARCH

Throughout history, friction has become evident between scientific inquiry and societal concerns. For example, issues such as genetics, cloning, invasive and non-invasive interventions, and treatment aimed at performance enhancement in sport have been sources of controversy. Unfortunately, there is no all-encompassing ethics theory accepted by philosophers and scientists in the natural and social sciences that distinguishes between societal-science conflicts and provides directions or guidelines to those who practice science (McNamee, Olivier, & Wainwright, 2007).

The quantitative paradigm, which aims at testing hypotheses driven from a sound theory, is divided into: (1) correlational methods, where no interventions or manipulations are taking place; and (2) experimental methods where causality is inferred by manipulating conditions, environments, and individuals. The main ethical concerns here relate to the people, instrumentation, and interventions. The researcher must ethically select the sample for the study, inform the selected participants about their rights, risks, and expected behaviors, and not force them to take part in the research or use any manipulative measures which cause them to make decisions and take actions against their will. The instruments must be reliable and valid, the interventions must be humane and neither invasive nor harmful, data must be honest and not be unethically altered, and lastly, results and conclusions must be presented truthfully and published as such. The AASP, APA, and ISSP ethical guidelines and principals cover these aspects of ethical conduct in more detail.

Once researchers decide to carry out a research plan, they must consider the ethical requirements and consequences at each phase of the research implementation. Figure 15.2 illustrates a logical sequence of research plan phases, which together constitute the research framework. At each stage, the researcher must consider ethical issues.

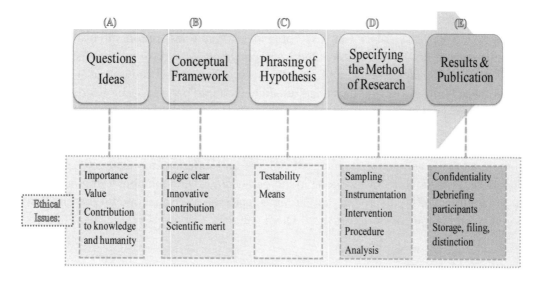

Figure 15.2. Sequence of Research Plan and Associated Ethical Issues

A research plan starts with an idea and question(s). At this stage, the researcher must consider the *importance* and *value* of the imposed questions to humanity and the environment at large. Once a conceptual framework is established, the researcher must consider its *logical argumentation* and the *innovative contribution* required for this stage of hypothesis testing. At this stage, it is important to appraise the theoretical considerations related to ethical issues of *scientific merit*. Once hypotheses are stated, one must consider how *testable* they can be, and by what *means* one can test them. The research method is a plan aimed at testing the hypotheses. As previously stated, some research paradigms do not consider hypotheses and sound theory as a foundation for a research plan (we considered these research plans as *exploratory*), and thus have a different set of ethical standards and considerations by which to abide. For the quantitative-positivistic paradigm, the method entails *sampling, instrumentation, intervention, procedure,* and *data analysis*. Each of these segments has ethical considerations associated with participant safety which are outlined in this section. Finally, when the research is completed and the hypotheses tested, a set of ethical rules applies to its *honest publication, debriefing the participants,* and *managing files* (*storage and distinction*).

A prominent issue in considering research ethics is the risk-benefit ratio, in cases where risk may be physical, emotional, behavioral, or any other form of discomfort, which may potentially harm the participant. To what degree one exposes humans to risks or potential benefits, is a philosophical issue with serious implications. With the risks and benefits comes the issue of *protection,* which ethics committees must consider carefully and responsibly. The research benefit must be considered from both personal and societal perspectives; the utility versus societal acceptance of the research topic is a question that deserves much attention. For example, the incidence of death while exercising is extremely small as compared to its benefit. Consequently, society is more likely than not to accept the risks associated with such research endeavors. Protection of participants and awareness of the risk/benefit ratio necessitate:

> a) voluntary informed consent to participate, b) the overarching goal to bring fruitful results to society, c) historical knowledge of the domain, d) avoidance of undue suffering, e) prevention of research with possible incidence of death, f) risk that does not exceed the humanitarian benefits, g) proper protection, resources, and facilities to avoid injury or disability, h) guidance by highly-skilled researchers, i) free will to withdraw from the research at any time, and j) readiness to terminate the experiment in cases of serious risk of injury, disability, or death. (McNamee et al., 2007, pp. 24–25)

In the following section, we summarize the ethical issues encountered by positivist researchers and provide comprehensive guidelines to deal with them. In line with McNamee et al. (2007), the positivistic approach consists of several research paradigms: *basic, strategic, applied, scholarship, consultancy,* and *professional practice*—all termed "scientific." We present ethical issues inherent at each stage of the research process and then outline the measures that should be considered and how participants should be informed (when applicable). The issues and measures to be taken are based on a review of literature including the APA, AASP, and ISSP ethical principles, as well as the principles outlined by The British Pediatric Association

(1992) and The Medical Research Council (1991). Additional suggestions have drawn upon the works of Jago and Bailey (2001), Nicholson (1986), Watson, Etzel, and Vosloo (2010), Berg and Latin (2008), and the brainstorming session of a number of graduate student members of the performance psychology lab at the Florida State University.

ETHICAL ISSUES RELATED TO SAMPLING

Sample selection and determination take place before implementing the intervention and administrating measures. The researcher must consider ethical issues pertaining to both selection and personal matters at this stage. The ethical issues, along with specific recommendations, are summarized below.

Selection (Sampling) Issues:

Fair representation

- When possible, and in cases where a specific sample is required, employ either: (a) completely randomized, or (b) stratified random sampling procedures.

Fair selection of minorities

- Include minorities in the sample despite cultural and/or language barriers.
- Make an effort to adjust the research procedures to minorities' needs.
- Provide an explanation for the sample size.
- Include all relevant details in the consent.

Safety

- Secure the research environment.
- Train assistants.
- Develop and implement regulations.
- Ensure ongoing monitoring and assessment of research-related equipment.

Risks/honesty

- Minimize risks, and if still present, have plans to overcome them.
- State risks clearly in the consent.
- Ensure that participants clearly understand both the risks and benefits associated with the study.
- Provide honest expression of competencies as needed.
- Display willingness to make direct referrals as needed.
- Avoid ridicule and embarrassment.

Confidentiality

- Assign and use only ID numbers to represent participants.
- Keep informed consent and actual data separate.

- Assign different researchers for administering and evaluating the data.
- Inform participants that individual responses will be combined to form group findings for reporting purposes.
- Designate a secure location and pre-determined date to keep and destroy the collected data.

Rewards, compensation, and benefits

- State the criteria for receiving compensation clearly and up front.
- Do not offer compensation unless necessary.
- Pilot data first without offering compensation to see if data with compensation is skewed.
- Provide reasonable rewards—not so large that they bias participation. No incentives should compromise the dignity of any participant (e.g. cultural, individual norms).
- Ensure that all participants receive equal benefits.
- Limit any imbalance in benefits gained from participating (perhaps through repeated measures if one condition offers substantial benefits to participants).
- Provide honest weight of benefits and risks to the study.

Coercion and participation

- Do not provide coercive incentives to participate.
- Avoid presenting any clear authority.
- Limit social desirability, and when necessary provide a social desirability measure.

Awareness

- Only use deception when absolutely necessary for the study.
- Use only justifiable deception, and provide professional consultation (e.g., psychologist) following participation.
- Ensure that participants are aware of the risks/hazards and benefits associated with the study.

Age and health status

- Ensure that no participant has health conditions which should prevent their participation.
- Ensure the presence of medical support.
- If necessary, include appropriate financing and insurance coverage to the study.
- Implement appropriate follow-up procedures in cases of new treatment, drug administration, or training protocols.
- Understand the physical demands associated with participation and ensure that participants are able to cope with these demands without undue discomfort.
- Be aware and adjust accordingly to physical and mental disabilities.

- Provide appropriate training to the research personnel.
- Provide continual health assessments if needed (e.g., pain levels).
- Obtain assent forms and parental consent in studies including minors.

The issue of age may vary between countries or even between states within the same country. According to Nicholson, an alternative approach is to use a dual assent and consent procedure. Consent describes the positive agreement of a person while assent refers to acquiescence (British Pediatric Association, 1992). However, research involving children should be avoided if similar results could be obtained with an adult sample (Nicholson, 1986).

Before selecting participants for the research project, one should be aware to personal issues such as gender and sexual orientation. More specifically:

Gender/gender identity/sexual orientation.

- Consider gender identity and sexual orientation continuums in demographics (see the link http://counselingoutfitters.com/Reicherzer.htm).
- Practice self-awareness and carefully monitor gender-based stereotypes and prejudices and pre-determined attitudes.

Socio-Economic Status (SES).

- If applicable, ensure participation from a range of SES, consider compensation to low SES populations in need of transportation, transportation-related expenses, meals, etc.

Ethnicity/multicultural issues

- Refrain from ethnicity-based stereotypes and attitudes toward participants.
- Practice self-awareness and respect toward multicultural disparity.
- If needed, receive training on multicultural relevance to minority participants.
- Practice genuine respect and consideration to multicultural differences in research.
- Offer informed consent and questionnaires in alternative languages.

Exercise and health habits

- Do not disclose health and rehabilitative information
- Avoid involving unprofessional health or rehabilitative services in the research.

Nutritional requirements

- Consider nutritional correlates to exercise testing.
- Inform participants about any confounding nutritional intake (e.g., necessary for the study when fasting prior to blood sampling).

Dependency/conflict of interest.

- Ensure that no financial or relationship-based conflict of interest exists between the researcher and the participants.

AWARENESS OF ETHICAL ISSUES AND INFORMATION TO BE INCLUDED IN THE CONSENT FORM

Informed consent should detail the ways in which the researcher is securing the individuals' and the protocol's safety and regularization. The informed consent should explicitly state risks related to the study, and also ensure that the participant understands the potential risks and hazards. The researcher should honestly state competencies and refer the participant elsewhere in case problems arise. The informed consent should define and ensure the confidentiality of participants. If relevant, confidentiality should be presented as extending beyond the study's timeline, and consent should ensure the protection of relevant data. The informed consent can include a section for the participant to confirm they have read, understood, and approved the consent. It should also detail any breaches to confidentiality relevant to the study (McNamee, Olivier, & Wainwright, 2007).

Rewards, compensation, and benefits should be clearly defined in the consent. Accordingly, negotiation or departure should also be considered in terms of financial rewards and benefits. Scientific benefits to the study should be clearly laid out in the consent. In cases where there might be subtle elements of coercion (e.g., researcher is the employer, teacher of the participant, etc.), the consent should address these issues by clearly stating participants' choice to participate, or freely withdraw at any time. Participants should also be ensured that all identifying markers will be removed from all forms. To avoid deception or misunderstanding, the expectations and purpose of the study should be clearly stated.

For elderly populations, consider more than one way to convey the content to the participants due to hearing or vision loss, and other age-related impairments. For minors, consider converting information through the use of assent and parental consent forms. For children, use age-appropriate language while conveying the content. Avoid gender-biased language in formal and informal communications. Demographic information forms could be prepared to reflect more of a continuum of gender types, gender identities, gender expressions, and sexual orientations. If applicable, researchers should be discrete about sharing information related to SES. Researchers should refrain from making comparisons and biases drawn upon SES differences. This cautionary practice should be communicated to participants in the consent form. Furthermore, one should consider that in some cultures it may be normal for the head of the household to have the responsibility to decide whether or not his/her spouse will be participating in the study. One should be prepared to recognize unspoken reluctance of participants and respect it accordingly.

The consent form should clearly state the ways in which the information collected from the participants will remain confidential, will only be used for research, and will not be given to any third parties. The consent should clearly state and specify pre-conditions in research involving an exercise regimen. Participants' understanding of the requirements should be confirmed and participants' signature or initials should be obtained prior to performing the task. For all cases (e.g., illiteracy) where the consent form might not be applicable to sharing information with the participants, oral consent can be acceptable even though this necessitates prior approval from the Institutional Review Board (IRB).

ETHICAL ISSUES RELATED TO INSTRUMENTATION

The selection of appropriate instrumentation is an essential element to ethical and sound research. The major ethical issues to consider when deciding upon the instrumentation for a research project includes ensuring that it is valid and reliable, appropriate for the research participants, represents the current state of the art, and is within one's realm of competency to utilize and score.

Reliability

- Experimental protocols should be consistent across time, conditions, and individuals, especially for longitudinal and pre- post designs.

- Inter-rater agreement should be considered in cases where there is more than one expert rating.

- All questionnaires and surveys should possess high internal consistency.

- Questionnaires should assess latent traits equally across genders and cultures.

- The language of the instrumentation should be easily understood by all participants.

- A careful review of the demographic questions should be conducted to ensure that the procedures adopted are valid and reliable for the specific sample.

- The researcher must be aware of possible testing errors, and thus make decisions cautiously.

Validity

- Keep an objective quality and consider high face validity to avoid deception or confusion.

- Consider if measures of the same trait exist that are more valid and reliable in some populations.

- Assess the instruments across multiple forms of validity (content, convergent, divergent, criterion, etc.).

- Avoid modifying the content of psychometrically valid instruments.

Sample-appropriateness

- Minor or minority-appropriate language should be adopted in forms and questionnaires when necessary.

- Information in all questionnaires should be conveyed in layman language.

- Task-related expectations should be aligned with age-related competencies.

- A differential item function analysis must determine whether test items function consistently amongst different sub-populations.

- Physical and developmental capacities should be considered in advance.

- Alternative forms of test materials may be necessary for people with certain disabilities (e.g., visually impaired, hearing impaired).

- Biased or offensive language should be avoided.

- For standardization of scales not originally written in English, or designed for American culture, appropriate standardization to the specific culture and values must be developed or used.

Current instrumentation

- All instruments including questionnaires, rating scales, forms, and exercise testing equipment should be state of the art (if available to the researcher).
- For instruments and apparatus new to the researcher, the researcher should make sure to know how it is operated. Awareness to testing errors: For situations involving physical testing, physical exertion errors or missing data in testing should be quickly identified and compensated for.

ETHICAL ISSUES RELATED TO INTERVENTION

In experimental studies the researcher applies some kind of an intervention. Usually some participants are selected to be part of the intervention while others are selected as controls or as a placebo. The aim of these studies is to test the effect of the intervention on one or more dependent variables, while controlling others. Interventions may involve physical and physiological components; therefore, several ethical considerations must be taken into consideration in order to protect the participants from risks and harms.

Physical effort/skills

- To avoid harm and injury, request relevant medical/fitness history and design appropriate interventions based on physical activity and fitness levels.
- Ensure all physical tasks conform to the individuals' age-related competencies, and implement appropriate follow-up procedures to ensure participants' well-being for ongoing protocols.

Psychological skills

- Obtain information on possible confounds to physiological competencies (e.g., depression, mental relatedness).
- Promote an environment of free speech, and experiment with realistic boundaries in mind (e.g., realistic goal setting and appropriate encouragement).

Risks

- Obtain and offer a realistic assessment of risks in advance of testing.
- Minimize the risks and inform participants of risks in an explicit manner.

Deception

- If possible avoid deception.
- If deception is necessary, debrief the participants and explain the purpose of the deception, develop a protocol for mediating problems caused by the deception.

Training

- Do not overload the number of participants in training sessions, and avoid providing too many hours of training which may cause psychological or physical harm.

Scheduling

- The length and number of visits to the research center and total time required should be explicitly stated to participants within the consent.

- Participants' age and competencies should be considered in designing reasonable durations and total time limits.

Fair treatment procedures

- Ensure that any control groups have access to the treatment following the study.

- In cases where there are psychological ramifications to placebo procedures, offer professional counseling if needed.

ETHICAL ISSUES RELATED TO DATA

Research consists of data collection first, and data treatment and handling second. To secure appropriate procedures of data collection and use, the data must be reliable and unbiased, appropriately analyzed, interpreted, and reported.

Reliable/trustful

- Ensure triangulation of data by utilizing more than one way to assess and to collect the data (e.g., random assignment of participants).

- Use appropriate statistics and account for the family wise error rates (i.e., adjust significance levels appropriately).

Fabrication and falsification

- Do not fabricate research data. Employ multiple methods and raters when possible.

- To increase accountability, have more than one person collect data, and present data in an objective and detailed manner.

- Present the shortcomings of the study authentically.

- Report effect sizes and not just the alpha values.

- Report non-significant findings.

- Present all results regardless of their impact on the hypotheses.

Obfuscation

- Refrain from reporting only positive or expected outcomes, and present exceptions to the data.

Missing data

- Identify missing data as quickly as possible and design strategies to overcome the missing data (e.g. checking participant's responses following research).

Private data/archives

- During and following research, keep all data locked in locked and private folders. Identify these locations prior to testing and convey to participants that the data will be secure.

ETHICAL ISSUES RELATED TO PUBLICATION

In most cases the research results are published in journals, books, reports, and other communication channels. To avoid confusion and secure appropriate reports the research must follow several procedures, which are outlined below.

Reliability of results report

- Double check data input (e.g., have a third party examining coding).
- Adapt a theory-based approach where supporting statistical findings with appropriate theoretical background.

Plagiarism

- Refrain from taking credit for the work of others.
- Present the literature in the area of study authentically, and avoid presenting articles that are only supporting the case of your study.
- Highlight weaknesses, unknowns, and paradoxes truthfully.
- Do not use the same data from other research without proper acknowledgment.

Dissemination of important results

- Ensure that participants have access to results if they so choose.

ETHICS AND RESEARCH COMMITTEE

Ethics committees—local, regional or national—must approve research proposals and/or plans. Committee members are people who are not directly involved with the research they are evaluating for potential *risks, benefits,* and *scientific merit.* The evaluation process must be done as objectively and impartially as possible. In addition to evaluating all the detailed aspects of the research, the consent form given to participants to read and agree upon is ethically and legally crucial (Nicholson, 1986). Since research in the exercise (and sometimes sport) sciences may involve invasive methods such as blood sampling, pulmonary gas analysis, electrode attachment, psychological testing, and other similar and different procedures, consent must be provided to prevent legal prosecutions. Consent must be provided freely (Alderson,

1995), and any physical or mental coercion should be avoided. Pressure and indications of preferential treatment or benefits (in the form of grades, monitory/financial, health, enjoyment, and others) in other aspects of life must be completely forgone (Jago & Bailey, 2001).

Approval by the ethics committee is granted if the right questions are asked, and if the study consists of the appropriate methods to answer the questions. Consent forms must detail the background of the research and consist of relevant scientific evidence, precedents, previous trials, the usefulness of the research (Greenwald, 1982a, 1982b), and its scientific validity (Jago & Bailey, 2001). According to Jago and Bailey, both consent and assent forms must be checked to guarantee that the language is appropriate for children and guardians when the research involves minors. In addition, adequate insurance for the research institution must be considered for the researchers' safety and interference-free research.

SUMMARY

This chapter has outlined the main ethical issues associated with conducting research in the sport and exercise domain. It also recommended measures researchers should take to meet ethical standards that secure the safety of their participants and contribute to the quality of their research. The commonly accepted stages of research development were used to conceptually generate ethical standards. Additionally, a number of ethical guidelines were recommended for researchers using qualitative inquiries, which differ in nature and scope from quantitative inquiries. However, a more comprehensive perspective on ethics associated with qualitative methodology must be developed in the future. Though research in our domain draws its ethical standards from the larger domain of behavioral and social sciences, the ethical guidelines in exercise science still remain unique in that they involve processes of physical effort, psychobiological variables, social confrontations, assertive and aggressive actions, and sometimes violence and immoral behaviors. Researchers must be aware and cautious in planning, executing, and presenting research that involves such issues. There are many legal issues related to moral and ethical codes of research conductance. It was not our intention to cover these issues in this chapter, but we mention their existence to increase awareness of their importance. We hope that this chapter will encourage researchers to learn and teach ethics in research methods classes, and will be used as a catalyst for discussion about ethical perspectives and ethics-related considerations.

REFERENCES

Alderson, P. (1995). *Listening to children: Children, ethics, and social research.* Ilford, UK: Barnados.

Anders, A. D., & Diem, J. (2008). *Rejecting the claim of collaboration and learning to follow the unnamable.* Paper presented at the American Educational research Association (AERA), New York, NY, USA.

Belmont Report. (1979). The National Commission for the Protection of Human Subjects of Biomedical and Behavioral Research.

Berg, K. E., & Lating, R. W. (2008). *Essentials of research methods in health, physical education, exercise sciences, and recreation* (3rd ed.). Philadelphia, PA: Wolters Kluwer/Lippincott Williams & Wilkins.

British Pediatric Association (1992). *Guidelines for the ethical conduct of medical research involving children.* London, UK: BPA.

Fisher, L. A., & Anders, A. D. (2010). Critically engaging with sport psychology ethics. In T. V. Ryba., R. J. Schinke., & G. Tenenbaum (Eds.), *The cultural turn in sport psychology* (pp. 101–126). Morgantown WV: Fitness Information Technology.

Greenwald, R. A. (1982a). General principles of IRB review. In R. A. Greenwald, M. K. Ryan, & J. E. Mulvill (Eds.), *Human subject research: A handbook for institutional review boards* (pp. 51–62). London, UK: Plenum Press.

Greenwald, R. A. (1982b). Informed consent. In R. A. Greenwald, M. K. Ryan, & J. E. Mulvill (Eds.), *Human subject research: A handbook for institutional review boards* (pp. 79–90). London, UK: Plenum Press.

Helsinki Declaration (1974). *Regulations and ethical guidelines: Ethical principles for medical research involving human subjects.* World Medical Association declaration of Helsinki, National Institute of Health, USA.

Jago, R., & Bailey, R. (2001). Ethics and pediatric exercise science: Issues and making a submission to a local ethics and research committee. *Journal of Sport Sciences, 19,* 527–535.

Maughan, R., Nevill, A., Boreham, C., Davidson, R., Linthorne, N., Stewart, A., . . . Winter, E. (2007). Editorial. *Journal of Sport Sciences, 25,* 617–618.

McNamee, M., Olivier, S., & Wainwright, P. (2007). *Research ethics in exercise, health, and sport sciences.* New York, NY: Routledge.

Medical Research Council (1991). *The ethical conduct of research on children.* London, UK: MRC.

Medical Research Council. (1992, December). New MRC guidelines on research ethics. *Bulletin of Medical Ethics, 84,* 18–23.

Nicholson, R. N. (Ed.). (1986). *Medical research with children: Ethics, law, and practice.* Oxford, UK: Oxford University Press.

Nuremberg Code. (1949). *Trials of war criminals before the Nuremberg military tribunals under Control Council Law* No. 10, Vol. 2, pp. 181–182. Washington, DC: U.S. Government Printing Office.

Pojman, L. J. (1995). *Ethics: Discovering right and wrong.* Belmont, CA: Wadsworth.

Reicherzer, S., & Anderson, J. (2006). *Ethics and gender continuum: A lifespan approach.* Retrieved from http://counselingoutfitters.com/Reicherzer.htm

Ryba, T. V., Schinke, R. J., & Tenenbaum, G. (Eds.). (2010). *The cultural turn in sport psychology.* Morgantown WV: Fitness Information Technology.

Watson, J. C., & Clement, D. (2008). Ethical and practical issues related to multiple role relationships in sport psychology. *Athletic Insight, 10*(4). Retrieved from http://www.athleticinsight.com/Vol101ss4/104IssueHome.htm

Watson, J. C., Etzel, E. F., & Vosloo, J. (2010). Ethics: Assessment and measurement in sport and exercise psychology. In G. Tenenbaum, R. Eklund, & A. Kamata (Eds.), *Handbook of measurement in sport and exercise psychology.* Champaign, IL: Human Kinetics.

Young, I. (2004). Five faces of oppression. In L. Heldke & P. O'Connor (Eds.), *Oppression, privilege, and resistance* (pp. 37–63). Boston, MA: McGraw Hill.

CHAPTER 16

ETHICS IN ASSESSMENT AND TESTING IN SPORT AND EXERCISE PSYCHOLOGY

Edward F. Etzel, Michael Yura, Frank Perna, and Justine Vosloo

INTRODUCTION

The purpose of this chapter is to discuss several of the core ethical issues concerning assessment and testing in our rapidly changing field. These challenges will likely arise when one is involved in the processes of teaching, consulting, or conducting Sport and Exercise Psychology (SEP) research or overseeing the work of others engaged in these practices. Specifically, information will be offered on test and assessment instrument use, competence, test-user qualifications, use of obsolete instruments, computer-based interpretations, test-taker welfare, confidentiality and informed consent, and cultural and gender issues, as well as psychometric and normative properties of assessment devices.

ETHICS IN ASSESSMENT AND TESTING

There have been discussions about ethics in the recent SEP literature (e.g., Andersen, Van Raalte, & Brewer, 2001; Aoyagi & Portenga, 2010; Brown & Cogan, 2006; Etzel, Watson, & Zizzi, 2004; Parham, 2010; Stapleton, Hays, Hankes & Parham, 2010), but fewer specific considerations about issues concerning SEP ethics and assessment and testing (Gardner & Moore, 2006a; McCann, Jowdy, & Van Raalte, 2002; Nideffer & Sagal, 2001). The use of various

---

[1]Portions of this chapter were published in Duda, J. L. (Ed.). (1998) *Advances in sport and exercise psychology measurement.* Morgantown, WV: Fitness Information Technology.

psychometric methods and instruments has historically distinguished psychologists from other helping professionals (e.g., counselors, social workers, psychiatrists). Many resources are available concerning the nature and availability of psychological and psychoeducational instruments (Hogan, 2005). "Testing" appears to be frequently employed by professionals across the broad range of SEP settings and clientele. Within SEP settings, "tests" are often used for four purposes:

1) Clinical/counseling (e.g., evaluation of mood or transitional career-related interests).

2) Health and exercise (e.g., mood changes as a function of participation in aerobic activity or self-reported behaviors in the physical domain).

3) Performance enhancement (e.g., motivation, sport-related imagery capabilities).

4) For special purposes (e.g., talent identification, neuropsychological testing; Heil, Henschen, & Nideffer, 1996; McCann et al., 2002; Nideffer & Sagal, 2001).

In the past, some SEP professionals have seen testing as a controversial practice (Heil et al., 1996; Silva, 1984; Vealey & Garner-Holman, 1998) and may eschew testing (Orlick, 1989). However, many appear to employ systematic assessments and integrate testing as regular elements of their professional functions (Ostrow, 2002). Those who employ tests and other assessment devices do so for several reasons:

a) to efficiently and accurately assess the psychological characteristics and concerns of test takers;

b) to create hypotheses about the appropriate intervention methods (Kanfer & Goldstein, 1986);

c) to measure the progress of behavioral change in their clients' functioning (Sagal, Sagal, & Miller, 2004);

d) to be accountable for their professional work; and

e) to gather information for teaching and research purposes.

It is necessary that professionals and "professionals in the making" be acutely aware of the many ethical and legal issues associated with the development and use of assessment devices (e.g., questionnaires, inventories, interviews) and the rich information they provide. Further, SEP educators, researchers, and clinicians must follow the ethical principles and standards governing the assessment and testing processes.

TESTING AND ASSESSMENT

Before proceeding, it seems useful to define some key concepts for the reader. What do we mean when we use the terms *test* and *assessment* in the following discussion? Anastasi (1988) defined a psychological test as "an objective and standardized measure of a sample of behavior" (p. 23). Tests are "standardized" because the test content, administration, scoring, and interpretation procedures are consistent and comparable. Standardized and unstandardized tests can be useful to the process of psychological assessment, which can be thought of as "the set of processes used . . . for developing impressions and images, making decisions and checking hypotheses about another person's pattern of characteristics that determines his or her behavior in interaction with the environment" (Sundberg, 1977, p. 21). Assessment methods come in various forms and may include surveys and questionnaires, interviews, standardized tests and observations (Bennett et al., 2006; Fisher, 2009).

TESTING CONCERNS

Tests are typically administered to the benefit of clients, students and research participants by professionals in SEP and allied professions. Koocher and Keith-Spiegel (2008) observed that testing and assessment methods have unfortunately been misused over time; they likely will continue to be intentionally or unintentionally misused by professionals who are unaware of the potential for misuse. Nideffer (1981) identified several avoidable testing and assessment improprieties, such as

- not informing athletes about the purposes of testing,
- compelling them to complete tests,
- not informing test takers of the results,
- not revealing how the results were to be used and by whom,
- unqualified people (e.g., coaches, management) using tests,
- using tests for screening and team selection purposes that likely overextended the predictive validity limits of the instruments, and
- inappropriate test selection and administration.

These behaviors are commonly considered to be unethical and should be avoided (AASP, 1996; APA, 2010; Fisher, 2009).

In view of the above and other challenges (e.g., repeated requests to test athletes and teams, breaches in confidentiality, high costs, time), it is no wonder that many athletes, coaches, and organizations appear wary about testing. For example, some time ago, controversies surrounding test misuse led the National Football League Players Association to limit the administration of personality tests to their athletes (Nideffer, 1981). The pervasive use of the Wonderlic Cognitive Ability Test in professional football is an example of an instrument that remains controversial (DeLoureiro, 2011). Perhaps today, given revolutionary developments like the Internet, testing may be more prevalent than in past years. Heil (1993) observed that astute sport psychologists should be alert to "strong preconceptions" about psychological testing that may exist in consultation environments (p. 96). These biases may adversely influence their professional credibility and possibly jeopardize the effectiveness of their work with others (see APA Standard 9.01a).

PROFESSIONAL TEST AND ASSESSMENT INSTRUMENT USE

No specific ethical standards governing the professional use of tests in SEP settings have been universally embraced. In the absence of common guidelines, the most recent APA and AASP ethical guidelines concerning evaluation and assessment will be relied upon in this chapter to provide some practical parameters for these functions (AASP, 1996; APA, 2010). Due to the space constraints, only selected APA and AASP guidelines relative to evaluation, assessment, and testing will be discussed.

TESTING IN PROFESSIONAL RELATIONSHIPS

According to APA Ethical Standard 9.02, assessment and testing should be undertaken only within the context of a clearly defined professional or scientific relationship (e.g., when one is conducting a research project, providing counseling or consulting services, teaching sport psychology). Because the potential for harm to test-takers exists, it is considered inappropriate to administer tests without a clear professional or scientific purpose. Psychological tests are not to be frivolously administered to friends, family members, spouses, partners, students, team members, or others. People may be harmed by misinterpretation of results, the test-takers may be made aware of things about themselves that they do not want to know, and/or the test-givers may become aware of information that the test-takers do not want them to know. The test may also lead to the formulation of a loose diagnosis based upon limited information.

Testing is a serious undertaking. Matarazzo (1999) tells us, "The testing by one individual of another human's intellectual, personality and related characteristics is an invasion of privacy to an extent no less intimate than that involved in an examination carried out on that same individual's person or resources by a physician, attorney, or agent of the Internal Revenue Service" (p. 331). Therefore, testing should be used only when there is a specific research question(s), referral question(s), or instructive reason. Selection of instruments should be done with care. The context and appropriateness of the instruments as well as their validity and reliability should be considered. The modification of instruments should also be done cautiously, if at all. The SEP professional would benefit from consulting APA guidelines for guidance on appropriate modification techniques (APA, 2010; APA Standard 9.02b).

TESTS USE BY UNQUALIFIED PEOPLE

APA Standard 9.07 cautions professionals to prohibit the use of assessment techniques by unqualified people. Inexperienced people (e.g., students, inexperienced professionals, coaches) should only be allowed to employ such techniques under the direct supervision of a competent professional. When SEP professionals agree to supervise the use of assessment devices, they are ultimately responsible for the actions of those they oversee (Canter et al., 1994). Professionals who choose to oversee the use of tests by unqualified others must be very clear about the competencies of subordinates, monitor their work closely, and appreciate the serious implications of the decision to supervise them.

Relatedly, APA Standard 9.04 points out that it is unethical to release "raw" psychological data (e.g., numerical scores, written reports, notes about the testing situation, specific test-taker responses) and findings to those who are not qualified to interpret them (Tranel, 1995). The purpose here is to avoid the potential misuse of data that may cause harm in some way to test-takers. Therefore, SEP professionals should refrain from releasing such information to coaches, management, teams, students, or other third parties. Rather, they should provide carefully constructed, insightful interpretations of the data within the context of the reason(s) for having administered testing in the first place (e.g., to understand an athlete's emotional response to injury, aspects of his or her personality, or leadership potential).

TEST SECURITY

APA Ethical Standard 9.11 advises professionals to maintain the security and integrity of tests and other assessment procedures they may use. They should not release test items, test manuals, or protocols because doing so may jeopardize the validity and reliability of an instrument when administered to those familiar with its content (i.e., test takers would no longer be naive). Test security is particularly important to protect for those instruments that are copyrighted or are intended for restricted use vis-à-vis legal regulations. For example, an SEP professional should not share a copy of the *Profile of Mood States* (McNair, Lorr, & Droppleman, 1971), a copyrighted, restricted-use test, with an athletic team with which he or she is working to educate them about their mood. The test-taker's responses should be securely stored in the professional's locked office or by using computer files that are securely protected using a password (Nagy, 2005).

Ethical principles, such as AASP's Principle D and APA's Principle E, emphasize the importance of respecting an individual's rights and dignity (AASP, 1996; APA, 2010). Thus, test-takers should be informed about the basic nature of instruments and the possible findings obtained from testing, except in rare cases involving deception in research, when research participants must be debriefed as soon as possible, post-testing. People have the right to know why they are being asked to complete an instrument, how the results might be useful to the professional consultation, and any other pertinent questions involved with their voluntary agreement to participate in the assessment process.

Every test-taker must provide "informed consent" to participate in assessment and testing activities, or provide "assent" in the case of those who are not capable of providing consent by law (e.g., minors). Additionally, test-takers involved in research should be able to withdraw participation without consequences at any time (APA Standards 3.10 and 9.03a). Professionals should also be careful not to reveal specific test content, especially that which includes the use of copyrighted instruments that involve "contractual obligations" with publishers (APA, 2010).

COMPETENCE

Competence implies that SEP professionals develop, clarify, and maintain their professional expertise. Expertise is obtained not only from education and training experiences, but also from regular continuing education and training, and consultation to maintain and/or enhance expertise. Professionals must remain knowledgeable about the process of assessment and psychometrics in general. Further, APA Ethical Standard 2.03 indicates that to be considered competent, it is the responsibility of test users, or supervisors of test users, to stay current with any developments surrounding the applicability, psychometric properties (i.e., validity and reliability), and normative information concerning any instruments or methodologies they use (APA, 2010). Remaining competent through focused continuing education, reading, attending meetings, and professional consultation is not an easy thing to do over time; it is associated with the professional risk described as "practitioner decay" (Bennett et al., 2006).

When specific training in these areas was not seen as necessary or was not possible during one's initial education and training, one must obtain appropriate training, supervision, or consultation from another qualified professional before the less-qualified individual administers these unfamiliar instruments. Moreover, it is crucial that untrained students or other less-qualified professionals obtain close supervision on an ongoing basis for two reasons: (a) to ensure the provision of high-quality services, and thereby avoid test misemployment of existing instruments; and (b) to obtain training and guidance from qualified supervisors in the use of certain unfamiliar or new assessment devices.

As noted above, SEP professionals must also provide appropriate supervision to others (e.g., students, trainees, less-qualified professionals seeking supervision) in the proper use of particular assessment instruments. Professionals are responsible for: (1) obtaining permission to use and administer psychological instruments; (2) maintaining confidentiality and privilege associated with the results provided by instruments; and (3) overseeing the nature and quality of the interpretation of these results provided by supervisees to those tested (APA, 2010; Fisher, 2009).

Lastly, because they have the ethical obligation to maintain the highest level of psychological practice within their discipline, those who have knowledge of the misuse of tests by unqualified persons are ultimately responsible for such misuse. Notifying an individual about potential or apparent test misuse would be the first (typically uncomfortable) step a professional should take to attempt to intervene in such matters.

TEST USER QUALIFICATIONS

Who is "qualified" to administer and interpret tests? Anastasi (1988) observed several years ago that ". . . with the diversification of the field and the consequent specialization of training, no psychologist is equally qualified in all areas" (p. 51). However, for those who wish to be well-informed about, or claim to be competent in, the ethical practice of assessment and the use of psychological tests in sport and exercise settings, useful information can be found in the *Standards for Educational and Psychological Testing* (American Educational Research Association [AERA], American Psychological Association, 1999). Specifically, the above-mentioned publication provides information for users on central issues such as: (a) methods of evaluating the quality and applicability of tests; (b) the practice of testing; and (c) the consequences of test administration and interpretation. The knowledge contained in the Standards is indispensable to test users and students who wish to become proficient in this area.

Some user qualification standards also exist for the employment of certain types of tests, questionnaires, and other instruments. These standards date from the early APA system of test complexity classification (APA, 1954). Three basic levels of tests were identified and are still in use today, particularly by commercial test publishers (e.g., Consulting Psychologists Press; see Table 16.1).

Table 16.1. Levels of Test Use and Their Qualifications

Level Symbol	User Qualification
A	Non-psychologists who understand the instrument they administer and the general reasons for testing
B	Knowledge of psychometrics, statistics, test construction, and appropriate psychology course work
C	Advanced degree in an appropriate profession or membership in state professional associations, professional state licensure, or professional national certification

USE OF OBSOLETE INSTRUMENTS

Although tests usually undergo few modifications over time, many are revised on a regular basis (Ostrow, 2002). From an ethical perspective, APA Standard 9.08 directs test users to avoid developing hypotheses or making recommendations from old data and/or outdated instruments (APA, 2010). In the first instance, professionals should not utilize information about test-takers that is probably not characteristic of them presently, unless one is comparing past data with current data for some good reason. Second, the basic purpose of a test is to validly and reliably measure the construct(s) or behavior(s) it is supposed to measure. If one chooses to use an instrument that is obsolete (i.e., an older edition), it may not be as useful a measure as a newer form, unless there is evidence supporting the use of older versions with special populations (Canter et al., 1994).

COMPUTER INTERPRETATIONS

With the advent of sophisticated computer-assisted assessment programs and Internet-based testing capability, the use of detailed interpretations of test-taker responses can raise the quality of feedback when provided by individuals trained in their use and application. However, it is also possible that people who have neither the academic training nor the practical experience to employ these instruments may cause harm to test-takers. Putting complex and sometimes sensitive personal analyses in the hands of untrained or undertrained individuals can have negative emotional, legal and ethical implications. For example, if an untrained person merely provides an athlete, team, or organization with "automated" interpretation printouts, without taking into consideration information about the person's reasons for seeking assistance, the purpose for having taken the test (various contextual/life factors; personality characteristics; attitudes toward the testing experience; and other special considerations such as age, gender, and ethnicity), the potential exists for misinterpretation of results and harm to the test-taker. Those who are less well-trained may overlook useful background information and possibly miss important data provided in a computerized interpretation. It is essential that computer-generated reports be used and monitored with the same scrutiny as if they were scored and interpreted by the professional administering the instrument(s) and that the professional remains responsible for all aspects of the assessment (APA, 2010).

CLIENT WELFARE, CONFIDENTIALITY, AND INFORMED CONSENT

Respect for people's rights and dignity is seen as the primary goal of psychological ethics codes (Whelan, Elkin, & Meyers, 1996, 2002). To protect the welfare of consumers, the most recent AASP statement of ethical principles indicates that members should "do no harm . . . to ensure the dignity and welfare of individuals we serve and the public" (Meyers, 1995, p. 1). This principle is directly related to SEP professionals' responsibility to protect the right to privacy and confidentiality of those they serve.

Confidentiality is an ethical concept, and in some professional relationships, states, and institutions it is a legal right. It refers to the ethical agreement by professionals not to reveal information about the clients, students, research participants, or others with whom they work without the permission of those being served, or in some extreme legal instances (noted below) without their permission. Confidentiality differs from "privilege," which refers to communication between clients/patients and specific persons, typically professionals, that is prevented from revelation by law (Koocher & Keith-Spiegel, 2008).

The issue of confidentiality is also very important regarding the use of technology to conduct assessments with clients (Watson, Tenenbaum, Lidor, & Alfermann, 2001). This form of communication can be more easily intercepted; thus, when the professional relationship involves assessment over the Internet, the limitations of confidentiality should be clearly communicated to the client (Watson, et al., 2001; see also Chapter 12 in this book).

The nature of information surrounding the reason(s) for testing or information obtained from testing must not be disclosed to anyone (e.g., coaches, parents, management) except in the following three circumstances: (1) if the test-taker provides written permission to do so, or the permission of a parent or guardian is obtained in the case of a minor or someone who is somehow incapable of making decisions for himself or herself; (2) if information obtained indicates that the test-taker is dangerous to himself or herself (i.e., suicidal) or to others (i.e., homicidal); or (3) if test information is subpoenaed by the court.

In advance of any assessment activities, the aforementioned information must be clearly communicated to, understood by, and agreed upon by test-takers as part of the act of providing informed consent. Since it is unethical to require or compel athletes, teams, or other clientele to participate in testing, informed consent or assent must be provided by participants in sport and exercise settings (e.g., research projects, performance enhancement consultations, clinical relationships). Additionally, one must be careful to address these and other challenging and sometimes competing demands of organizations, their cultures and their members (e.g., management, coaches, etc.) whose values may differ from those of the SEP professional (Gardner & Moore, 2006b).

In every situation in which a professional agrees to conduct assessments, one must be clear about who the "real client" is (Ogilvie, 1979). One can ethically best serve only one party and may share information about assessment and testing activities and findings only with that person unless given permission to talk with others. To avoid problems with credibility and trust, as well as ethical binds associated with so-called "multiple relationships," professionals must set and respect specific boundaries.

Consistent with current AASP and APA ethical guidelines, the SEP professional's primary responsibility must be to serve the person(s) whom the professional is evaluating or studying. It is crucial that the roles and responsibilities of the professional are outlined and agreed upon for the athlete client(s), research participant(s), and/or third parties (e.g., coaches, management, sports medicine staff) at the onset. Although a referral for testing may have been made by a third party (e.g., management, parents, coaches), it is imperative that the nature of the assessment consultation, and its limitations relative to the boundaries of confidentiality, be clearly stated and agreed upon by all involved parties during the initial consultation at and before the onset of any professional testing activities.

An ethical/legal exception to the foregoing is important to note. Confidentiality is not guaranteed when one is testing a person under the age of 18. Because a young client is legally considered a minor, privilege is held by the parent(s) or legal guardian(s) of that athlete. Privilege cannot be waived by a minor; it may be waived only by the parent or guardian of the young person. It is imperative that privilege be understood by all parties prior to any data-gathering interactions between a professional and an athlete. Any limits on the information gathered during assessments must be agreed upon with parent(s) prior to testing and understood by the young athlete if he or she and the SEP professional are to establish and engage in an open, trusting relationship.

SEP professionals need to be careful not to reveal the identities of persons or organizations associated with testing consultations and/or the data obtained from these activities (Sachs, 1993). When discussing or reporting any type of information dealing with evaluations (e.g., in scholarly writings, for educational purposes, presenting at conferences), the identities of test-takers must be disguised. The focus should be on the results, not on individual client or team identities.

Test-takers should provide written evidence of their understanding of the conditions surrounding assessments by signing an "informed consent" document. This is a contract that serves as a clear and fair agreement between the testing professional and the test-taker. This agreement assumes that the athlete has the right to know whatever conclusions or results are drawn from the assessment data. Moreover, test-takers should know that the information obtained from testing is their "property" and, thus, is the subject of privilege and confidentiality issues. Test-takers also need to be made aware of the limits of test results. Depending on the purpose of assessment, such data are intended to provide information on the psychological attributes of clients, to test research hypotheses, and/or to acquire information that may be useful to behavior change.

TEST FEEDBACK

Test-takers have the right to know about the results of testing and related information. Such feedback should be provided to test-takers in understandable language that avoids using labels and technical jargon that may not be comprehensible to laypersons. As recommended by APA Standard 9.06, professionals should also be sensitive to the language they use and the backgrounds of test-takers, and adjust their interpretations to consider the various aspects of the test-takers' backgrounds (e.g. gender, race, age, ethnicity, etc.; APA, 2010). All test takers have the right to receive feedback related to their performance on assessment tools and the ways in which test results could be personally useful or possibly useful to third parties (if written permission was granted by the test-taker for others to know about assessment information). This is true even if the purpose of testing involves analyzing group attributes or behavior (e.g., motivation, attitudes toward sport, performance anxiety). Group assessment does not preclude the SEP professional from providing individual interpretations to each test-taker. That is, it is appropriate to offer a follow-up appointment to interested athletes who want to obtain an individual interpretation of their test results.

It is also the ethical responsibility of researchers to provide individual interpretations to research participants as requested, particularly to those whose test results reveal a potential problem. For example, if a test administrator discovers that the anxiety level of the particular athlete is high enough to hamper normal functioning, it is the administrator's responsibility to contact that participant and offer to assist him or her to develop an appropriate strategy for dealing with that anxiety or to offer a referral (APA, 2010).

RELEASES OF INFORMATION

All test-takers should be made aware of their rights concerning the dissemination of personal test data prior to any assessments. Because trust is one of the key factors in the relationship between SEP professionals and their clients, it is important that athletes know that their test results will not be used in decisions associated with their athletic performance, team status, or other aspects of their sport participation without their permission or the permission of parents or guardians.

However, certain exceptional situations may exist that preclude the provision of feedback to test-takers (e.g., when they waive the right to see information obtained from testing). These exceptions are based upon written agreements made by test-takers (e.g., prospective professional athletes) before testing with organizations (e.g., sport teams), or in the case of forensic evaluations (see APA Standard 9.10).

CULTURAL AND GENDER ISSUES

Cultural Considerations

Culture has deservedly garnered greater recent attention in SEP (Schinke & Hanrahan, 2009). Contextual concerns are vital and pertinent to the development, administration, and interpretation of assessment devices with SEP-related populations. Some publications can be particularly useful to the ethical assessment and testing of people from various backgrounds (e.g., APA, 1993). Both the APA and AASP ethical codes encourage respect for human differences (e.g., AASP Principle 3 and APA Principle E) and awareness of our limitations/biases regarding multicultural issues. Whenever possible, one should carefully select an instrument to minimize potential biases. Because SEP practitioners employ various instruments when working with diverse populations, using instruments appropriate for a particular group of people is paramount. Fisher (2009) recommends that professionals should avoid the use of assessment methods that have not been developed for a specific population. If no alternative exists, the results or testing and recommendations that emerge should be made cautiously and acknowledge this limitation.

Unfortunately, efforts to develop "culture-fair" or "culture-reduced" tests have generally been unsuccessful; there are no "culture-free" tests. Therefore, it is the responsibility of the SEP professional to: (a) use instruments that minimize potential cultural bias; (b) take into consideration the background of the population that an instrument was designed for and "normed" on the general nature of the population one is testing; and (c) weigh any limitations of certainty that may be associated with the use of a test with people from diverse backgrounds (APA, 2010; Sachs, 1993).

Paniagua (1998) provided some guidelines that can be used to minimize bias in assessment with multicultural groups:

1) Professionals should examine any of their own biases and prejudices before evaluating people who are from different racial or ethnic backgrounds than their own;

2) Professionals should evaluate any socioeconomic variables and culturally related syndromes that may affect test use;

3) Professionals should ask culturally relevant questions; and

4) Professionals should attempt to use the least potentially biased instruments available. (pp. 107–108)

Professionals' backgrounds and skills in the areas associated with assessment and treatment are essential to effective and ethical practice (Watson, Etzel, & Shapiro, 2009). Assessment of culturally diverse populations can be effective if the test administrator displays both cultural sensitivity and competence when working with diverse sport and exercise populations. It is crucial to develop and refine this sensitivity as best one can and communicate these sensitivities when teaching assessment to others (e.g., students, supervisees). Whenever possible, the ethical professional should avoid evaluating persons with special backgrounds that have not been included in their training or experience. If they are compelled to do so, they should seek consultation

Gender Issues

Gill (1995) contends that the consideration of gender issues and their professional implications are not commonplace in exercise and sport psychology practice. Nevertheless, they probably influence everything we do. APA Standard 9 indicates that test users need to be sensitive to gender considerations when selecting, administering, scoring, and interpreting any assessment techniques (APA, 2010).

An example of an assessment area in which many SEP professionals are likely to be involved with female athletes is that of interest testing (i.e., relative to various transitions, such as major selection, occupational choice, and retirement). Betz and Fitzgerald (1987) discussed the problem of attempting to integrate interest-inventory results in a society of gender-role socialization and occupational gender segregation. The process involves the socialization of women into traditional occupations and roles, as well as personality traits, interests, and skills. These phenomena may also affect male response styles on various instruments. Although some changes have been made in the construction of certain instruments, careful consideration needs to be made to develop sensitivity to response patterns of women who are more similar to their male counterparts (and vice versa), rather than making the false assumption that all women or men respond similarly. Walsh and Betz (1995) suggested that these patterns may lead to the interpretation of test results that perpetuate female overrepresentation in traditional roles. They provided two useful suggestions relative to the minimization of unethical gender bias in testing. First, test users must regularly consult test reviews to see that language bias and test-item content bias has been addressed and minimized. Second, testing consumers need to be sensitive to gender-role socialization for males and females that may adversely affect test-response patterns. Professionals also need to regularly self-assess any gender biases or prejudices that may undesirably impact their work with test-takers and take efforts to minimize their effects.

PSYCHOMETRIC AND NORMATIVE PROPERTIES OF ASSESSMENT DEVICES PSYCHOMETRIC ISSUES

As was previously noted, there are some SEP professionals who appear to refrain from using any type of formal psychological assessment devices or inventories in their normal practice. However, many do regularly rely on the use of such instruments to teach or to do research, to understand presenting psychological concerns, and to develop interventions. For those SEP professionals who employ testing, it is important that they clearly understand the unique psychometric properties of the test(s) they administer and interpret. It is essential that test properties (i.e., validity and reliability) be understood and examined before the administration and interpretation of any instrument (see APA Standards 9.02 and 9.05).

TEST NORM ISSUES

Another issue concerning the ethical use of psychometrically sound instruments involves normative data associated with the instrument. Although an SEP professional may use an instrument or measure in a manner consistent with the intent of the test developer, the use of outdated norms and test use with populations different from those the tests were normed on is unethical. Further, it is advisable to develop local norms and establish the instruments' criterion validity for previously under-sampled groups (e.g., athletes, ethnic minorities, women).

COMMON INTERPRETATION ISSUES

Several issues and/or conditions may have an impact on the understanding and usefulness of test results that have ethical implications. Given the limitations of this chapter, we will briefly discuss two: 1) assessment anxiety, and 2) styles of responding to test content.

Assessment anxiety. Conditions affecting the test-taking athlete or exerciser at the time of an evaluation (e.g., test setting, test-taker characteristics) must be considered with sensitivity if we are to understand the scores test-takers produce. Indeed, to understand how a person takes a test, it is probably as important to attend to the client's test-taking behavior as it is to know what test she or he took (Sundberg, 1977). To illustrate, ethical professionals need to be attentive to a common, natural artifact of the evaluative process (i.e., test anxiety). Just as performance anxiety may affect performance on the field, on the court, or in the pool, conditions such as test anxiety can adversely affect test-takers' performance when completing an instrument.

Response styles. Another factor that may influence the validity or reliability of test data in sport and exercise settings concerns response styles to test questions (Nideffer, 1981). Issues such as "faking good" (minimization) or "faking bad" (exaggeration) impact the accuracy and usefulness of test scores. For example, athletes may not want to reveal certain things about themselves for fear that such revelations may have an impact on their team status or "draftability," in the case of professional prospects. If an SEP professional has chosen an appropriate and sound instrument for use with a particular athlete or group of athletes, and if the circumstances or goals associated with the assessment appear consistent with the purpose of the instrument, it seems logical that the results could be used in a valid manner. However, if a test-taker responded to this instrument with an exceptional response style (e.g., responding consistently indifferently on a 5-point Likert scale), this may technically invalidate the results for that particular athlete. Such response patterns must be noted by the sport psychology professional when conducting any evaluation.

CONCLUSION

The issues surrounding the ethical use of tests and other assessment methods are critical to many applied sport and exercise psychology consultants in their functioning across professional roles. Within the limits of this chapter, the authors have tried to provide an overview of general ethical guidelines relevant to professionals involved in psychological assessment and testing in sport and exercise settings. Such a task is a formidable one. Clearly, this chapter is not in any way an all-encompassing reference. However, we would hope that the reader would look at the chapter as an ambitious attempt to provide some useful information on the subject at hand and would consult one or more of the many references that follow to assist in thinking about ethics in testing and general professional practices.

REFERENCES

American Educational Research Association, American Psychological Association, & National Council on Measurement in Education. (1999). *Standards for educational and psychological testing.* Washington, DC: American Psychological Association.

American Psychological Association. (1954). *Technical recommendations for psychological tests and diagnostic techniques.* Washington, DC: Author.

American Psychological Association (1993). Guidelines for providers of psychological services to ethnic, linguistic and culturally diverse populations. *American Psychologist, 48*(1), 45–48.

American Psychological Association. (2010). Ethical principles of psychologists and code of conduct. Retrieved from http://www.apa.org/ethics/code/index.aspx#

Anastasi, A. (1988). *Psychological testing* (6th ed.). New York, NY: Macmillan.

Andersen, M., Van Raalte, J., & Brewer, B. (2001). Sport psychology service delivery: Staying ethical while keeping loose. *Professional Psychology: Research and Practice, 32,* 12–18.

Andersen, M., Williams, J., Aldridge, T., & Taylor, J. (1997). Tracking the training and careers of graduates of advanced degree programs in sport psychology, 1989 to 1994. *The Sport Psychologist, 11,* 326–344.

Aoyagi, M., & Portenga, S. (2010). The role of positive ethics and virtues in the context of sport and performance psychology service delivery. *Professional Psychology: Research and Practice, 41*(3), 253–259.

Association for Applied Sport Psychology. (1996). Ethical principles and standards. Retrieved from http://applied-sportpsych.org/about/ethics

Bennett, B. E., Bricklin, P. M., Harris, E., Knapp, S., Vandecreek, L., & Younggren, J. N. (2006). Assessing and managing risk in psychological practice: An individualized approach. In Bersoff, D. (Ed.), *Ethical conflicts in psychology* (2nd ed.). Washington, DC: American Psychological Association.

Betz, N., & Fitzgerald, L. (1987). *The career psychology of women.* New York, NY: Academic Press.

Briggs, K., & Myers, I. (1962). *Myers-Briggs Type Indicator.* Princeton, NJ: Educational Testing Service.

Brown, J. , & Cogan, K. (2006). Ethical clinical practice and sport psychology: When two worlds collide. *Ethics and Behavior, 16,* 15–23.

Canadian Society for Psychomotor Learning and Sport Psychology. (1982). *Ethical standards for sport psychology educators, researchers, and practitioners.* Unpublished manuscript.

Canter, M., Bennett, B., Jones, S., & Nagy, T. (1994). Ethics for psychologists: A commentary on the APA ethics code. Washington, DC: American Psychological Association.

Coppel, D., Hanson, T., Hart, E., Gould, D., & Rotella, R. (1993). Professional issues influencing ethical behavioral choices. In *Proceedings of the Association for the Advancement of Applied Sport Psychology Conference* (p. 30). Montreal, Quebec: Association for the Advancement of Applied Sport Psychology.

DeLoureiro. L. (2011). Cold hard facts: The unreliability of the Wonderlic test. Retrieved from http://sportsillustrated.cnn.com/2011/football/nfl/03/24/wonderlic-test/index.html

Dodson, J. (1995, May). The brain game. *Golf Magazine,* pp. 20, 24, 33.

Ethical standards for provision of services by NASPSPA members (1982, Fall). NASPSPA *Newsletter,* pp. ii–vi.

Etzel, E. F., Watson, J. C., & Zizzi, S. (2004). A Web-based survey of AAASP members' ethical beliefs and behaviors in the new millennium. *Journal of Applied Sport Psychology, 16,* 236–250.

Fisher, C. (2009). *Decoding the ethics code: A practical guide for psychologists* (2nd ed.). Thousand Oaks, CA: Sage Publications, Inc.

Gardner, F., & Moore, Z. (2006a). Assessment in clinical sport psychology. In F. Gardner & Z. Moore (Eds.), *Clinical sport psychology* (pp. 43–61). Champaign, IL: Human Kinetics Publishers.

Gardner, F., & Moore, Z. (2006b). Ethics in clinical sport psychology. In F. Gardner & Z. Moore (Eds.), *Clinical sport psychology* (pp. 199–220). Champaign, IL: Human Kinetics Publishers.

Gill, D. (1995). Gender issues: A social-educational perspective. In S. Murphy (Ed.), *Sport psychology interventions* (pp. 205–234). Champaign, IL: Human Kinetics.

Hardy, C. (1993, Winter). President's message. *AAASP Newsletter,* pp. 1, 3.

Heil, J. (1993). Diagnostic methods and measures. In J. Heil (Ed.), *Psychology of sport injury* (pp. 89–112). Champaign, IL: Human Kinetics.

Heil, J., & Henschen, K. (1996). Assessment in sport and exercise psychology. In J. Van Raalte & B. Brewer (Eds.), *Exploring sport and exercise psychology* (pp. 229–255). Washington, DC: American Psychological Association.

Heil, J., Henschen, K., & Nideffer, R. (1996). Psychological assessment in applied sport psychology. *Journal of Applied Sport Psychology, 8,* S32.

Hogan, T. (2005). Sources of information about psychological tests. In G. Koocher, J. Norcross, & S. Hill, (Eds.), *Psychologist's desk reference* (2nd ed.; pp.101–104). New York, NY: Oxford University Press.

Kanfer, F., & Goldstein, A. (Eds.). (1986). *Helping people change: A textbook of methods* (3rd ed.). New York, NY: Pergamon.

Mattarazzo, J. (1999). Computerized clinical psychological test interpretations: Unvalidated plus all mean and no sigma. In D. Bersoff (Ed.), *Ethical conflicts in psychology* (2nd ed.; pp. 331–333). Washington, DC: American Psychological Association.

McCann, S., Jowdy, D., & Van Raalte, J. (2002). Assessment in sport and exercise psychology. In J. Van Raalte & B. Brewer (Eds.), *Exploring sport and exercise psychology* (2nd ed.; pp. 291-305). Washington, DC: American Psychological Association.

McNair, D., Lorr, M., & Dropplemen, L. (1971). *Profile of mood states.* San Diego, CA: Educational and Industrial Testing Services.

Meyers. A. (1995, Winter). Ethical principles of AAASP. *AAASP Newsletter,* pp. 15, 21.

Nagy, T. (2005). *Ethics in plain English: An illustrative casebook for psychologists* (2nd ed.). Washington, DC: American Psychological Association.

Nideffer, R. (1981). *The ethics and practice of applied sport psychology.* Ithaca, NY: Mouvement Publications.

Nideffer, R. (1987). Applied sport psychology. In J. May & M. Asken (Eds.), *Sport psychology: The psychological health of the athlete* (pp. 1–18). New York, NY: PMA.

Ogilvie, B. (1977). Walking the perilous path of the team psychologist. *The Physician and Sports Medicine, 5,* 62–68.

Nideffer, R., & Sagal, M. (2001). *Assessment in sport psychology.* Morgantown, WV: Fitness Information Technology.

Ogilvie, B. (1979). The sport psychologist and his professional credibility. In P. Klavora & J. Daniel (Eds.), *Coach, athlete, and the sport psychologist* (pp. 44–55). Toronto, Canada: University of Toronto.

Orlick, T. (1989). Reflections of sportpsych consulting with individual team sport athletes at summer and winter Olympic games. *The Sport Psychologist, 3,* 358–365.

Ostrow, A. (Ed.). (2002). *Directory of psychological tests in the sport and exercise sciences* (3rd ed.). Morgantown, WV: Fitness Information Technology.

Paniagua, F. (1998). *Assessing and treating culturally diverse clients* (2nd ed.). Thousand Oaks, CA: Sage.

Parham, W. D. (2010). Ethical considerations in applied sport psychology: Culture, communications, and going the extra mile. *Professional Psychology: Research and Practice, 41,* 151–152.

Petitpas, A., Brewer, B., Rivera, P., & Van Raalte, J. (1994). Ethical beliefs and behaviors in applied sport psychology: The AAASP ethics survey. *Journal of Applied Sport Psychology, 6,* 135–151.

Rotella, R. (1992, Fall). Sport psychology: Staying focused on a common and shared mission for a bright future. *AAASP Newsletter,* pp. 8–9.

Sachs, M. (1993). Professional ethics in sport psychology. In R. Singer, M. Murphy, & L. Tennant (Eds.), *Handbook of research in sport psychology* (pp. 921–932). New York, NY: Macmillan.

Sagal, M., Sagal, P. T., Miller, G. E. (2004). Assessment in sport psychology. In C. Spielberger (Ed.), *Encyclopedia of applied psychology* (pp. 177–190). New York: Academic Press.

Salmela, J. (1981). *The world sport psychology sourcebook.* Ithaca, NY: Mouvement Publications.

Schinke, R., & Hanrahan, S. (2009). *Cultural sport psychology.* Champaign, IL: Human Kinetics Publishers.

Silva, J. (1984). Personality and sport performance: Controversy and challenge. In J. Silva & R. Weinberg (Eds.), *Psychological foundations of sport* (pp. 59–69). Champaign, IL: Human Kinetics.

Silva, J. (1989). Toward the professionalization of sport psychology. *The Sport Psychologist, 3,* 265–273.

Silva, J. (1996). A second move: Confronting persistent issues that challenge the advancement of applied sport psychology. *Journal of Applied Sport Psychology, 8,* S52.

Singer, R. (1993). Ethical issues in clinical services. *Quest, 45,* 88–105.

Stapleton, A. M., Hays, K. F., Hankes, D. M., & Parham, W. D. (2010). Ethical dilemmas in sport psychology: A dialogue on the unique aspects impacting practice. *Professional Psychology: Research and Practice, 41*(2), 143–152.

Sundberg, N. (1977). *Assessment of persons.* New York, NY: Prentice-Hall.

Taylor, J. (1994). Examining the boundaries of sport science and psychology trained practitioners in applied sport psychology: Title usage and area of competence. *Journal of Applied Sport Psychology, 6,* 185–195.

Tranel, D. (1999). The release of psychological data to non-experts: Ethical and legal considerations. In D. Bersoff (Ed.), *Ethical conflicts in psychology* (2nd ed.; pp. 303–307). Washington, DC: American Psychological Association.

Vealey, R. (1993). Imagery training for performance enhancement and personal development. In J. Williams, (Ed.), *Applied sport psychology: Personal growth to peak performance* (pp. 201–224). Mountain View, CA: Mayfield.

Vealey, R., & Garner-Holman, M. (1998). Applied sport psychology: Measurement issues. In J. Duda (Ed.), *Advances in sport and exercise psychology measurements* (pp. 433–446). Morgantown, WV: Fitness Information Technology.

Walsh, B., & Betz, N. (1995). *Tests and assessment* (3rd ed.). Englewood Cliffs, NJ: Prentice Hall.

Watson, J. C., Etzel, E., & Shapiro, J. (2009). Ethics and counseling practice with college student-athletes. In E. Etzel (Ed.), *Counseling and psychological services for college student-athletes* (pp. 85–112). Morgantown, WV: Fitness Information Technology.

Watson, J. C., Tenenbaum, G., Lidor, R., & Alfermann, D. (2001). Ethical uses of the internet in sport psychology: A position stand. *International Journal of Sport Psychology, 32,* 207–222.

Wechsler, D. (1981). *Manual for the Wechsler Adult Intelligence Scale—Revised.* New York, NY: Psychological Corporation.

Whelan, J. (1994, Summer). Considering ethics. *AAASP Newsletter,* pp. 24, 27.

Whelan, J., Elkin, T., Etzel, E., & Meyers, A. (1995, September). Ethics in exercise and sport psychology: Consideration of specific guidelines. Workshop conducted at the annual meeting of the Association for the Advancement of Applied Sport Psychology, New Orleans, LA.

Whelan, J. Elkins, T., & Meyers, A. (1996). Ethics in sport and exercise psychology. In J. Van Raalte & B. Brewer (Eds.), *Exploring sport and exercise psychology* (pp. 431–447). Washington, DC: American Psychological Association.

Whelan, L., Meyers, A., & Elkins, T. (2002). Ethics in sport and exercise psychology. In J. Van Raalte & B. Brewer (Eds.), *Exploring sport and exercise psychology* (2nd ed.; pp. 503–524). Washington, DC: American Psychological Association.

Williams, J. (1995). Applied sport psychology: Goals, issues and challenges. *Journal of Applied Sport Psychology, 7,* 81–91.

Williams, J., & Scherzer, C. B. (2003). Tracking the training and careers of graduates of advanced degree programs in sport psychology, 1994 to 1999. *Journal of Applied Sport Psychology, 15,* 335–353.

Wilson, L., & Ranft, V. (1993). The state of ethical training for counseling psychology doctoral students. *The Counseling Psychologist, 21,* 445–456.

Windt, P., Appleby, P., Battin, M., Francis, L., & Landesman, B. (Eds.). (1989). *Ethical issues in the professions.* Englewood Cliffs, NJ: Prentice-Hall.

CHAPTER 17

ETHICAL DECISION MAKING

Jack C. Watson II and Edward F. Etzel

"Knowledge comes, but wisdom lingers."
Tennyson, *Locksley Hall*

INTRODUCTION

So far, the reader has hopefully encountered some useful knowledge about the often distinctive ethical challenges one may likely encounter in the various aspects of SEP consulting, research and teaching. With a bit of luck and some diligence, this knowledge will translate into wise and enduring ethical thinking and practice. In this closing chapter we will attempt to communicate some general views and specific guidelines for identifying and making sound ethical decisions. Perhaps disappointingly, none of these guidelines are perfect or applicable in every challenging incident. As you will see below, there are some reliable models for engaging in these processes—both formally and informally. Other sources are available to the reader for more in-depth information on these topics (Hadjistavrolpoulos & Malloy, 2000; Harris, Visek, & Watson, 2009; Markkula Center for Applied Ethics, 2004; Moore, 2003).

IS IT REALLY A DUCK? AM I REALLY FACING AN ETHICAL PROBLEM?

Before we discuss decision-making approaches and models, it seems appropriate to consider how one becomes aware of ethically troublesome situations. Like ethics in general, this can be a confusing process. For example, students or new professionals may not know or be sure of when they are facing a questionable professional behavior, practice, or situation. It holds true to say "You don't know what you don't know." What might you need to know to have your ethical "antennae" raised?

The first step in this process is sensing that something is possibly awry and, by some means, deciding that you are probably facing a problematic situation. What are some keys to developing and applying such awareness? In her discussion of moral reasoning, Kitchener (1984) identified a pair of approaches that seem to have relevance to ethical awareness and subsequent action. She proposed that one may have some sort of intuitive sense of encountering and subsequently addressing a morally challenging situation. Just how one acquires an "intuitive sense" of the existence of ethical concerns is rather difficult to determine; perhaps it comes from personal history (i.e., extensive training and many hours of practice) or a feeling/ concern that something is inherently wrong (i.e., violating the "Golden Rule" that presents a risk or seems to have caused harm to another). We kind of know that if it looks like a duck and walks like a duck it probably is a duck. Hypothetically, we then act on our intuitive sense of what is the right thing to do. More on various approaches will be provided later in the chapter.

Kitchener's other view is that ethical sense and logical action are rooted in values. As the reader knows from earlier chapters and other sources, our ethical codes stem from organizational (e.g., AASP, ACA, APA) values, often identified in the introductions and preambles of codes. So, if one accepts Kitchener's second point of view, one probably becomes aware of something and responds as a result of knowing that what the codes say are values-based prescribed and proscribed practices. This approach may make more sense to people.

Practically speaking, SEP professionals and students need to be knowledgeable about what a code says in order to know when a duck has entered the room and perhaps how to appropriately respond to its being there. This suggests that we need to read our code(s) carefully—and probably at least yearly. It also seems prudent to ensure that the codes are readily accessible. Have the code(s) of your professional organization(s) bookmarked on your computer. Print a copy of the code(s) and have a file readily available—for example, a red folder an arm's length away. Read about ethics, even if the area is not your preferred cup of tea. Attend workshops at conferences and take continuing education courses on ethics.

All professionals, even the most well-intentioned, make ethical mistakes. Some of the most beneficial conference workshops that the authors have attended have included presenters describing some of their most glaring ethical blunders and their perceptions of the reasons for making these mistakes. These occur because practitioners are human, and humans make mistakes. Extensive knowledge of the pertinent ethical codes and the motivation to behave ethically is not enough to elude questionable professional behaviors (Harris et al., 2009). Therefore, the use of ethical decision making models is encouraged to help increase the likelihood of making ethically sound decisions (Koocher & Keith-Spiegel, 1998).

MODELS OF DECISION MAKING

Ethical decisions are made by practitioners each and every day. While some of these ethical decisions may seem commonplace and mundane (e.g., Should I talk with a coach about what was discussed in a session with one of their athletes?), others are more challenging (e.g., Should I breach confidentiality when a client of concern reveals repeated thoughts of self-harm?). These ethical decisions are difficult because they often involve new situations/information, and have multiple resolutions that are difficult and/or uncomfortable to follow and that are either at odds with each other or seem equally appropriate. As Kitchener (1984) has indicated, an ethical dilemma is "a problem for which no course of action seems satisfactory. The dilemma exists because there are good, but contradictory ethical reasons to take conflicting and incompatible courses of action" (p. 43). While such decisions can be difficult to make, practitioners can make quality decisions if they possess an understanding of the pertinent ethical codes of conduct, personal and professional values, moral principles, and the factors that may influence decision making. An understanding of one or more ethical decision-making models, and posses a personal philosophical approach to ethical decision-making (Kumpf, 2012). It is important to note that use of ethical decision-making models does not always lead to clear-cut resolutions to difficult situations. However, if followed, these models provide practitioners with a path to reduce bias by helping to account for and process important information and influential factors.

As noted earlier in this book, codes of ethics are themselves based upon moral principles of behavior often referred to as the ethical principles. While codes of conduct rarely identify black and white behaviors and specifically instruct a professional on how to react in a specific situation, ethical principles are designed to provide practitioners with underlying information about the philosophical underpinnings on which the more enforceable codes of ethics were developed. Therefore, they serve as inspirational guides to help practitioners better understand how the code was developed. The ethical principles upon which the American Psychological Association (2010) bases its ethics code include: (1) Beneficence and Nonmaleficence; (2) Fidelity and Responsibility; (3) Integrity; (4) Justice; and (5) Respect for People's Rights and Dignity. The Canadian Code of Ethics for Psychologists (2000) has weighted the ethical principles on which its code of ethics is based, putting them in an order by which psychologists should consider these principles if they are in conflict with each other: (1) Respect for the Dignity of Persons; (2) Responsible Caring; (3) Integrity in Relationships; and (4) Responsibility to Society.

Our personal and professional values develop over time as we grow our professional identity and become more experienced (Kumpf, 2012). These values develop based upon how we as practitioners view and react to ethical situations. The growth of these personal and professional values is strongly affected by our interpretation of the ethical principles and how we view their role as a practitioner. Therefore, these values may carry over from the values that we held prior to entering the field, but are also strongly influenced by the experiences that we have encountered since entering the field as a student/trainee.

Whether or not we like to believe this, our decisions are affected by many factors that we interact with in our environment (Hadjistavropoulos & Malloy, 2000). Understanding the factors that are likely to influence our decision making and trying to take them into account while progressing through a decision-making model can help us as practitioners make good and rational decisions. The factors identified by Hadjistavropoulos and Malloy (2000) that might influence the decision-making processes of psychology practitioners include: individual influences (e.g., influences created by our personal make-up related to demographics, ethical orientation and development); issue specific influences (e.g., influences affected by our personal moral perception of the current issue); significant other issues (e.g., the influence that important others have upon us as a decision maker in terms of our thinking and behavior); situational influences (e.g., influences affected by the culture and climate of one's work organization); and external influences (e.g., influences from the world around us that affect us from outside of our work setting).

The ethical theory/philosophy subscribed to by an individual influences the decision-making styles of that individual. The ethical theory/philosophy utilized by a practitioner often evolves over time. However, the *teleological* and *deontological* perspectives appear to be the most influential theories with regard to the ethical decision-making models used in psychology (Hadjistavropoulos & Malloy, 2000; Whelan, Meyers, & Elkins, 2002). In general, teleology can be viewed as an outcome-oriented perspective whereby the ethicality of an action is judged solely by the outcome of that action. Deontology takes an action-oriented perspective whereby the ethicality of an action is based upon the intentions and quality of actions taken by an individual rather than the outcome of those actions. While a complete description of these theoretical perspectives is beyond the scope of this chapter, readers are encouraged to pursue additional readings related to these theories.

THE ETHICAL DECISION-MAKING PROCESS

To date, no ethical decision making model that is specific to the field of sport and exercise psychology has been proposed. However, the concept of sport and exercise psychology practitioners using ethical decision-making models developed for use by other helping professions has been suggested by Harris et al. (2009). A commonly used, practice-based ethical decision-making model will be outlined below. This model will be followed by a case presentation and a discussion of that case using the model as a guide.

The decision-making model presented was developed by Hadjistavropoulos and Malloy (2000). It has been recognized as an excellent model for resolving ethically challenging situations in the field of sport and exercise psychology (Harris et al., 2009), and is closely related to the current 10-step model proposed within the Canadian Psychological Association's (2000) *Canadian Code of Ethics for Psychologists*. This multi-stage model involves seven steps that include: (1) identifying the relevant ethical issues and practices that are specific to the situation; (2) developing multiple alternative courses of action for dealing with the situation; (3) analyzing the short- and long-term risks and benefits of the identified alternative courses of action on all of the groups involved; (4) selecting a course of action after considering the appropriate principles, values and standards; (5) carrying out the selected course of action with a willingness to assume responsibility for any resulting consequences; (6) evaluating the results and consequences of the action; and (7) assuming responsibility for the results of the action and taking steps to correct any negative consequences or to restart the decision-making process if necessary.

While not specifically contained in the Hadjistavropoulos and Malloy (2000) model, practitioners are strongly encouraged to seek consultation from those persons affected by the ethical situation as well as independent colleagues and/or advisory boards who might be able to add objectivity to the process of making a decision. However, when consulting with individuals external to the situation, ensure that "the decision for action remains with the individual psychologist, [and] the seeking and consideration of such assistance reflects an ethical approach to ethical decision making" (Canadian Psychological Association, 2000, p. 3).

Ethical decision-making is a complex process that cannot always be effectively accomplished by following a step-by-step process. The models presented above should be used as a guide to help practitioners reach an appropriate decision that utilizes a great deal of information including the relevant codes of ethics, ethical principles, personal and professional values, ethical philosophies, and knowledge of the internal/external factors that might affect us. However, one should note that situations and personal experiences regularly affect our view of self and how we view the world and our professional responsibilities. Therefore, we should expect that our resolution to a specific ethical dilemma might change based upon where we are in our professional careers and the internal/external factors that influence us. However, it should be our goal to identify the best possible resolution to an ethical dilemma based upon the information that we have available to us at that specific point in time.

CASE EXAMPLE

Johnny is a 23-year-old basketball coach working for a basketball training center in New York City. Johnny recently graduated from college after playing four years of basketball at a large Division I university with a rich history of basketball success. His dream upon graduation was to play professional basketball. Johnny tried all of the routes upon graduation—NBA, D-League, playing overseas, etc.—but was unsuccessful at landing a spot on teams in any of these leagues. Having played against players who are currently playing in all of the these leagues while in college, he knew in his heart that he had the skills to make it in some, if not all of these leagues. In his mind, the reason why he did not make it was because his performance was influenced by the anxiety that he experienced during important games. So, Johnny decided to take a job at a basketball training academy as a coach so that he would have an opportunity to train and could continue to work on his skills, while being able to stay connected with the basketball community.

One day after practice while picking up her son from basketball camp, Dr. Jordan met Johnny and they talked for a little while about her son's progress. During this conversation, Johnny found out that Dr. Jordan was a licensed psychologist who specialized in sport psychology after completing a graduate program with a specialization in this area. While her practice was only about 30-40% athlete clients, it was her goal to transition her practice in a way that would allow her to work only with athletes. Given his history, Johnny was very interested in learning more about sport psychology and asked Dr. Jordan a lot of questions about the field and how it works. Through this conversation, he became even more convinced that he would benefit greatly from sport psychology services. However, Johnny was surprised to learn that she charged her clients over $200 for a one-hour session, and knew that he would never be able to pay this fee on his current salary.

The following week, Johnny saw Dr. Jordan again while she was waiting to pick up her son from training. He approached her and told her that her son had been making great progress. Johnny indicated that Dr. Jordan's son would benefit even more from individual lessons, and that with these lessons Johnny was pretty sure that he would not only make his school's basketball team, but possible be one of the star players. Johnny told Dr. Jordan that he would be able to provide these lessons and wondered if Dr. Jordan would be willing to work out a deal where he provided her son with basketball lessons in exchange for her providing him with sport psychology consultation services to help him perform at his best and hopefully earn a spot to play professionally. He told her that he wanted to learn how to better handle his emotions during important situations, as he had a history of not dealing well with anxiety during big games. Johnny indicated that while he knew that her consultation fee was higher than his fee for lessons, he would be willing to give more lessons than he received sessions. Johnny was also hoping that "maybe they could work out a deal" where he paid her more money if he earned a professional contract. Further, Johnny revealed to Dr. Jordan that he knew a lot of professional basketball athletes that he played with and against. He said that he would be vocal about singing her praises and sending other athletes to see her.

Dr. Jordan was very interested in this proposal since she had noticed the improvements that her son was making. She wasn't sure if there was anything wrong with the proposed arrangement since bartering is not always a problem. She told Johnny that she would think about his offer and let him know her decision the next time that they saw each other.

Decision Making Process

Dr. Jordan was not sure if it would be a good decision or not for her to take Johnny up on his offer. While the offer sounded potentially useful to her and her growing sport psychology practice, she just did not feel totally right about it. This initial feeling of uneasiness and questioning was something that she had experienced in the past when she sensed that she might be facing an ethical dilemma. In fact, this feeling had helped her to avoid several questionable ethical challenges in the past, so she always took this reaction seriously. Because of this feeling, she decided that it was best for her to make use of a decision-making model she had learned in graduate school to help her make her final decision. Below is the outline of a seven-step model she employed and the answers that she developed to each of the prompts (Hadjistavropoulos & Malloy, 2000).

(1) Identify the relevant ethical issues and practices that are specific to the situation. Having been trained with a specialization in sport psychology, Dr. Jordan felt as if she was probably competent to help Johnny deal with anxiety issues. However, she was less clear about some of the payment issues, so she turned to Section 6 of the APA Ethics Code (2010). Here, she read about bartering for services and tried to determine if it was advisable in this situation. She was also not at all sure about his plan involving repaying her additional money if he fulfilled his dream and signed a professional contract. Dr. Jordan felt as if doing such would not allow her to arrange a fee structure early on, and also felt as if she would need to check the law to ensure that this was appropriate. Finally, Johnny seemed to suggest that he would give referrals to other athletes as a means of payment for her giving him discounted sessions. Dr. Jordan was not sure if this would be the same as paying for referrals. She wondered if by agreeing to do this if she might be paying him for false advertising—especially if she was agreeing to allow him to do this even before he met with her. Finally, Dr. Jordan sensed that she might be establishing a potentially unethical, multiple relationship with Johnny if she went along with his proposed payment structure. So, she also reviewed Section 3.05 of the APA Ethics Code and tried to determine if this relationship would likely result in impairment, exploitation or harm.

(2) **Develop multiple alternative courses of action for dealing with the situation.** Dr. Jordan came up with the following alternative courses of action based upon the information that she gathered: (a) Decide not to provide services for Johnny, because it was probably unethical, but offer to find him services from another provider that he might be able to afford; (b) to barter services, but to work out the costs of the trade so that they were equivalent in both directions (e.g., three of his training sessions for each of her sessions), so that he would not owe her more money if he signed a professional contract and would not need to pay her additional money or be required to help her recruit additional clients; (c) to trade services, but to be willing to trade session for session (e.g., each of his one hour training sessions was equal to one of her one hour sport psychology sessions), and allow him to pay her additional money if he signed a professional contract;, (d) to trade for services in such a way that she would benefit (e.g., four of his training sessions for four of her sport psychology sessions), because Johnny needed services a great deal; and (e) work with Johnny and ask him to pay a reduced rate for services that he can afford.

(3) **Analyze the short- and long-term risks and benefits of the previously identified alternative courses of action on all of the groups involved.** Many alternative short- and long-term risks and benefits seemed to exist. To start with, Dr. Jordan perceived the individuals involved in this case to be herself, Johnny, and potentially her son. While providing the risks and benefits to each of the aforementioned options would be too long for this section, below you will find a brief overview of some of her perceived short- and long-term risks and benefits, which involved the following questions: Would she be acting unethically by providing these services? Would the quality of her work or Johnny's progress affect his relationship and training with her son? Would her son's progress affect the quality of her relationship and work with Johnny? Would bartering put her in a position of authority or control over Johnny either now or in the future? Who would this relationship benefit the most? Why would she want to establish this relationship? Might any of these payment options be illegal? Would all of these payment options be pushing or overstepping the spirit of the ethical principles? Would she be opening herself up to legal or ethical actions in the future.

(4) **Select a course of action after considering the appropriate principles, values, and standards.** Based upon her evaluation of the potential courses of action and the results of a consultation with an experienced colleague about the appropriateness of the situation, Dr. Jordan decided that she would be willing to provide services to Johnny. However, she was not sure about how to proceed, so she discussed two potential options with Johnny to determine which would be best for him. Both of these options seemed ethical to her. These options were

to: (1) either charge him a discounted rate that he could afford to pay for services without trading services, or (2) trade services with Johnny, but to do so at a level that is based upon a fee structure that is equitable and benefiting both parties (e.g., trading three hours of Johnny's teaching ($60/hr) for one hour of her sport psychology services ($200/hr).

(5) Carry out the selected course of action with a willingness to assume responsibility for any resulting consequences. After some discussion with Johnny, Dr. Jordan decided that it would be best to not barter with Johnny. However, she decided that based upon other business models that she had looked at, that it would be best to discount his services to a level that he could afford. This would help to continue building the sport psychology portion of her practice while still bringing in some funds to support her efforts. She did, however, keep her son in group basketball lessons and started private lessons for him. These private lessons were conducted by Johnny, and she paid him the full hourly rate for the provision of these lessons for her son.

(6) Evaluate the results and consequences of the action. Dr. Jordan was well aware of the potential for a negative multiple relationship to develop as a result of the agreement she had developed with Johnny. She consulted with a fellow psychologist about the arrangement. She regularly evaluated and processed her relationship with Johnny to ensure that she was not taking advantage of him, and that this relationship was not affecting the services that she provided to him.

(7) Assume responsibility for the results of the action and take steps to correct any negative consequences or to restart the decision making process if necessary. Through her recurring consultations with her colleague, Dr. Jordan made sure that she took full responsibility for her decision. She continued to process her work and relationship with Johnny. She was prepared to discontinue the consultation and take action if any developments suggested that this was not working out accordingly. Fortunately, the situation continued to work out well, and they continued to work together for the next year.

SUMMARY

All practicing sport psychology professionals will face ethical challenges throughout their careers. Many times these ethical dilemmas will be obvious, and clear-cut answers will be available to the practitioner. Other times these ethical dilemmas will be much more difficult to identify, and will not be associated with clear-cut actions for dealing with them. This chapter has attempted to outline options to help practitioners become more aware of ethical dilemmas before they result in problems. This chapter also outlines selected ethical knowledge and a decision-making model to help sport psychology practitioners better understand a proven method for dealing with ethical situations.

It should be noted that ethical situations are difficult to identify and do not come with easy-to-follow instructions for dealing with them. All practitioners make ethical missteps at one point or another, so making a mistake does not qualify a practitioner as being unethical. It is important for practitioners to take steps and precautions that allow them to identify potential ethical quandaries and take steps to make good decisions related to these dilemmas.

According to Kumpf (2012), the ability to consistently make good decisions is facilitated when we possess a solid understanding of ethical codes of conduct, understand our own personal and professional values and moral principles, have knowledge of ethical decision-making models, and employ a personal philosophical approach to ethical decision making. Along with these previously mentioned qualities, effective ethical decision makers are also likely to consult with fellow practitioners about their views related to a specific situation, and document their discussions and the steps taken to make specific decisions.

REFERENCES

American Psychological Association. (2010). *Ethical principles of psychologists and code of conduct.* Washington, DC: Author.

Canadian Psychological Association. (2000). *Canadian code of ethics for psychologists* (3rd ed). Ottawa, ON: Author.

Kumpf, C. I. (2012). Frameworks and models in ethical decision making. In C. M. Jungers & J. Gregoire (Eds.), *Counseling ethics: Philosophical and professional foundations* (pp. 47–70). New York, NY: Springer Publishing.

Hadjistavropoulos, T., & Malloy, D. (2000). Making ethical choices: A comparative decision-making model for Canadian psychologists. *Canadian Psychologist, 41*(2), 104–115.

Harris, B. S., Visek, A. J., & Watson II, J. C. (2009). Ethical decision-making in sport psychology: Issues and implications for professional practice. In R. Schinke (Ed.), *Contemporary sport psychology* (pp. 217–232). Nova Science Publishers.

Kitchener, K. (1984). Intuition, critical evaluation and ethical principles. *The Counseling Psychologist, 12,* 43–55.

Koocher, G., & Keith-Spiegel, P. (1998). *Ethics in psychology: Professional standards and cases* (2nd ed.). New York, NY: Oxford University Press.

Markkula Center for Applied Ethics. (2004). A framework for thinking ethically. Retrieved from http://www.scu.edu/ethics/practicing/decision/framework.html

Moore, Z. (2003). Ethical dilemmas in sport psychology: Discussion and recommendations for practice. *Professional Psychology: Research and Practice, 34,* 601–610.

Whelan, J. P., Meyers, A. W., & Elkins, T. D. (2002). Ethics in sport and exercise psychology. In J. L. VanRaalte & B. W. Brewer (Eds.), *Exploring sport and exercise psychology* (pp. 503–523). Washington, DC: American Psychological Association.

Index

About the Editors

Dr. Edward F. Etzel, PhD, serves as a professor in the Department of Sport Sciences within the WVU College of Physical Activity and Sport Sciences. Ed is a licensed psychologist in the state of West Virginia and a staff member of Well WVU's Carruth Center for Counseling and Psychiatric Services. His duties include being the liaison between the center and the WVU Department of Intercollegiate Athletics. Ed is involved in the provision of counseling services for personal, career, and sport performance enhancement concerns, consultation with WVUIA staff on mental health issues.

Ed is listed as a consultant on the U.S. Olympic Committee's Sport Psychology Registry. He served as Chair of the American Psychological Association's Division 47 Education Committee and served as Chair of the Association of Applied Sport Psychology's Ethics Committee from 1998 to 2007. Ed is a Fellow in the Association of Applied Sport Psychology and received the American Psychological Association's Division 47 Distinguished Contribution to Education in sport and exercise psychology award in 2009. Ed is an avid exerciser, animal lover, DJ on WWVU-FM radio, golfer, amateur cook, gardener, guitar player, and water color painter. He is married to G. Anne Cather, MD. They reside in Morgantown, WV.

Dr. Jack C. Watson II, PhD, is the acting assistant dean in the College of Physical Activity and Sport Sciences at West Virginia University, where he has been a faculty member for 13 years. Dr. Watson is a CC-AASP and a licensed psychologist in the state of West Virginia. He has a small private practice in Morgantown, West Virginia where he sees athletes for issues of performance enhancement. He was also the president of the Association for Applied Sport Psychology from 2012-2013.

As a researcher, Dr. Watson has focused much of his attention on the topic of professional issues in sport and exercise psychology, with a very specific focus on the topic of ethics. He is the former Chair of the Association for Applied Sport Psychology, Ethics Committee, and served as a member of this committee for many years. He has published 13 articles, 7 book chapters, and given 24 presentations at national and international conferences on the topic of ethical issues in sport and exercise psychology.

About the Authors

Mark B. Andersen is a professor in the College of Sport and Exercise Science at Victoria University in Melbourne, Australia. He also coordinates the Master of Applied Psychology program in the College of the Arts and is a member of the Institute of Sport, Exercise, and Active Living (ISEAL). His research interests include supervision, mindfulness-based practice, exercise and chronic disease, and injury prevention and rehabilitation.

Mark Aoyagi is Director of Sport & Performance Psychology and an assistant professor in the Graduate School of Professional Psychology at the University of Denver. His areas of interest include theories of performance excellence and professional, training, and ethical issues in sport psychology.

Tiz Arnold, EdD, works in a military sport psychology program, and also does consulting work with athletes and teams. Her areas of interest include developing mindfulness, attention, and confidence.

Patrick Baillie, PhD, LLB, is a clinical psychologist and lawyer, based in Calgary, Alberta. His research interests include issues arising at the intersection of law and mental health, including ethics, criminal responsibility, risk assessment, and laws governing the practice of psychology.

Lindsey Blom, EdD, is an associate professor in the School of Physical Education, Sport, and Exercise Science at Ball State University. Her research interests include the psych-social aspects of youth sport, the athletic triangle, group dynamics, and coach-athlete relationships.

Joe Frontiera, PhD, is managing partner of Meno Consulting, and an adjunct professor in Leadership Studies at West Virginia University. He writes a regular column for The Washington Post, and co-authored Team Turnarounds (2012).

Marjourie Fusinetti, MA, is an AASP Certified Consultant. She conducts performance enhancement training with a variety of populations, including military and sport, in the Louisville area. Her areas of interest include leadership, burnout, injury, and stress management.

Lael Gershgoren, PhD, is a lecturer in the college of Physical Education & Sport at the Wingate Institute, Natania, Israel. In addition, Lael serves as a performance enhancement consultant of elite athletes. His research interests include individual & team decision making, shared mental models, and motivation.

Douglas M. Hankes, PhD, is the director of Student Counseling Services at Auburn University and is the applied sport psychology consultant for the Auburn University Athletic Department. His areas of professional interest include training, supervision, student-athlete development, and welfare and the ethical practice of applied sport psychology.

Brandonn S. Harris, PhD, CC-AASP, is an assistant professor in the Department of Health and Kinesiology at Georgia Southern University. His research interests include professional and ethical issues in sport and exercise psychology, youth sport participation, and athlete and coach burnout.

Kate F. Hays maintains an independent practice in sport, performance, and clinical psychology, "The Performing Edge," in Toronto. Her research interests include the application and intersection of sport psychology to other areas of performance, as well as the mental benefits of physical activity.

Doug Hirschhorn, PhD, is the chief executive officer of Edge Consulting LLC, a firm specializing in peak performance coaching for the financial industry. He is a frequent contributor in the media and author of several books: *The Trading Psychology Playbook* (2013); *8 Ways to Great* (2010); and *The Trading Athlete* (2001).

Dan Leidl, PhD, is a managing partner of Meno Consulting, and co-author of the book Team Turnarounds. He writes regularly for publications that include The Washington Post and Psychology Today, and his research and writing interests include leadership, motivation, team development, and achievement.

Mary Jo Loughran, PhD, is an associate professor of psychology at Chatham University, where she serves as the Director of Training for the PsyD program in Counseling Psychology. Her research interests include health promotion and the psychology of distance running. Dr. Loughran also maintains a private practice where she specializes in work with collegiate student-athletes.

John Lubker is the Associate Dean of Students in the Graduate School and an Associate Professional Specialist in the Department of Psychology at the University of Notre Dame. His research interests include professional issues in sport and exercise psychology, transitions in sport, and student-athlete adjustment to college.

James Moncier is an assistant professor in Family Medicine and Psychiatry at the University of Alabama School of Medicine, Huntsville Regional Medical Campus. His research interests include performance anxiety, mental toughness, and sustaining excellence.

Moon Mullins, MS, is a retired United States Army Lieutenant Colonel and aviator who serves as the Site Manager for a military sport psychology program in Louisville.

Steve Portenga, PhD, is President of iPerformance Psychology and an assistant professor at the University of Denver. His research interests include the ethical practice and training of applied sport psychologists, the intersection of leadership and team dynamics, and the theoretical foundations of human performance.

Selen Razon is an assistant professor of sport and exercise psychology in the School of PE, Sport and Exercise Science at Ball State University. Her research interests include exercise promotion in healthy and chronically ill populations, and effectiveness of poly-sensory stimuli in modulating attention and decreasing exertion in effort-expenditure settings.

Michael Sachs is a professor in the Department of Kinesiology, College of Health Professions and Social Work, at Temple University. He is interested in the psychology of running as well as motivation and adherence, especially technological approaches to countering excuses for not exercising.

James P. Sampson, Jr., is the Mode L. Stone Distinguished Professor of Counseling and Career Development and co-director of the Center for the Study of Technology in Counseling and Career Development. His research interests include the content and process of career decision making, the design and delivery of cost-effective career resources and services, and the design and appropriate use of information and communication technology in counseling.

Robert Schinke is a professor and Canada Research Chair in Multicultural Sport and Physical Activity at Laurentian University. He has co-edited and authored 14 books in the areas of cultural sport psychology and sport for peace and human development. His research has been funded by the Social Sciences and Humanities Research Council of Canada, the Indigenous Health Research Development Program, the Canadian Foundation for Innovation, and Health Promotions Canada.

Vanessa Shannon is a mental conditioning coach at IMG Academy. She has previously held positions as an assistant professor at West Virginia University, and as an assistant professor and department chair at Tennessee Wesleyan College.

Mark Stonkus, EdD, CC-AASP, LMHC, CSCS, is the owner/founder of MBX Training, a performance facility in Massachusetts that combines physical and mental training into one comprehensive approach to athletic training. He also established Clutch Athlete, a program specializing in mental toughness training skills for enhancing athletic performance under pressure.

Gershon Tenenbaum, PhD, Benjamin S. Bloom Professor of Educational Psychology, is a professor of sport and exercise psychology at the Florida State University, USA. He published extensively in psychology and sport psychology in areas of expertise and decision-making, psychometrics, and coping with physical effort experiences. Gershon received several distinguished awards for his academic and scientific achievements, and is a member and fellow of several scientific and professional forums and societies.

Amanda J. Visek, PhD, is an assistant professor in the Department of Exercise Science in the School of Public Health and Health Services at The George Washington University. Her research interests include pediatric sport psychology, retention and attrition factors related to sport participation, aggression in sport, professional issues, and the application of sport psychology to issues of public health relevance.

Justine Vosloo is an assistant professor in the Department of Exercise and Sport Science at Ithaca College in Ithaca, NY. She is active in research which focuses on coach-athlete interactions, mentoring and work-life balance issues in coaching, professional issues in sport and exercise psychology, applied sport psychology practice and the psychosocial issues related to childhood obesity.

Dr. Keith Wilson works with soldiers in the United States Army. He trains soldiers to use sport psychology techniques to enhance their personal and Army-related performance and mental strategies to develop their mental and emotional resilience.

Michael T. Yura, PhD, is a Biometrics SME for International Biometrics Group. His research interests are in biometics and forensics, professional issues in sports psychology, and sport behavior.

Sam Zizzi is a professor of sport and exercise psychology at West Virginia University, and an adjunct professor in public health. His research interests include applied sport psychology and physical activity promotion. He and his colleagues coordinate one of the largest insurance-sponsored obesity prevention and treatment programs in the US, the PEIA weight management program.